NINETY YEARS ON

The New Book of the A3 Pacifics
By
Peter Coster

FLYING SCOTSMAN in 1968, in her early days in Alan Pegler's ownership, with two corridor tenders, passes Marshmoor signalbox at full speed on a positioning run from Doncaster to Kings Cross. In composing the photograph I used the *contre-jour* view of the train used so successfully by Cyril Herbert on many occasions with Atlantics and Pacifics in pre-war days. No doubt the crew were enjoying a nostalgic trip! The second tender was converted to carry only water. Boiler 94A(27058) Corridor tenders (5325 and 5327) (P J Coster)

Irwell Press Ltd.

First published in the United Kingdom in 2013
by Irwell Press Limited, 59A, High Street, Clophill,
Bedfordshire MK45 4BE
Printed by *Melita Press*,
KW3, Corradino Industrial Estate,
Paola PLA 3000
Malta

Contents

PREFACE

In endless sweeps for that elusive In endless sweeps for that elusive print, scouring the archives held in the dungeons beneath Irwell Castle, the Editor has accumulated a number of A1 and A3 photographs. These have been passed to me, together with the Revd Arthur Cawston's excellent photographs kindly lent from his bequest by my old friend Canon Brian Bailey, plus some more recent offerings, for a gentle meander back to those days when a train looked like a train, Scotland was on the other side of the world, the departure of a great express was a ceremony attended with careful detail, and its passage was something thrilling and exciting.

A number of supplements to *The Book of the A3 Pacifics* (Irwell Press 2003) in the same style as *The Book of the A4 Pacifics* had been planned using these illustrations, but these are now combined in a second volume of A1s and A3s. At the time of writing, it is a century since the Great Northern Railway appointed a young 35 year-old as Chief Mechanical Engineer, H.N. Gresley. In April 2012 it was 90 years since home-going passengers at Kings Cross were astonished at the presence of a huge, handsome express steam locomotive standing on the empty stock

roads, the like of which they had never seen before. It was GREAT NORTHERN, awaiting inspection by the GNR Directors. This year will be the 90th year since the third of these locomotives emerged from Doncaster Works – 'The Plant' – 1472, later 4472, soon to be named FLYING SCOTSMAN. These three anniversaries we hope to commemorate with this New Book of the A3s.

The story of the Gresley A1s and A3s was thoroughly covered in the original book, and with the illustrations available it is an opportunity, indeed an excuse to take a closer look at individual locomotives. In doing so we have set out to maintain the standard of production and illustration of the original, at the same time reaching into the retreating past to recall the sight, sound and railway culture in which a class of fine locomotives operated.

The story of the class was set out in the original 'Book Of' the A3s, and it is what it is. However, I have put down the history of each individual locomotive, summarising events, together with personal comments. Even now, while the history of the class is generally complete, there is a trickle of new information on the details of individual locomotives, revealing more

about their use and particularly during the sad business of withdrawal and disposal. Brian Bailey has spent time examining the Engine Record Cards at the NRM, and has contributed to the detailed histories. I am also grateful to Tony Wright for his help with the captions and other observations and advice in connection with this reprinted edition, enabling a number of corrections and adjustments. Tony, as an experienced modelmaker, has a very keen eye for detail and has built a number of remarkable A3 4mm models. I must include Peter Townend, a good friend for longer than either of us care to think about, for his reminiscences and anecdotes.

I have used information from a number of sources, acknowledged in the first book, principally W.B. Yeadon's A3 *Register*, first published by Irwell Press and now by Book Law Publications, in order to summarise the history of each locomotive. Inevitably there is a degree of repetition but it allows us to examine each locomotive separately. So we look at a much-loved class of locomotives, that embodied the analogy with the horse, even to the extent that they were mostly named after them.
PJC 2013.

FLYING SCOTSMAN, specially prepared for the Wembley exhibition by Doncaster in 1924, with polished bright work and the company's coat of arms on the cabside. She has her original A1 Diagram 94 boiler (7693) and her GN tender (5223). It was substituted a few weeks later by a shorter K3 tender (5378); space allotted at Wembley, it turned out, was insufficient for the full length of loco and eight wheeled tender.

Chapter One
Photography

Here are another hundred and fifty or so pictures of Sir Nigel Gresley's class A1 and A3 Pacifics from both well known and not-so-well-known railway photographers. It has been progressively more difficult to find new illustrations of every A3, and the triumvirate of FIRDAUSSI, GALOPIN and NIGHT HAWK, which were the most elusive, have eventually succumbed. Quality not quantity. The really difficult A3s to track down physically, such as FLAMINGO and CICERO were in fact easy, since most photographers tended to be southerners who rarely saw them, and when they eventually had them in their viewfinders, they made no mistake.

Railway photography has changed enormously over the years covered in these collections. Today there are electronic cameras of all sorts that have roughly elbowed the conventional box with a lens and film into the museum, and with a few plastic memory cards the size of postage stamps, one could have photographed literally everything at Stratford Shed and Works. Today we have specialised cameras such as underwater and infra-red for natural history work. The latter would have been useful to photograph the Night Scotsman striding north behind its Gateshead A1 in the 1950s!

It was not so when GREAT NORTHERN and her sisters were new. The Tideys, Hebrons and their contemporaries had to haul a great pack of glass plates with them, as well as a plate camera and tripod. Equipment tended towards wood rather than aluminium; there was no plastic in those days and everything was made of metal or hardwood such as mahogany. It was very heavy. A day's photography would probably comprise 12 shots or so. Then a carefully chosen location, and the equipment was set up with reverence. The camera was aimed, and in those days one looked through the plate camera with the aid of a ground glass plate to compose the picture. Then the exposure was calculated. I wonder how, for I started with a celluloid disc calculator, and having dialled the film, shutter speed and weather (cloudy bright, etc) the aperture was specified. Then the experienced photographer, knowing his site and the speed of trains, would decide on the shutter speed, from which the aperture could be calculated, in 'stop numbers' – f4 or f5.6 for example.

The photographic artist, knowing the behaviour of his emulsion, would adjust the aperture by a quarter stop or so, depending on the angle of the sun, etc.

WINDSOR LAD pulls out of Waverley with an express for Glasgow, Perth or Dundee. It is June 1937 with a mixture of semaphore and colour light as the Waverley resignalling gets under way. Two trilbies are examining the contents of a location cupboard by the tender. The A3 has the prototype Diagram 94A boiler 8776 and A3 non-corridor tender No.5567.

SINGAPORE standing at Peterborough with a down stopping service. The period is late 1936 which means that the A3 was fairly new. The A3 has Diagram 94A boiler No.8783 (notable in that it has a true 'banjo' shape, only carried by the final nine A3s) and A3 non-corridor tender No.5582. (Rev. A C Cawston, courtesy Brian Bailey)

As many processed their own work, further control could be exercised in the darkroom. It was always a feeling of growing exhilaration mixed with relief at seeing one's photograph taking shape in the developer, and of course sadness when the focus or exposure was found to be wrong. When everything had been calculated, recalculated and rehearsed, the precious plate was inserted with care, and the protecting slide cover over the emulsion would be withdrawn. As the train came into view, the photographer, not knowing for certain what sort of picture it would make, had to decide whether to shoot or not. The exhaust was critical to a well-balanced composition. If he had got it right, the shutter was fired. Cars were a rich man's toy, and humping the equipment up Shap was more like native portering up Everest than today's photography.

I, and many like me, could not have survived. Half the plates would have been useless, having got the exposure wrong. In some cases the cover plate would have been forgotten. Some would

be blank, as the shutter had not been cocked ready for firing, and the shot lost. Some might well have been exposed twice by mistake. And so on. The advent of more modern cameras, roll film and, critically, interlocked shutters and film transport to prevent people like me from double exposing, must have been a wonderful advance to the older men. The advent of the 35mm camera brought films of greater capacity, and the smaller format brought lenses with larger apertures, making photography in poor weather easier. It prompted the larger formats to improve, and some fine work was done using the Rollei cameras, for example. The Rolls-Royces – the plate cameras with their Zeiss lenses – moved on to cut film and roll film. Equipment was getting lighter. With negatives now less than a quarter of the size of roll films and even smaller when compared with plates, the film makers had to advance into far finer grain emulsions to enable enlargement when printing. The finer the emulsion, the slower the film, and the bigger the lens aperture required to allow

shutter speeds high enough to 'stop' an express.

The name most associated with the use of 35mm format is Cyril Herbert – C.C.B. Herbert – of the LNER, who was one of the first railway photographers to use a 35mm camera. He was a member of the Chief Civil Engineer's staff, who thereby had access to locations unavailable to most others. CCB was a master of composition as well, and his contre-jour shots of Pacifics and Ivatt Atlantics going hard, especially those taken on the shadow side of the train giving greater use of light and shade, are among the very best. The 35mm camera is the world that I entered in the 1950s, having realised that the $1/30^{th}$ second exposure of the box camera would stop nothing. Now the speed of the film and the accuracy of the exposure were the limiting factors, although black and white film was fairly tolerant of poor exposure as I recall. One needed to use slower and fine grained films for large prints, as previously explained.

Then colour film came on the scene, one of the earliest being Kodachrome I, which in my view was excellent if exposed properly. However, at 10 ASA the film speed was far too low. The American Standard Association rating was the speed rating of the film, with which one set the light meter to get the exposure correct. Now it is ISO but the speed ratings are the same. The usual speed, before the electronic camera replaced the analogue, as it were, was 100-200 ASA. Only on a bright summer's day with a wide aperture could one hope to stop a train at speed, and then not too fast or at a wide angle from head-on. In poor light, colour films tended to disappoint, losing contrast and taking unpleasant colour casts. B&W was both better and faster. One could not always choose the weather. Gradually the principal manufacturers, Kodak, Agfa, Gevaert, Ilford and others brought out faster emulsions, although correct exposure needed to be much more precise, at least to a half stop if not even closer, and developing had to be spot on to avoid colour casts. I have seen quite a few of my own and friends colour films spoilt by poor developing. As for printing, well, one was in the hands of youngsters employed by the processing firms with only rough guidance, and

whether they had any idea of the correct hue for an A4 or a maroon 'Big 'Un', for example, was a matter of luck.

Interestingly, Gevaert produced a B&W positive film, *Gevapan*, quite slow at 25 ASA. The quality of the film was superb. There was always a dichotomy between those who used colour and those traditionalists who stuck to B&W in all areas of photography, of course. Railway photographers, particularly towards the end of steam, were not afforded the luxury of choosing the weather, and colour certainly lost a lot of its vitality when the sun went in. B&W did not vary so wildly with the sunlight, and correctly exposed, *Gevapan* produced some fine images in most weathers.

As the procession towards the scrap yards accelerated, photographic activity increased for many of us. One could certainly not choose the weather now. I decided to use a very fast – and expensive – colour film, High Speed Ektachrome, at 160 ASA, but it had to be developed with great care. With a friend I found a specialist laboratory which could develop it for double the rated speed, 320 ASA, which was excellent for expresses or subjects in poor light. Their work was excellent. The need for a well honed routine, checking the equipment,

buying a supply of film and making sure all the cameras and lenses were present and neatly packed was essential before travelling to a location. Even so, it didn't stop me from occasionally forgetting to wind on. The reward was a fine, clear picture recording a sight that was soon to go. Often, but not always.

Enter the cine camera, with the pathetically short 8mm and Super 8mm films, 2½ minutes and then reverse, 5 minutes total. Then there was 16mm, but one needed an inheritance or a job in a merchant bank to afford the running costs. Reproduction on video tape or CD/DVD required sound tracks, and we had to get used to the misuse of Peter Handford's superb recordings in the background, with two cylinder single blast A4s, three cylinder Black Fives and Castles, and so on, all at the wrong speeds. Difficult to get right.

It was the video camera which married sight and sound perfectly, and then came the digital camera. Now it is all very different, with small cameras, no film, and locomotives that are immaculate, as are the trains that they pull. A pity we didn't have it forty years ago! Our one famous A3 is safely at the NRM, having spent more time in private hands than in those of the LNER and BR.

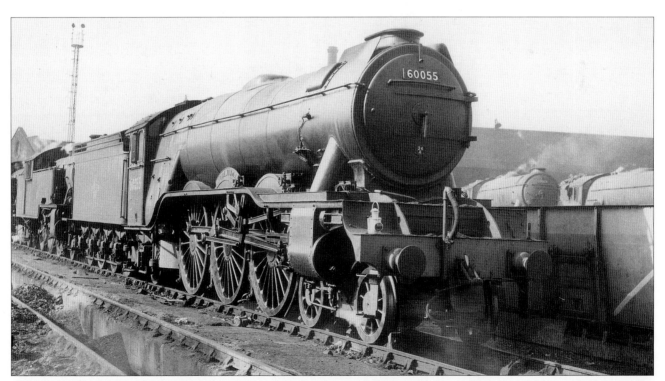

WOOLWINDER was one of the favourite Southern Area A3s and was well used at several sheds. She was the first A3 to be fitted with a double Kylchap post-war. Here she stands over the ashpits at Top Shed among the 'Concrete Mixers' (L1s) on February 21st 1960. The A3 has small chimneyside deflectors that were fitted in October 1959 as an initial attempt to control drifting exhaust when the regulator was eased. Experience indicated that something stronger was required, and trough type deflectors were fitted as a result, although, alas, not to WOOLWINDER which was a very early withdrawal, in September 1961. The slightly heavier A4 Diagram 107 boiler brought a premature end to a number of A3s. Sister A3 LADAS is in the background. The engine has a Diagram 107 boiler (29301) and a GN tender (5286). (David Idle, transporttreasury.co.uk)

60050 PERSIMMON works an up express through Doncaster in 1955. This loco spent many years post-war on the GC section, but in 1955 she was transferred to Kings Cross for three months for the summer traffic. She has a Diagram 94HP boiler 27078 and GN tender No.5259.

Chapter Two
The Locomotives

Thinking about these locomotives as I captioned the photographs brought back a number of memories. In my time post-war, the quality of fuel and the inclination of young men to fire large quantities of it for a poor pay, in conditions where danger was never far away, was far less than before the 1939-45 war, in the great days of the Gresley A1s and A3s – the Super-Pacifics as the LNER called the latter. They always had the strength to haul their trains, and ran well pre-war. After the war, steaming was not always as free as the drivers wanted, and the speed was not always that required with the normal level of delay on a congested main line. Timing runs was often disappointing. Locomotives were often scruffy, some filthy, even the Blue 'Uns, the A4s.

As one who grew up near the East Coast main line, naturally the A3s were a substantial part of the motive power fleet, and their appeal to a young boy was immediate. There was always a sense of being sold short when that familiar smokebox front had a Green

Arrow behind it and not an old friend with a name. A handsome and perfectly proportioned locomotive with a lusty exhaust, they had names, a very curious mixture that imparted a sort of personality. I well remember waiting, camera in hand, especially near a tunnel, listening to this approaching beast with its deafening exhaust muffled by the tunnel walls, until it burst out into daylight, released as it were from its previous confinement.

Those who worked on the railway, state or privately owned, will remember just how difficult it was to change the system. There was nothing so painful or unthinkable as a new idea. Of course, it was run by men in their early sixties, many of whom were content to leave things as they were. The present system worked, and while a new way forward might work better, it might not, and blame would be the result. Therefore the preference was to leave things as they were. If one pressed too hard, one was dismissed (literally sometimes) as obsessive, or bucking the system – 'not one of us' springs to mind. If one was

realistic and dropped the idea, ten years of doing the same pointless things beckoned.

I believe L.P. Parker, Motive Power Superintendent for the ER, had requested conversion of the single blast Gresley Pacifics to double Kylchap exhaust, but the CMEE at Doncaster, Kenneth Cook, had refused. Pressure had resulted in the problem of poor steaming being referred to Swindon of all places, where the ultimate panacea, the Dean blastpipe, had been tried. To report the results in service of an alteration such as this, the normal practice was simply to quote the observations of the Loco Inspector which, with all due respect, rarely got anything done. The Reports on the merits or otherwise of the use of Swindon proportions on the A4 Pacifics had been received and parroted forward in letters to the CMEE at Doncaster, which produced no reaction.

One of the letters was seen by Peter Townend, who knew that it would get nowhere without a recommendation. He amended the letter to include the

GALTEE MORE, fresh from general overhaul, pulls away from Grantham with a down slow train in 1932. It appears to be one of the immortal articulated sets that carried commuters into and out of London from the GN and GE suburbs. The boiler is a Diagram 94 boiler 27039 and the GN tender No.5283. (Rev. A C Cawston, courtesy Brian Bailey)

CENTENARY, with the up Yorkshire Pullman and bearing the old LNER headboard restored post-war, approaching Potters Bar on October 24th 1947. Here she was a Kings Cross engine, but most of her time was spent at Grantham. The A3 has Diagram 94A boiler No.27012 and GN tender No.5257. (Rev. A C Cawston, courtesy Brian Bailey)

recommendation to fit double Kylchaps, and made sure that it went to Parker himself for signature instead of the usual practice. Eventually the CMEE replied, undertaking to modify the Swindon proportions. The well-known saying about deckchairs on the Titanic would have been appropriate here. There was a prejudice in the LMSR team at the 'Kremlin' (Board HQ, Marylebone) against using double exhausts, despite the considerable improvement in the performance of DUCHESS OF ABERCORN on test in 1939. The double Kylchap seemed to be regarded as the work of the Devil, and the official view was that it would obstruct tube cleaning, and would be too complicated and time consuming to remove and replace. This was of course the view of people with little or no experience of the Kylchap exhaust; in fact its stronger draught made tube cleaning unnecessary. Indeed the quieter and less raucous exhaust reduced noise and vibration which actually reduced maintenance and servicing. It demonstrated the perennial truth that even in matters of science and engineering fact, there was nothing like a good personal prejudice to overrule good sense.

I believe Parker was inclined to express his views sharply, which was not well received at Doncaster. Things

were getting nowhere, attitudes became entrenched, and crews continued to struggle with poor steaming. The idea of using investment to secure improvement, justified by the saving in coal, came to Peter Townend when Shedmaster at Kings Cross. The tests had to be carried out without the help or equipment of the CMEE, but eventually the case was made, and the CMEE was directed to carry out the work. Even so, there was displeasure at the centre at an unauthorised design alteration – which one suspects would have been stopped had they known. So the achievement of having the single blast Gresley Pacifics fitted with double Kylchaps, even as late as 1957 for the A4s and 1958 for the A3s, and in the teeth of opposition from both the Kremlin and Doncaster, was one of the highest order. The names of Messrs. Townend, Fiennes and Miller and their colleagues are fondly remembered by engineers and enthusiasts alike for what was achieved. A member of the Eastern Area Board that authorised the expenditure was one Alan Pegler!

Before the war, firemen spent many years firing, and became more skilled as a result. After the war for a variety of reasons, firemen were changed, promoted or left. With the arrival of diesel traction and the need to release

footplatemen for training, large numbers of firemen were changed and their replacements came from almost anywhere. The fireman to Driver Duckmanton on Peppercorn A1 60156 GREAT CENTRAL came from Canklow, originally on the LM. He viewed 268 miles to Newcastle and back on an A1 as the easiest day's work that he had ever experienced. It just didn't compare with a slog from Somers Town to Masborough with a Black Five or a Crab; then, you really knew you had done a day's work. After 1957 when West Riding depots from the ER and LMR had been subsumed into the NER, LM crews at Holbeck used A3s on the hard Leeds-Carlisle route. Several found them the best steam locos they had used, with free steaming and fast running.

Locomotive repair and maintenance would have been regarded as revenue expenditure, an operational cost. New construction would have been charged against capital expenditure, but the use of capital investment to secure improvement and reduced expenditure in an area traditionally regarded as a maintenance function was novel. Would that it had been used earlier for such as manganese liners, roller bearings and servicing aids.

We were used to the idea that A4s were fast and powerful locomotives.

What I think we were not prepared for, was the enormous improvement in A3 running with that simple modification. It seemed to give the engines another 10-15mph. They had, after all, been swept aside by the Peppercorn A1s. What we saw was a reversal of that process, amazingly. The A3s, now with light loads and tight schedules, ran like the A4s very often. PAPYRUS demonstrated in 1935 that the A3 could run fast, very fast. FIRDAUSSI confirmed to Gresley that a 'green engine' could time the Silver Jubilee, and in 1939 TRIGO and SINGAPORE cut the schedule of the Coronation significantly. A particular joy for us in the south was the sight of gleaming A3s alongside A4s and A1s, on the top trains, running with the same ease as their newer sisters.

Later, I travelled in the cab many times over many years. It was the best place to assess one's track, to learn a fresh area, to familiarise oneself with the signalling and the power distribution system on electrified railways. It was unusual for the driver, even the younger ones, not to drift back to the early days on steam engines. I remember a driver on a Class 86 reflecting to me, as we lurched and bounced along the West

Coast main line at 100mph, that 'Any b****y fool can start a steam engine, but it takes a Driver to drive it and stop it.' Then there was the Penzance man, waiting for the road at St.Germans with his HST, emphasising to me passionately how his old Grange 6829 would pull anything and go anywhere. Or the ex-Haymarket fireman, driving his 4-CIG non-stop from Brighton to Victoria, talking wistfully about his runs on the Elizabethan, in the days when enginemen were not merely bus drivers.

The virtue of the steam locomotive was that one got out of it what one put in. Having mastered the skills of firing and driving this simple machine, it ran well. If you made a mess of it, well... there it was. Try again. There was a reward for a job done well as the machine responded, like the animal with which the steam locomotive is so often compared. In many thousands of miles with drivers over the years, it was surprising how many would reminisce about their earlier years on steam locomotives.

PRETTY POLLY was the unfortunate engine's name, and though it was a famous filly it was still most unsuitable for an express locomotive, by a short head (to coin a phrase) from one or two others. She was a hard working and regular performer however; almost an omnipresent sight whenever a camera was pointed at the GN main line. Everyone it seems had a shot at 60061. The illustration is unique for it is when the down main was temporarily slued into the new down slow alignment at Hadley Wood to pass through the new Hadley South Tunnel on April 21st 1959. 60061 only ran for a year with a double chimney before the small deflectors were added. Boiler: 94A(27033) Tender: GN (5290). (John F Aylard)

The driver of 2552 SANSOVINO gets the right away at Grantham with an up service. The large somersault bracket signal was rarely photographed – cameras were either pointed back towards locos standing in the station or southwards towards down trains arriving at the station. (T G Hepburn, Rail Archive Stephenson)

Chapter Three
An Outline of A3 History

The history of the Gresley A1s and A3s was set out in *The Book of the A3 Pacifics*, but for the sake of those without that access, a simplified and updated history is given below.

Sir Nigel Gresley introduced the first GNR Pacific on April 11th 1922, GREAT NORTHERN, followed by 1471 on July 10th 1922. The GNR ordered a further ten A1s, delivered during the LNER's tenure. The second A1 was named SIR FREDERICK BANBURY on November 10th of the same year, after the Chairman of the GNR. Looking back to 1922, it was perhaps surprising, remembering the later prominence of Top Shed at Kings Cross, that both of the Great Northern Railway's A1 Pacifics should be allocated to Doncaster. The latter's importance was reinforced subsequently when the ten A1s, ordered by the GNR but adopted by the LNER in 1923, were built. Five – half the batch – went to Doncaster, three to Grantham, and only two, 4474 AND 4475, were at Kings Cross.

The LNER then ordered forty A1s, twenty from Doncaster and twenty from the North British Locomotive Co, built to the Group standard profile as pioneered with 4481. The fifteen A1s built for the NE area were fitted with the Westinghouse braking system which was in use with NER rolling stock. The equipment, which had included trip gear as a sort of mechanical precursor to AWS, was removed in the early 1930s. One curiosity was that the newly built Pacifics at Doncaster were sent to Gorton for a few weeks running-in, and one wonders why and how. Clambering up to Woodhead would hardly seem like running-in. Gorton had a works adjacent, and the Beyer-Peacock works was nearby. Gorton had a good reputation, but one would have thought Doncaster Works and Carr Loco could have dealt with them. John Robinson and Nigel Gresley had an amiable friendship by all accounts, but I suspect that Percy McClure the Motive Power Superintendent, an ex-GCR man, might well have set the arrangement up. The NB-built A1s were run in at their first depots, as was the usual practice.

The allocations suggest to me that the GN main line was operated by A1s working up to London and returning with a down service. Most services could be covered in this way. Kings Cross was ill-prepared for the arrival of numbers of large locomotives, and much of the northern end of the terminus had only recently been rebuilt. That project included the construction of a station loco yard and turntable just west of the south portal of Gasworks Tunnel. Prior to that, Pacifics went out to Hornsey shed to turn. There was a turntable behind the depot and another on the down side, but from the available photographs a larger one appears to have been installed, presumably for eight coupled freight locos, just north of the depot on the up side at the time. Top Shed was restricted in capacity and an increase in allocation, especially of large locos, was considered unwise at the time.

The twenty A1s from Doncaster Works went to the old GN depots, and the twenty from the North British Loco Co were shared between Gateshead, Heaton and Haymarket. Kings Cross and Grantham had six each, while Doncaster gained a further eight, making fifteen in all. Gateshead received ten straight off, Heaton and Haymarket five each. The Doncaster Pacifics worked the express and fast freight services to and from Yorkshire, as it was not until the 1930s strengthening of the Calder

From May 1925 until early 1926, the new 2561 ran anonymously before being named MINORU. She was a stalwart over nearly 40 years on the GN section of the East Coast main line. The location is not specified, but the NE 4-4-0 in the background suggests York. The A1 has Diagram 94 boiler 7780, and her GN tender No.5271.

A rare photograph of LNER No.2553 in 1925-26, then named MANNA. See also PRINCE OF WALES page 80. The A1 has Diagram 94 boiler 7771 and a GN tender, No.5263.

Viaduct at Wakefield that they were allowed to work over the route to Leeds. Later two A1s were allocated to Copley Hill, 2553 PRINCE OF WALES and 2555 CENTENARY.

The names selected by the LNER for the A1s and subsequently the A3s, were mainly winners of horse racing classics, with exceptions; PRINCE OF WALES, CENTENARY, WILLIAM WHITELAW, FLYING SCOTSMAN, SIR FREDERICK BANBURY and DICK TURPIN. The last-named, despite the obvious equine connection, was not the name of a classic winner. Comparison with the lists of selected names and those actually used revealed some interesting possibilities, and while some were rejected understandably, one wonders why the better ones were not used in place of some of the more curious ones retained. Individual histories are annotated with intended and actual names for each A3. The names were not necessarily attached by the time of entering traffic in each case.

In 1925 the A1 was tested against the GWR Castle, and although the trials were too short to be of great value, it was clear that the Castle was the better engine by some distance. The broad piston rings were being replaced with narrow rings at Doncaster at the time, which reduced the amount of leakage. However, it was clear to Bert Spencer, Gresley's Technical Assistant, that the valve gear needed redesigning, and a modified arrangement was fitted to GAY CRUSADER in February 1926. The results were sufficiently encouraging for Spencer to continue pressing Gresley until it was agreed, a year later, to modify an A1 with a new design of valve

gear. The engine was CENTENARY, and it was immediately clear that her fuel and water consumption were significantly reduced. Gresley himself travelled on CENTENARY and authorised the conversion of the remaining 51 A1s.

The second improvement was less obvious, that of a higher boiler pressure, and to that end Gresley ordered five 220psi boilers in 1927. They were fitted to ENTERPRISE and LEMBERG in 1927 and HARVESTER, BAYARDO and SHOTOVER in 1928. The cylinders of LEMBERG were lined down to 18¼ins to give parity of tractive effort with the 180psi A1, while the other four retained their 20ins cylinders. LEMBERG was then tested against SOLARIO, a conventional A1, and it was no surprise that the results were almost identical. It was surprising that ENTERPRISE, with 20ins cylinders, was not included, but I doubt it would have made much difference in the long run. The new A1s were not received at Gateshead and Heaton with unalloyed enthusiasm at first, and there were a few occasions where the steaming was at fault. The three reboilered NE Pacifics were a help in that respect. At the time it was decided to classify the rebuilds A3/1 where the cylinder diameter was unchanged at 20ins, A3/2 in the sole case of 2544. The new A3s were to be A3/3. The subdivisions seem to have been more clerical than mechanical and were dropped a decade or so later.

Through working between London and Newcastle started in 1927, and the non-stop Flying Scotsman started in 1928. This precipitated a fairly extensive exchange of A1s in 1927-28. Three

Southern Area A1s selected, FLYING SCOTSMAN (Doncaster), DONCASTER and ROYAL LANCER (Grantham) were not at Kings Cross, and had to be transferred in exchange for PRINCE OF WALES (to Doncaster) and DIAMOND JUBILEE and HERMIT to Grantham. One can understand 4472 FLYING SCOTSMAN being selected but quite why the others in particular, one might ask? Low mileage, certainly, long travel valves and conversion to Group standard profile as far as 2547 DONCASTER, 4472 and 4476 ROYAL LANCER were concerned. The two other Kings Cross A1s, 4474 VICTOR WILD and 4475 FLYING FOX were not ready, but were converted to long travel valves by July 1928, although VICTOR WILD could not be used until converted to Group standard profile in 1933. I think we may assume that the two A1s were most recently outshopped, and sent with 4472 to bolster Top Shed's Non-stop team.

Just as the Southern Area engines selected had to be transferred to Kings Cross, those from the Scottish Area were loaned from Gateshead and Heaton. Only one of the Haymarket quintet, 2565 MERRY HAMPTON had been overhauled with long travel valves, while 2563 WILLIAM WHITELAW had received a light repair with valve conversion. The others were overhauled in the following months. So there was a similar need to that of Kings Cross for additional power. Two of the three Pacifics loaned were 220psi rebuilds, HARVESTER and SHOTOVER, while Gateshead were not impressed at the selection of their best A1, GLADIATEUR, as the third. The story of Gateshead's procrastination and the shambles involving tenders with vacuum and Westinghouse braking systems, followed almost inevitably by reversion to using Haymarket's A1s, was well told in the RCTS *Locomotives of the LNER*.

While at Haymarket, HARVESTER was used to establish clearance for wider Pacific operation in Scotland. WILLIAM WHITELAW was tested over the Waverley route with unconvincing results, but a later test with SHOTOVER was successful and, shortly after, three of the first ten A3s were sent to Carlisle Canal. Of the eight A3s built in 1930, three new A3s went to Haymarket, leading to the transfer of A1s to Eastfield, Tay Bridge and Ferryhill as well as St.Margarets in Edinburgh. Five more A3s, and then A4s from 1936 onwards brought Pacific power to many more services.

The 1930s were great years for the A1s and A3s. The work of the Doncaster engines on the Breakfast Flyer was good, but the two high speed trials revealed the locomotives' capacity for speed. The first run, which nearly finished before the south portal of Gasworks Tunnel, was justly famous, especially having reached 100 mph for the first time. The handling of FLYING SCOTSMAN at speed is interesting. Sparshatt's use of a cut-off as long as 54% at full regulator has been criticised by locomotive men as the hammering that it undoubtedly was.

The record card at the NRM is however endorsed to record the fitting of a 'special blastpipe' a few days before the trial run itself. Quite what that meant is unclear, and there is no associated correspondence to shed any light on it. A French variable blastpipe had been fitted to 4472 for about a year from May 1927, after which it was transferred to Gateshead's 2575 for nearly a further year. A type used on several railways in France, it functioned through the raising or lowering of a shaped choke (*trèfle*) inside the blastpipe. Apart from regulating the cross-section of the exhaust, it spread the exhaust into a number of jets. No record of its performance could be found, and I would imagine the file would have been endorsed 'Too Difficult'. It required an understanding of the mechanics of combustion that would have been beyond most crews of the day.

The GWR used a jumper blastpipe in which the exhaust pressure lifted a moveable cap to expose additional orifices. This would have been present on both CALDICOT and PENDENNIS CASTLE in the 1925 Exchanges. However, at the time Andre Chapelon was experimenting in France with different types such as the Kyläla, which led to the development of the Kylchap design. A Kyläla blastpipe was tested on a D49, and Chapelon himself rode on the engine. Peter Townend's recollection is that 4472's was said to be an adjustable blastpipe such as one with a jumper top. This was the pattern used in the A4s less than a year later. The blastpipe and chimney needed to work together so that the chimney was exactly filled with the exhausting steam in order to maintain the smokebox vacuum. If a column of exhaust steam was too large or too small, the vacuum reduced and the steaming rate was impaired. The use of such a long cut-off suggests that the A1 was at its maximum speed, but the back pressure would have tended to throttle her. Hitherto, reducing the orifice diameter and hence increasing the velocity of the exhaust was considered the best way to improve the evaporation rate, but in that it increased back pressure in the cylinders, it was counterproductive. However, Andre Chapelon's influence, through his friendship with Gresley, was being felt at Doncaster. Gresley served on a committee of the UIC (*Union Internationals des Chemins de Fer*) and was aware of the developments on the Continent, especially the work of Chapelon. Already, the Kylchap exhaust was being used on the Mikados. So possibly the orifice diameter was increased and not reduced. An intriguing puzzle.

Both the A1s and A3s were not hard on maintenance, so long as one understood the unique requirements of the 2:1 gear. A number of frame failures were dealt with by splicing new frame sections, while the Doncaster boiler in both 180 and 220psi forms was particularly reliable and economical. Occasionally an A1 or A3 would be fitted with a blastpipe with a half inch increase, that became standard in 1934. There

There was no finer sight than an express locomotive going hard on a rising gradient, and Hitchin was one of the best places to see up expresses working hard at speed. Many hours have been spent there by enthusiasts, and the sound of an up express was audible from south of Three Counties, the exhaust growing louder but just a little slower as it drew nearer. Peter Handford, in his Transacord series, made two wonderfully nostalgic recordings of up expresses here. The A3 is KNIGHT OF THISTLE, and judging by the passengers on the platform, it would be 773up, the 7.25 from Grantham. The picture illustrates a danger to all who went on or near the track: as we turned to admire the spectacle of a speeding train, hidden in the trailing exhaust is another train approaching, its sight and sound obscured by the first train both for us and the second driver. The date is March 28th 1959, and the A3 has a Diagram 94A boiler (27027) and a GN tender No.5285. (A E Bennett, transporttreasury.co.uk)

SCEPTRE with the 6.55 from Newcastle to Doncaster leaving Darlington on February 22nd 1953. The Diagram 94A boiler is No.27020 and the GN tender is No.5258. (R E Vincent, transporttreasury.co.uk)

were some engines which were indifferent performers. Certainly there were some which were less commonly seen, and which one heard poor accounts of from drivers and others.

As mentioned earlier, the magnificent run by PAPYRUS in 1935 showed the advance in performance that was achieved in the A3 design. It was confirmed by the performances of FIRDAUSSI on the Silver Jubilee in late 1935, and by the famous runs in 1939 by TRIGO and SINGAPORE. Indeed the two last-mentioned quite probably included high speeds in the descent of Stoke bank. Even the A1 could run fast, as witness the work on the Breakfast Flyer. SOLARIO made a famous run on the Scarborough Flyer, and in 1938, she worked the Coronation forward from Grantham and then through to Kings Cross from Edinburgh. The war and its aftermath cast a shadow over the more spirited A3 performances for a decade and nearly another after that.

As the number of Pacifics increased, supplemented in the late 1930s by new V2s, the LNER motive power authorities sought to use Pacifics in new areas and on new routes. The A1s had been used on the GC, and a number were sent to Gorton, Leicester and Neasden. With the outbreak of war, they were

returned, but a number went to New England and Gorton in the 1940s, possibly as a wartime measure to avoid the blitz. Post-war, in 1949, a dozen or so A3s were sent to Leicester and Neasden, and several others had shorter spells there. Returning A3s from Leicester seemed to be in excellent condition. The number of A3s and V2s, compared with the number of services on the GC, seemed quite out of proportion.

The same might be said of the quintet at Neville Hill. A3s were sent to Neville Hill before the onset of war, but were taken back. Again, after the war, the same A3s were sent back with two more. Neville Hill worked one leg of the Queen of Scots Pullman between Leeds and Newcastle, and part of the North Briton, plus some cross-country services. Later the through working was extended between Leeds and Edinburgh and Glasgow as part of an attempt to extend loco diagrams that was cut short by the wartime rostering. Nevertheless, visits to the depot usually revealed three Pacifics, if not more, on shed. One of the problems with steam traction was the large number of locos needed to cover not only the rostered duties, but inspections, maintenance and stoppages for repairs as well.

Carlisle Canal's Pacifics worked the Waverley route, and occasionally the Carlisle-Newcastle road, although the latter seemed to feature Gateshead Pacifics rather than Canal's. After tests with an A1, WILLIAM WHITELAW, in 1927 and an A3, SHOTOVER, in 1928, an A3, ENTERPRISE, was sent there in December 1928. She was returned six months later, unpopular and allegedly run down. This story deserves closer scrutiny. The unpopularity is understandable. The Waverley route was a hard route, and the arrival of a locomotive with her original 20in cylinders and hence a tractive effort some 50% greater than the usual express power was bound to ask questions of her drivers. The adhesive factor of the reboilered A1 had been significantly reduced which meant, bluntly, that the locomotive was more liable to slip. As to her condition, ENTERPRISE had a light and two heavy repairs before going to Canal, a light repair at Cowlairs during her time at Canal, and another heavy repair after returning to Kings Cross. I guess that the problem really lay more with poor steaming – remembering that Waverley route firemen were unused to a 41.25 sq.ft. grate – and a cracked frame. However, her allegedly poor condition was not such as to require general overhaul for another year.

CAPTAIN CUTTLE had already been sent new to Canal, followed by COLORADO and FLAMINGO as ENTERPRISE was sent south. A decade later, SIR VISTO joined the A3s, and a year it became a quintet later with the arrival of CORONACH. After the war, the number fell to four for over a decade until the arrival of diesel traction. In retrospect one wonders why the A3s were not replaced by V2s, which were regularly used from St.Margarets in any case. Speeds were restrained by gravity or line limits on the banks, and what was needed was pulling power at 30-40mph.

Other routes were circumscribed by the RA9 route availability of the A3s, but occasionally they worked from York to Scarborough or Hull, and over the Joint line from Doncaster to March. As the steam era closed, with routes having been strengthened over the decades, A3s were used on lines that would have been barred in times past. ST SIMON was on a railtour over the Southern Region in 1963, a long way from 1923! In preservation, FLYING SCOTSMAN has run over routes that would have seemed not merely impossible but ludicrous half a century before.

The original allocation of the A1s and A3s, Area by Area, remained broadly true until about 1950. The first twelve remained in the Southern Area, apart from three trial periods; GREAT NORTHERN on rebuilding, ENTERPRISE at Carlisle in 1928, and ST SIMON, new, in the north east. The twenty A1s built at Doncaster largely remained in the Southern Area, until the late 1930s when LEMBERG and THE TETRARCH moved to Gateshead and ORMONDE went to Haymarket. In the late 1950s a boundary change took four more, BLINK BONNY, PRINCE PALATINE, SANSOVINO and BLAIR ATHOL to Newcastle. PRINCE PALATINE, the last A3, actually finished running at St.Margarets, in January 1966.

The twenty A1s remained in the NE Area, provided one counts in Neville Hill, and later, Leeds in general, which worked north in the NE Area, with the exception of BAYARDO. Carlisle Canal was more of a Scottish depot rather than NE. The five Scottish A1s remained in Scotland until 1950, although SIR VISTO moved to Carlisle in 1940. The major change was the transfer for the other four, now rebuilt as A3s, to the Southern Area in exchange for A3s in 1950. This was in response to the Scottish Region, which wished to have only left-hand drive Pacifics. The reason was that the trade unions had pressed for left-hand drive locos in place of the ex-A1s, which were still right-hand drive. I suspect that this was driven by the conclusion of the Inspecting Officer, following an accident in which the right-hand driving position had been offered as a contributory cause, despite two decades of successful running with that alleged handicap on the A1s. Why the two remaining ex-A1s, ORMONDE and SIR VISTO were not sent south as well was a question asked by many at the lineside.

The first batch of ten A3s, as built, comprised seven Southern Area and three Scottish engines sent to Carlisle Canal. Interestingly, Haymarket, which one would have thought was a deserving case, received none. Two subsequently moved to the north, one NE Area (FAIRWAY) and one Scottish (CORONACH). In 1950/51 the remaining five Southern Area 1928 A3s were sent north in exchange for the four former A1s. Of the second 1930 batch, five went to the NE Area and three to Haymarket, that shed's first A3s. One NE engine, BLENHEIM, moved to Haymarket later. Of the final nine, five went to Haymarket and four to Gateshead. Subsequently SANDWICH moved to the Southern Area and CAMERONIAN to Gateshead, but the seven others remained in the same area.

****

Summarising. of the twenty-seven A3s as built, seven went to the Southern Area, nine to the NE Area and eleven to the Scottish Area. By 1950, the Scottish Region had seventeen, the NE Region still had nine, and the former Southern Area, now the Eastern Region, had only SANDWICH. But shed no tears for the Eastern and North Eastern, for

Carlisle's SIR VISTO rolls into Carlisle with an up express off the Waverley route on April 18th 1955. She has a Diagram 94A boiler No.27036 and a GN tender No.5224. (J Robertson, transporttreasury.co.uk).

An up Class H unfitted freight approaches Damdykes from the north behind NIGHT HAWK on November 8th 1952. This location is the same as for LEMBERG (on page 62) with the pre-war LNER mechanical single aspect colour light signals again well shown. This design in effect substituted the powerful Adlake lamp, with the coloured filters from the spectacle plate on the semaphore arm, as the driver's permission to proceed. The shortened semaphore arm can be seen to the right of the post. Boiler: Diagram 94A No.27014, GN tender No.5288. (Jim Smith)

they had twenty-two new Peppercorn A1s each! This resulted in the notebooks of young enthusiasts in the south having large yawning holes where the original A3s occurred, with only SANDWICH commonly seen and MANNA and BOOK LAW if they were vigilant! PAPYRUS and HUMORIST were sadly missed. Peter Townend told me that the latter would not have gone north if he had been at Kings Cross!

It was my original intention in Chapter 8 to provide constructive comment on each individual locomotive, but that was unrealistic. Many of the class continued to work steadily, unremarkably and uneventfully over the years, and there is little to say beyond their deployment and personal reminiscence. Lack of comment should not be assumed to imply that the loco was regarded as a black sheep. Certainly there were some in the earlier post-war years that were no loss when they were transferred away, but the subsequent recovery was marvellous to see. As had been said many times to me, 'the number of the cab side no longer mattered'.

The arrival of the A4s and the streamliners was such a publicity coup for the LNER that the impression took hold that the A3s had been surpassed and the Gresley A1s were very much second rate traction. It was not said of course, but the transfer of A1s to the

GC section was seen to be evidence of that fact. However, the A3s, as they all became, were not so far behind the A4s as all that. They were a smooth riding locomotive, no different in handling or firing from the A4, fleet of foot but less powerful. Once freed from the limitations on steaming, with lighter trains from 1956, the A3s ran well. Post-war, classification as 7P, in contrast to the Peppercorn A1s and A4s which were 8Ps, kept the A3s off the principal turns which were rostered for an 8P locomotive. This restriction was observed more closely by some than others, but if time was booked against a 7P, there would be awkward questions from Control or Motive Power! With the reduction in loading in 1956/57, the A3s were nearer parity with the A4s, and the classification system seemed less important.

To trace Pacific movements hereon, one needs to study the *Register* of W.B. Yeadon, a remarkable and comprehensive record mentioned in the Preface. I acknowledge readily that I have quoted from it, a far larger and more authentic archive than my own, in assembling histories of each locomotive. I have added the life mileage for each locomotive to the details, conscious of the shortcomings of the system and its vulnerability to typing errors. The records kept are often incomplete, for example, noting when

a new blastpipe was fitted (sometimes at the shed) but failing to note if or when it was removed. A number of the transfers recorded were in fact short term with the loco returning to her previous home shed subsequently. This was often because cover was required for a Pacific away at shops, possibly for unforeseen repairs – unclassified or casual repairs. Overhauls took an engine out of traffic for far longer in those days. For example, MELTON went from Grantham to Doncaster for just over a week when two months old, followed by a week at Gorton but returned to Doncaster. Likewise she went to Grantham for two months and Kings Cross for three in 1930. One needs to remember that in the absence of an A1, either a K3 or Ivatt large Atlantic would have to deputise back then.

The one contentious event that stands out in the history of these fine locomotives involved the first one, GREAT NORTHERN. Edward Thompson, on succeeding Sir Nigel, made a number of basic changes, the most important being the future eradication of the conjugated valve gear. The P2 Mikados required urgent attention, and the opportunity was taken to incorporate separate valve gear and divided drive in the rebuilt loco. The order for the last batch V2s was amended so that the last four were built at Darlington as Pacifics. Thompson had introduced a series of standard classes intended, amongst other benefits, to reduce the variety of different parts that were needed by depots for maintenance. Encouraged by the assumed success of his ten Pacifics, he produced an outline design for the new standard express passenger locomotive which would, in due course, displace the Gresley Pacifics.

In principle it was faultless. It associated the 41.25 sq.ft. grate, a double Kylchap exhaust and the excellent A4 boiler, with a new front end including divided drive and three cylinders with enlarged piston valves. On paper it would have been the best Pacific on the old LNER. That Pacific was of course GREAT NORTHERN. There is an irony here, in that Thompson's arguably best Pacific was a Gresley engine in nearly all respects other than the most significant. The critical change was the move away from unified drive with conjugated valve gear. This latter arrangement limited the diameters of the cylinders and valves, whereas divided drive allowed the use of 10ins piston valves and 19ins cylinders. Thompson was of course intent on eliminating the conjugated gear, which resulted in the infamous extended front end. Although the main frames of Gresley's big engines could well have been stronger, his favoured layout with cylinders in line abreast, 2:1 gear and

unified drive was fairly robust. Unfortunately for Thompson, the change to divided drive left the loco chassis significantly weaker, which impacted on the riding and need for maintenance attention. The insistence on equal length connecting rods simply made the problem worse. A further consequence was the arrangement whereby exhaust steam from the outside cylinders reached the blastpipe which had all the appearance of a last-minute lash-up, and was a constant leakage problem.

The eleven new Pacifics – six ex-Mikados, four based on V2s, and 4470 – were strong and free steaming, but they were prone to wheelslip. Although on test GREAT NORTHERN returned economical figures for coal and water, in practice the Thompson Pacifics all too often were driven with longer cut-offs and their appetites were excessive as fires were ripped apart by the powerful exhaust. With only six Gresley Kylchap engines in service, there was not a great deal of experience in handling Kylchap engines among footplate crews other than in the senior links at Kings Cross. It was strange that Thompson, who cared very much about the appearance of his locomotives and produced several handsome designs, was not concerned to improve the appearance of his Pacifics.

The main problem lay in the manner of the creation of the new standard express locomotive. This was done not by new construction but by rebuilding an existing locomotive, and Thompson chose to rebuild Gresley's first Pacific, GREAT NORTHERN. Whether he regarded the conversion of Gresley's first Pacific as a sort of messianic act, a first step in removing the 2:1 gear that he disliked, we will never know. No doubt Thompson considered his design an improvement on the 180psi A1, and there is no doubt that he was quite correct. There were eighteen of the 180psi Pacifics left, now classified A10, but despite advice and appeals from his assistants, Thompson was not for changing.

GREAT NORTHERN was a historic locomotive which, all other things being equal, would have graced the National Railway Museum along with its GNR predecessors, such was its importance. For an earlier generation, GNR 1470 was a very special locomotive indeed, an icon as one might say today, and Thompson's decision to rebuild her was regarded as an act of vandalism or worse. There was a great deal of anger both outside and inside the LNER, which, for a long while coloured opinions on Thompson's work. The received wisdom for my generation was that this was the destruction of a

The early morning express from Sunderland coasts down through Greenwood behind Heaton's SUNSTAR on June 11th 1951. Heaton Pacifics worked up to London on this turn, returning on the 17.35 Newcastle in the evening, remanned at Grantham, until the winter book of that year. The A3 is in BR blue; Diagram 94A boiler No.8780 and A3 non-corridor tender No.5476. (Rev. A C Cawston, courtesy Brian Bailey)

perfectly sound locomotive. The rebuilt locomotive had reduced cab sheets, a long smokebox, a stovepipe chimney and even a new straight nameplate, which made it look very much a cartoon of the original A1 Pacific. Shortly after a Gresley cab was fitted, together with a pair of enormous smoke deflectors, improving the appearance somewhat.

GREAT NORTHERN, after the initial years of fame, had become an unremarkable but hard working member of the Gresley A1 class. By the time of rebuilding her accrued mileage was in line with her sisters. However, by all accounts the old A1 of the 1940s was not an impressive performer, and by that time much of the original had been replaced or renewed. There was no doubt that, rebuilt, GREAT NORTHERN was a far better locomotive. However, many both inside and outside the industry respected Sir Nigel Gresley and resented the choice of his first Pacific. It did not help that 4470 looked as she did. By all accounts Thompson was not a good man manager and alienated a number of staff, which might explain the quality of some of the design and construction work on the elongated front end.

The importance of the rebuilt GREAT NORTHERN emerged after the retirement of Edward Thompson. Under his leadership, in 1945 he had secured LNER Board agreement to a post-war five year plan which included no less than 75 Pacifics, perhaps somewhat excessive for a company that already possessed over 300 Pacifics and V2s. I often wondered whether this plan envisaged the eventual withdrawal of the earlier A1s, for the LNER certainly did not need so many large locomotives. Thompson's successor, Arthur Peppercorn, thought differently, and restored the bogie to its normal position for the second batch of A2 Pacifics, and for the subsequent build of 49 A1 Pacifics. The A1 differed from Thompson's prototype in that the new Diagram 118 boiler had a 50 sq.ft. grate. Although their capabilities were masked in the earlier years by post-war mediocrity, the A1s were a very capable and successful class, worthy successors to the Gresley A1s and A3s. In a way, the loss of GREAT NORTHERN was compensated by the emergence of Peppercorn's A1s.

The rebuilt GREAT NORTHERN, its dark blue livery, worked along with the other newer Pacifics. Later its livery changed to apple green, then BR blue, and finally dark green. The nameplate was embellished with the GNR coat of arms, and later fitted with a rimmed chimney. After working from Gateshead and Haymarket, she settled down to main line work from Kings Cross, until displaced by Peppercorn A1s. She went to New England, which tended to be something of a home for Thompson Pacifics – hardly a vote of confidence – but was then sent to Grantham where she was used on main line work.

With the reorganisation of the Grantham top link with regular manning, GREAT NORTHERN was one of the six locomotives chosen. She was replaced early on by another Peppercorn A1, and was used as a pool engine from then on. Her reliability was rather lower than the Peppercorn A1s that succeeded her and her visits to Doncaster Works were slightly longer due to her uniqueness. There was a period when she worked the slow service to Doncaster following the down Flying Scotsman, returning later in the afternoon. I remember seeing a plate in her cab with the words 'Grantham Pilot. Return to Grantham immediately.' It was said that there was some trouble with the coupled wheels shifting on the axles, and she was under observation from Doncaster Works. GREAT NORTHERN continued to work as a pool engine like many other A1s, both at Grantham and Doncaster, from where she was withdrawn in late 1962.

ST FRUSQUIN, a NE engine throughout its life, at York with an ECS train. The date must after May 1961 when it received the A4 boiler but, through an oversight, no trough deflectors. Those of us who didn't have to drive them were less keen aesthetically on the deflectors, but safety was paramount. The A3 has Diagram 107 boiler 29324, and her GN tender was No.5257 or 5287.

THE WHITE KNIGHT coasts through Doncaster with an express from Tyne Commission Quay on May 23rd 1959. No doubt the photographer was waiting for SIR NIGEL GRESLEY with the 112mph railtour on that famous day. Boiler 94A (27048) Tender A3 non-corridor (5581). (R Wilson, transporttreasury.co.uk)

One of the rarest of visitors to the south in post-war years, BLENHEIM gets under way with an Aberdeen or Perth express on July 5th 1959 through Princes Street Gardens in Edinburgh. 'Express' was a somewhat relative term on the Perth line, constituted as it was with odd bits of route originally built as parts of other railways, and infested with permanent speed restrictions (PSRs) and a heavy climb to Glenfarg. Although Haymarket worked most services, in later years ex-LMSR 4-6-0s from Perth shared in the work; 44720 and 44721 were regular visitors with the occasional Jubilee. The A3 has Diagram 94A boiler No.27006 and an A3 non-corridor tender No.5572. (J Robertson, transporttreasury.co.uk).

Chapter 4
Names

The A3s, as witness the fame of FLYING SCOTSMAN, had, and still have a special place in people's affections. Of course one is conditioned by one's own memories, and there may even be people who recall fondly Ivatt's Class 4 2-6-0 or Bulleid's Q1 0-6-0 with affection. And why not indeed? The A3s, like the A4s, Duchesses, Scots, Castles, Kings and the Peppercorn A1s were all part of a wonderful collection, a veritable treasury, and all valuable in sentimental terms. No doubt those who struggled in the smoke, heat, wet, cold and filth to keep them going would have regarded that as nonsense, but the army of locomotive engineers in preservation is evidence that the steam engine has been forgiven its shortcomings and is rightly prized today.

The names of the A3s are fascinating. The names owners bestowed on their champions are many and various, and some downright eccentric. My old friend Dr Geoffrey Hughes, former Editor of the *Gresley Observer* and expert in matters LNER, has for a long while sought to find who actually put their hand to the racing world's equivalent of Wisden in order to select the names.

While we might wonder who should bear the blame for not having the sense to reject some of the most unsuitable, the ranks of classic race winners contain far worse that could grace a loco. At one time 2596 was to be named COMMON, but fortunately wiser views prevailed and she became MANNA.

Whether for many those odd names actually emphasised the link between the iron horse and the living animal I cannot say, but it did for me, and that feeling has never quite gone. I still remember reading about the retirement in 1962 of CHARLIE, the last shunting horse, at Newmarket. That would have sat oddly on an A3! In Cornwall as in many parts of the country, working horses such as Suffolk Punches, Shires and Percherons are kept by such as retired farmers, and these magnificent animals, typical of those that actually worked alongside their iron brethren in small railway yards, resound to the names of CAPTAIN, BLUEBELL, BOBBY, ROBIN, etc. These too, might have sounded strange on an A3, especially to those more used to Castles, Granges, Manors and Halls! To some from another part of the country, without the link of

familiarity, the names must have seemed not just odd but incredible. SANDWICH may have been fine for a golf course, but a strange name for a horse, and a silly one for 150 tons or so of machinery. Perhaps it was not so plain daft as PRETTY POLLY, but horses often had the sort of name that one might hesitate to apply for example, to an ocean liner.

Local A3s such as SOLARIO, MINORU, CENTENARY, etc were almost old friends, and even the less happy names had the same familiarity about them. And then one stumbles over locomotive names in quite unexpected places. For example, musing some while ago among the ruins of Dunkeld Cathedral, I suddenly realised that the marble memorial that I was looking at was dedicated to 'Niel Gow' a 'fine Scottish fiddler' (sic) born in the district. Memories of one of our rarer North Eastern visitors, Heaton's 60082, came flooding back quite inappropriately. In fact the name of the racehorse was mis-spelt as *NEIL* GOW, since the name was an abbreviation of Nathaniel. The A3 is correctly named after the animal if not the musician.

BOOK LAW with the relief to the 7.52 from Sunderland, just south of Retford, on August 7th 1956. The A3 is well cleaned, her Diagram 94A boiler is No.27004, and the GN tender is No.5263. The track is being repaired as witness the heaps of chippings in the six-foot. (B K B Green, Initial Photographics)

TRIGO was the first of the 1930 batch of eight A3s shared between Gateshead and Haymarket sheds. After the 1939-45 war she spent most of her time allocated to Neville Hill, and was rarely seen south of Leeds. Here she is at Neville Hill, about to go off shed on September 29th 1961. In the distance is the new diesel depot, and it was the allocation there of Type 4 diesel-electrics D345-D349 for comprehensive new diagrams that brought TRIGO and her sisters to the Metropolis. The A3 has Diagram 94A boiler 27076 and A4 non-corridor tender No.5645. (Bryan Wilson, transporttreasury.co.uk).

Chapter Five
Reminiscences

My first memories of the A3s are from the lineside when visiting my Grandmother during the war and early post-war years, with my cousin and friends on the bank above Ferme Park South Down signalbox. We sat and peered and argued as to the identity of the passing dirt-encrusted A3 or A4, as lads did. Many of the freight locos were quite indecipherable, and the decision by BR to attach a numberplate to the locomotive smokebox door earned the grateful thanks of schoolboys. We gradually learnt the names, unaware of which loco came from where – indeed it was the advent of the *abc* that transformed our understanding of railways. Haymarket, Heaton and the Hills, Copley and Neville, were names unknown to us. The A4s were not at their best in a coating of grime, but the filthy but elegant A3s, with those huge coupled wheels and perfectly balanced proportions, remained in the mind – TRACERY, FELSTEAD, SOLARIO, SANDWICH and many more.

The first memory of an A3 in the full glory of the LNER apple green livery was at New Southgate, going home in the darkness of a winter evening. Almost silently, with the rumble of wheels on the rails, this vision emerged ghost-like into the station lights – FLYING SCOTSMAN herself, gleaming in apple green, rolling slowly past on the down slow with a freight. Over the years later, from the platform, the signalbox or from visits to Doncaster Works, I saw all of the class, mostly old friends but some strangers such as BAYARDO and CORONACH on the famous 19.10 parcels to York. It was always a treat to see the shining round smokebox and fresh paint, whether it was a stranger such as BROWN JACK, or one of our own. Trips to Hadley Wood were on Sundays when the service was sparse, the highlights being the 10.00 and 11.30 from Kings Cross. One memory was of an apple green PAPYRUS on the 10.00, thundering round the bend from New Barnet, seen from the down side path between New Barnet and Hadley Wood. It was a greatly impressive sight, enough to inspire many a young lad to find a career with the railway.

Greenwood was an idyllic spot to watch trains. The rustle of wires, the clank of the down main somersault, later sadly replaced, each heralded the sound of the express clearing New Barnet, swinging round the bend and approaching, the sound of the exhaust becoming louder and louder. Then there was the anxious peering to see whether it was an A4, A3 or V2, or one of those new Pacifics. One learnt to listen for the exhaust beat in

BAYARDO had been a Heaton Pacific from delivery, and her mileage suggests that she was a hard working member of the fleet there. Here she has the heavy 13.20 Kings Cross-Edinburgh approaching the top of the long climb out of London at Potters Bar. The date is June 1937, and the extra tractive effort will have been helpful, although the cylinders may well have been reduced to 19ins by that date. The A3 has the first Diagram 94HP boiler, off ENTERPRISE, No.8027 and her original GN tender No.5288.

SIR HUGO as an A1 on a down express at Greenwood in the 1928-30 period. Diagram 94 boiler and a GN tender No.5291.

case what promised to be an A3 turned out to be a V2. Then there was the rasping Kylchap exhaust, usually of the new Pacifics, but sometimes one of our local trio of A4s, or HUMORIST, the latter then a London engine. I remember seeing some of the Coronation stock in its original livery, far from clean, hauled by an A4 unseen before, the fourth Kylchap A4 bearing No.5, SIR CHARLES NEWTON.

Cecil J Allen's classic book *The Gresley Pacifics* was compulsory reading, and one learned of the great days of the A3s. Lads became word perfect, to a standard but dreamt of by our English teachers. Perhaps it raised expectations too far, for when a journey was undertaken behind an A3, it was often an anticlimax. It was not Bill Sparshatt and the days of the streamliners. The best part of a decade had to pass before the A3s started to run as in the days of yore. When I started work, I enrolled in the University of Platform 10 at Kings Cross, which was a superb educational establishment in the world of railways presided over by Eric Neve, learning what happened, why, and with whom. Gradually one learnt about engineering and operating, aided by study at college, and began to appreciate that there was more to it than met the eye. The expresses, hauled by Peppercorn's A1s in relative silence, or

the A4s of Top Shed represented the railway operation at its best. On summer Saturdays, the higher mileage A3s and V2s from New England and Doncaster were pressed into express work. The occasional reluctant New England or Doncaster V2 was painfully obvious, all black smoke and running late with half a dozen expresses tied to her tail lamp. This was the reverse of the coin. It took all sorts.

Trials were carried out on the Talisman with A3s in good condition, which led to the reintroduction of A3s on through services to Newcastle. I remember seeing WOOLWINDER with the dynamometer car heading the down Talisman in good style. A reduction of train loads in 1956/57 helped. They seemed to run well, and I recall a good trip with GAY CRUSADER on the down Morning Talisman with speeds in the 80s and rising to over 90mph several times on the run to Newcastle.

Then came the surprising moment. At York in summer 1958, spending a day photographing, I positioned myself for a shot of the up Scotsman at the north end of the main up platform, by the crossings where the Scarborough line swung away. It was headed by an A3, but as she rolled her train slowly in towards the station, I saw that it was WOOLWINDER, and from the sight, and the sound of the familiar hissing

exhaust, it was clear that she had been fitted with a double Kylchap. The A4s were being fitted with double Kylchaps and most running were modified, but while on the grapevine it was rumoured that the A3s would be redraughted, there was no certainty, so we thought. Now it had come true. In time more and more A3s emerged, and before long they were running turn and turn about with the A1s and A4s.

One of the finest sights for the GN commuter in this magnificent finale of the steam era was the down Yorkshire Pullman, which departed at a time when many of us were travelling home. The A4s had been replaced by their older sisters, and the A3, cleaned to perfection, was a sight for sore eyes as she set off for the north. One of the oddities of this period was that the oldest of the class ran as well as any, in particular ROYAL LANCER and ENTERPRISE at Grantham, FLYING FOX, GAY CRUSADER and HERMIT at Top Shed. The last-named made an amazing 73 consecutive return trips on the Yorkshire Pullman. We waited each day for the 9.50 from Leeds, half-expecting a replacement for the previous night's departing HERMIT, but she emerged yet again, gleaming, from the swirling smoke around Gasworks Tunnel without fail.

There were some duties on which the A1s and A4s were preferred, but occasionally a gleaming A3 appeared on the Scots Goods, the Talisman or the Flying Scotsman. One evening waiting for Bill Hoole on the Up Flying Scotsman from Grantham, the train emerged from Gasworks Tunnel headed by none other than 60103, FLYING SCOTSMAN. Of course she was ten minutes early.

In the north there was the same transformation, with the A3s making some remarkable running. St. FRUSQUIN made that run from Newcastle to Edinburgh in 1959, taking 113 minutes for the 124.45 miles. Harry Knox remembers firing to Driver Peter Robertson with SPION KOP on the Talisman, making a run but a minute or so slower.

But the tidal wave of diesel traction was running, and before long the cleanliness abated, and the lines of old favourites stopped gradually lengthening. 'Stored' gradually became 'Withdrawn', and lines of condemned Pacifics formed at Doncaster, Darlington, at depots, and at two spectacular dumps at Bathgate and Carnbroe in Scotland. It was all over.

At the west end of Waverley station an evening service for Glasgow is about to leave behind HUMORIST in mid-1956. The only double Kylchap A3 for nearly 20 years, she is in her final form with Peppercorn smoke deflectors. I always felt them to be quite inappropriate for an A3, always needing to be brought forward, and it was a pity they were not replaced with trough deflectors. She has a Diagram 94A boiler No.27079 and a GN tender No.5265. (J Robertson, transporttreasury.co.uk).

I have little doubt that apart from FLYING SCOTSMAN herself, the most photographed A3 was HUMORIST, by virtue of the number of alterations to the A3's appearance. Here is HUMORIST, in original condition, on the 1 in 200 climb out of London at Hadley Wood with a down express. The Doncaster A3 appears to be in almost new condition and certainly it is before the 1933 modifications. The boiler would be Diagram 94HP No.8082 (original) or new No.8254; the GN tender is No.5265.

Chapter Six
Individual Performances

Melton, Flying Scotsman, Minoru, Tracery

Early adventures into train timing, encouraged by C.J. Allen's monthly articles in *The Railway Magazine*, were not encouraging. For one from the fair county of Middlesex, the occasional burst of speed was exhilarating but all too rare. 60mph looked fast, and so trips to Hitchin left a deep impression of high speed. Schedules in the late 1940s and early 1950s were not challenging, although TSRs (Temporary Speed Restrictions) and signal checks usually conspired to make arrivals late even so. Most early main line runs were with A4s or Peppercorn A1s, and what little experience of A3 running was gained was not inspiring.

There was a driver at New Southgate I came to know, a pleasant and quiet man who retrieved his ancient bicycle from the parcels office and rode slowly home. In fact his disappearing figure fascinated me, for as he cycled uphill, his speed was so low that he must have been in danger of stalling and falling off. He seemed to be in need of what

the Signalling Regulations described as 'assistance in the rear'. I suspect that he looked older than he actually was. His bicycle looked even older. Men appeared much older in those days, no doubt due to cigarettes, coal dust and ash in the working environment. His name was Farrington, similar in spelling but critically different from Ted Hailstone's colleague on SILVER LINK – Frank Ferrington. I later learnt that Driver Farrington, who was a senior man in the second link at Kings Cross, was known to the irreverent firemen as 'Daisy'. The second link was formed of men who had the necessary seniority, but preferred not to lodge for one reason or another. Some were senior to the newer top link men. They were able, and just how able I was to find out later.

In 1956 I had to go to Newton Heath concrete works to inspect some bridge beams with a senior colleague. I was apprehensive of another dreary run and late arrival at Euston on the LMR, and it was an opportunity to sample the relatively new Manchester-Sheffield-

Wath 1500v DC electrification. So I managed to persuade a gullible travel clerk that I needed Regional passes to travel back via Sheffield and Retford. After a boisterous ride over the recently realigned 1500V DC route from Manchester to Sheffield, destroyed by the poor riding of the EM1 and EM2 electric locomotives, and then a spin to Retford with a B1, I waited for the heavy express with portions from everywhere in the East and West Ridings, from Hull (13.30) to Harrogate (13.15).

The up Flying Scotsman came through at speed behind, very unusually, EARL MARISCHAL before the up platform road signals cleared. As the arrival time came and went, from the north came that ringing knock, 'the Gresley knock', only several tens of decibels louder than one would have preferred. The familiar, friendly face of an A3 drew in, but making a very uncomfortable mechanical noise. It was MELTON, an old friend, but one that had been seen on humble turns of late, and had not been to Doncaster Works

The original GRAND PARADE, recently overhauled, one suspects, in summer 1933, with an A3 corridor tender (No.5331) and a 'personal' set of headlamps. The location looks more like Haymarket from the roof line of the shed rather than Kings Cross. Note the single coal rail above the corridor, just visible. The Diagram 94HP boiler is No.8076, and the A3 corridor tender is No.5331. The old orthochromatic emulsion tended to darken the apple green livery.

since returning from a spell on the GC section. The driver, to my surprise, was Driver Farrington – Daisy – who grinned a greeting at me. Over the years our conversation cannot be recalled with any accuracy, but the gist was that it was going to be a hard run, as this engine was waiting shops and very run down. I remember wondering whether it might be wiser to alight at Grantham for a better run to London.

The Retford start was not all that hard, but with a short reverse curve and a greasy rail, the stiff Gresley pull-out regulator often caused a rather explosive getaway. From my window in the front coach, I heard him get the old girl away with a slip or two, yet driving her quite hard, to judge from the bark from the chimney. As we slipped, the coupled wheels seemed to shift slightly to and fro in the frames as we swung across to the up main. The single blast A3 had a lusty exhaust when working hard, and we certainly thundered up to Markham, albeit with a somewhat irregular and ragged exhaust beat. Farrington was not afraid to let her run, and there was a certain irony as we shot past an overheated EARL MARISCHAL and her train cooling their heels in Egmanton loop!

The handling of the A3 was absorbing, and I decided to stay with her. My reward was a splendid start away from Grantham, again slightly greasy from the number of locomotives changed there, yet not a slip. With a heavy train, 14 on, the A3 might have been spared a little on the climb to Stoke,

but it didn't sound like it. All the time one could hear the heavy knocking from the engine. Down the bank, again she was made to run, reaching 86 as I recall, before coasting, taking water, and the Peterborough stop. The southbound start there was bad, rising on a curve towards the Nene Bridge, and many a time have I heard drivers struggling to maintain speed and adhesion. The restart from Peterborough was magnificent; again, not a slip, the regulator opening judged to perfection, and the A3 accelerating with her heavy train noisily over the Nene and round the curve to Fletton, away to London. The long climbs to Leys and Stevenage, and the faster section in between, all were handled well, and we ran into Kings Cross, after the signal checks, obligatory it seemed, within ten minutes late. Not remarkable on the face of it, but this was a very run-down locomotive: that was audibly obvious. Again, I forget Farrington's exact comment afterwards, but it was something like 'Well, she was rough but we didn't do too badly, did we?'

It is interesting to compare MELTON's run with later experiences. On July 27th 1957, Brian Bailey and I travelled down the main line to Grantham. I was surprised to see FLYING SCOTSMAN, for although I was well up with the grapevine, I hadn't realised that she had been away at Doncaster Plant. The heavy 17.15 Leeds changed engines on Saturdays, and the replacement was none other than FLYING SCOTSMAN. This was hardly

a running-in turn. The running was quite good, despite several delays, but what was remarkable was the sound of the A3, working hard. I referred in *The Book of the A3 Pacifics* to this run. The improvements that had been made at Doncaster, principally to the re-erection of the repaired locomotive, had resulted in almost silent running when coasting. The valves had been set by an expert, and I hadn't heard an A3 with such a clear and even beat for a long while – if ever. The 17.15 was a heavy fifteen coach train, 530 tons in all, but FLYING SCOTSMAN seemed to have no difficulty in working this big train back up to 60-70mph after three TSRs and a signal check. Not a remarkable run, but it was a treat to hear an A3 in such fine condition, a very stark contrast to my previous experience with MELTON.

On December 29th 1959 I had the opportunity to experience the work of an A3 now fitted with a double Kylchap, one of the old favourites at Kings Cross, MINORU. The 14.00 from Kings Cross was 400 tons, and MINORU had been running for nine months since her last overhaul. The running was quite different, however. The start was not far short of streamliner quality, 10-15 mph faster out to Hatfield, 70 at Woolmer Green and 80 at Arlesey. We passed Biggleswade in less than 'even time' – 41.1 miles in 40mins 9secs. A long signal check to walking pace at St.Neots was followed by 90 at Holme, and we stopped at Peterborough in seconds under 80 minutes. The net time was 69½ mins, quite comparable with

SPION KOP with an up express at Langley troughs in 1947-8. At the time she was a Kings Cross engine, with the 94HP boiler off FELSTEAD and standard non-corridor tender No.5481.

Joe Duddington's famous run with SOLARIO in 1936. MINORU went on to Grantham in just under 36 minutes, 31net, despite having accelerated to 74 by Tallington before a heavy signal check at Essendine on Stoke bank. Again, a good run; not necessarily out of the ordinary, but unrecognisable when compared with earlier single blast running.

The down Morning Talisman in June 1960 was first stop Darlington, and the load was nine coaches, 350 tons. By this time A3s were running to Newcastle, and I was pleased to find TRACERY at the head, though this is not the run tabulated in the Appendix. The running was very similar to MINORU with 84 at Arlesey, 60 over Stoke, and a steady 70-75 for much of the way. The time to Darlington was 227 mins 45 secs, 217 mins net. Once again, TRACERY hardly seemed to be extended other than accelerating quickly from the various checks and restrictions. It all felt so easy, not simply because Kylchap locos were quieter, but because the acceleration was more rapid and the exhaust beat more even and less laboured.

My last run with an A3 was the railtour to Darlington with FLYING FOX and FLYING SCOTSMAN when preserved. This was also described in the first book. The abiding memory, apart from 6 miles with the speedometer on 100mph, is how very much fast running had been restored to the A3s, and indeed how they had been enhanced in the process.

CORONACH, with the early morning Leeds-Kings Cross express, at Stoke summit in February 1932. The A3 has Diagram 94HP boiler No.8082 and GN tender No.5272. (Rev. A C Cawston, courtesy Brian Bailey)

60095 FLAMINGO going steadily past Bowland in the early morning mist with the overnight Anglo-Scottish express from St Pancras on August 6th 1951. The A3 has a Diagram 94A boiler 27017, and GN tender No.5224. (Rev. A C Cawston, courtesy Brian Bailey)

SIR FREDERICK BANBURY, then a Leicester GC engine, a wonderful sight fresh from the Paint Shops at Doncaster on June 15th 1955. Doncaster Paint Shop always did a good job with their paintwork. She had been held at the Works during the 1955 ASLEF strike, prevented from running-in. The engine has a Diagram 94HP boiler (27000) and a GN tender (5292). (Phil Lynch)

Chapter Seven
Trainspotting

Although the last of the class was withdrawn over four decades ago, in the curious way that memories work, those of days long ago spring readily to mind; younger days, days when no amount of effort mattered in the interests of our hobby, work, or both. At school, collecting train numbers was the current mania, although in the culture of the time and with wartime restrictions there was little enough time for it. As previously mentioned, locomotives were generally filthy for years after the cessation of hostilities which, unless the locomotive had a name, made numbers a work of some imagination! As a result of an interest in railways, many of us gained an understanding of how this vast organisation worked, and indeed went on to join it.

Collecting numbers was in itself harmless, but quite illogical. It was a masculine thing, at least largely so far. No doubt some psychiatrist would find a disorder to encapsulate the symptoms – Trevithick's Syndrome for example. It is a wonder that it hasn't been a subject for the odd PhD or so. The hobby, a

word from the 1950s, split into two sub-divisions, one being purely the accumulation of numbers seen, and the other being the acquisition of knowledge and understanding. In one case there would be enjoyment in seeing a different loco on the same train every day, and in the other, satisfaction in seeing the same loco complete a rostered week's work successfully. Steam locomotives usually had plain bearings and lubrication systems that, without regular inspection and maintenance, could fail. Those with roller bearings were considerably more reliable, but even they could not match the reliability of today's diesel and electric traction. Regular running by steam was more of an achievement in those days. It was greatly helped by regular manning and demanding drivers seeking a high standard of maintenance.

Today it is something that would be sneered at, if understood at all. This is very much the age of the sneer, in which a simple outer garment like the anorak has become an epithet. With the transformation of traction from steam days, much has gone from the simple

pleasure of watching a dramatic evocation of power. With peer pressure, computer games, drink, etc, anyone showing interest in such as railways is regarded as being unusual. It cannot be long before train spotting becomes either a security issue or a sign of some medical condition!

I suppose that if the locomotive became personified (easy enough when one thinks of it as the iron horse) then the desire to see each different locomotive could be understood. But the engines weren't different other than in name and number, and in some odd cases, technically. Yet small boys in hundreds and thousands stood by the lineside on the chance of seeing the unusual visitor. I remember the close boarded fencing at Harringay carefully inscribed 'Died waiting for SILVER KING', to which kindred spirits had added their own Pacifics – FLAMINGO, CICERO, etc, as a sort of prayer list.

One could understand, however hard-bitten an engineer, and there was certainly something about the sight of a stranger. I remember waiting on the old footbridge at New Southgate,

The Glasgow-Kings Cross express enters York on August 18th 1959 behind ENTERPRISE, now one of Grantham's stalwarts. Although only two months out of Doncaster Works, the A3 has acquired a coat of grime. The trackman is a good example of why the introduction of high visibility vests had been long overdue. She has retained Diagram 94A boiler No.27025 and A3 non-corridor tender No.5569. (E Goscote)

hearing a hiss and that trundling noise from the track that a steam locomotive made when it was moved slowly, and was suitably thunderstruck to see WINDSOR LAD, a vision in blue livery, emerge from behind the signalbox with an up parcels service. It was an A3, just like all the others, but it had an unique name and an arrangement of numbers that fascinated. Of course I was widely disbelieved by my peers back at school!

The LNER and its successors were quite parochial in the use of their locomotives, unlike the LMSR, largely as a result of the engine changing policy of the former. Looking back, the post-war situation had changed little after the 1922 Grouping in many respects. It was the failure to amalgamate depots that gave rise to some of the curiosities of operation. At Leeds, where the old LNER needed one express locomotive depot, it had two, Copley Hill for the old GN, and Neville Hill for the old NER. The old LMSR had more. That was without Ardsley and Bradford wanting express duties and engines as well. They were in two different Regions of BR, and if Neville Hill were short, they borrowed from the senior depot miles away at York and not from Copley Hill a few miles away. So the Neville Hill A3s were as rare as unicorns south of Leeds, and Copley Hill Pacifics likewise in the north-east. As for the Carlisle Canal quartet, well...

At Newcastle, with depots at Gateshead and Heaton, the route knowledge was similar in the senior links. Both knew the road from Kings Cross to Edinburgh. They borrowed from one another, and Gateshead provided the Darlington pilots. At Carlisle there were at least three depots working away as if the Grouping had never happened, never mind Nationalisation. Of course the size of the depot was relevant, the fact that each had different patterns of route awareness and different routes were worked. Then there were the depot traditions, with irrational animosities and rivalries, and the often unhelpful contribution from trade unions. So I suppose it is no wonder that management decided that there were more fruitful subjects for modernisation, and walked away.

As a result, we had a railway where a visit to the north-east, or Scotland enabled us to see an entirely different group of locomotives. Then the close boarded fences would have read 'Died waiting for DONOVAN, CENTENARY,' or any number of the local A3s down south.

A Leeds to Kings Cross express races under the old intersection bridge at Sandy behind Grantham's VICTOR WILD on June 26th 1954. Despite its apparently overwhelming provision of motive power, keeping up with servicing, repairs and inspections always seemed a problem, and some idea of the situation on the main line as a hectic Saturday wore on can be appreciated here. VICTOR WILD, having worked up to London overnight, was on the 10.18 from Kings Cross to Leeds earlier in the day, and within just over an hour at Grantham was turned and coaled, and sent back with the 11.15(SO) from Leeds. She went into Doncaster for a general overhaul a week later! The bridge carried the Cambridge-Oxford line over the main line, and only had a single line for parliamentary reasons, I believe. It was renewed in 1959 but the line, which in retrospect might have been useful (like many of the 'Beeching' closures) was shut within the decade. The A3 has a Diagram 94A boiler No.27051 and her original GN tender No.5225.

Viewed from the front, the A3 was an enormously handsome and impressive locomotive, and the lipped double chimney added to that impression. Yet broadside, the double chimney sat too far forward – necessarily – and the original single chimney was a far more pleasing alternative, aesthetically. The use of snap head rivets instead of countersunk was a Thompsonian innovation. HERMIT waits in the old platform 10 with the 16.05 Kings Cross to Leeds and York on June 17th 1960 – the fireman has yet to fit the second headlamp. The A3 has Diagram 94A boiler 27029 and GN tender No.5271. (D C Ovenden)

BLINK BONNY pulls away from Newcastle Central on August 8th 1964, a few months away from withdrawal. She had worked a railtour to Derby and Crewe on 18 April 1964 – hence the white-painted hingestraps and buffer heads. Newcastle had power signalling with electro-pneumatic point motors, with the motor numbers on the compressors to enable motor testing. The A3 has Diagram 94A boiler 8081 and an A3 non-corridor tender, No.5580. (John Goss)

Chapter Eight
Statistics and Individual Histories

As mentioned in the Preface, the history and work of the Gresley A1s and A3s was covered in the original book, and with the illustrations available it is an opportunity to take a closer look at individual locomotives. Looking back at a class of locomotives, especially one whose members are so fondly remembered, it is inevitable that people have favourites, for a variety of reasons that tend to be personal rather than mechanical. It is worth saying that unless there are mechanical variations, each locomotive of the same class should be the same as the next at building, and that is largely true. Locos were built and repaired by gangs, which explains why some were released to traffic at building out of numerical order. The day-to-day condition, especially due to accrued mileage or servicing may mean that there were indeed variations between locomotives at a point in time. General overhauls normally returned each

locomotive to a near-pristine condition and eliminated those variations. Well, usually.

The A3s and the A1s before them had four boilers over the years, the original 180 psi diagram 94, the 220 psi 94HP fitted to five A1s and 18 A3s, the 220 psi 94A first used on WINDSOR LAD, and the diagram 107 A4 boiler working at 220 psi. Four tenders were also used, the GN coal rail tender, the standard high sided first used with TRIGO, the A4 version of that design, and the corridor tenders. The valve travel was increased from 1927 onwards, and the right-hand drive engines were converted to left-hand during 1952-54.

A number of small changes to locomotives occurred over the years which are not necessarily referred to in the captions but can be seen in the illustrations. Access to the conjugated gear was available at the front between the frames, but to protect the gear from

smokebox ash and char, a cover was provided. It was occasionally left open which defeated its purpose. The characteristic bogie axlebox guards were removed as versions of ATC and then the standard AWS were fitted with the protecting plate in front of the AWS receptor. The four Carlisle engines were never fitted with AWS. The Pacifics had two sets of guard irons, one bogie mounted and the other frame mounted. Post-war, over a long period the frame mounted irons were removed. Also post-war, possibly as part of the new BR regime, works plates of a more minimal design were fixed to the front frames. These duplicated the original brass plates on the smokeboxes or occasionally, the cab sides, which remained in position (quite rightly). Later, sporadically, they were removed. Over the life of the locomotives, the original nameplates were changed for a longer and more robust design. The

A trio of A3s line up at Kings Cross, with a Grantham A1 in platform 2. The date is late summer 1958, and TRANQUIL, with the up 8.00 from Newcastle, is the nearest A3, (Diagram 94A boiler 27065 and GN tender No.5291). DIAMOND JUBILEE, just fresh from Doncaster Works, is on the 9.00 from York, (Diagram 94A boiler 27069 and A4 non-corridor tender No.5644). The third, I believe, was ROYAL LANCER from Grantham on another NE express, the 7.53 from Newcastle, still single blast. (Diagram 94A boiler 27039 and GN tender No.5267). (P J Coster)

BR No.	LNER No.	BUILT	WITH-DRAWN	RECORDED MILEAGE	MILEAGE Date	MILEAGE LIFE (YRS)	AV. ANN. MILEAGE
60035	2500	10/07/34	04/09/61	1,617,000	W	27.16	59,536
60036	2501	09/07/34	23/11/64	1,535,000	10/63	29.29	52,407
60037	2502	25/07/34	12/12/63	1,695,000	12/62	28.30	59,894
60038	2503	11/08/34	18/11/63	1,637,000	W	29.27	55,928
60039	2504	09/09/34	14/03/63	1,577,000	W	28.52	55,295
60040	2505	27/10/34	06/07/64	1,535,000	10/63	29.00	52,931
60041	2506	19/12/34	04/12/65	1,577,000	12/62	28.02	56,281
60042	2507	01/12/34	30/07/64	1,509,000	7/4/63	28.36	53,209
60043	2508	09/02/35	14/05/64	1,552,000	12/62	27.88	55,667
60044	2543	28/06/24	16/06/63	1,992,000	W	38.96	51,129
60045	2544	26/07/24	24/11/64	1,907,000	10/63	39.25	48,586
60046	2545	09/08/24	16/06/63	2,039,000	W	38.86	52,470
60047	2546	30/08/24	08/04/63	2,089,000	W	38.60	54,119
60048	2547	30/08/24	08/09/63	1,907,000	W	39.03	48,860
60049	2548	27/09/24	29/12/62	2,005,000	W	38.25	52,418
60050	2549	25/10/24	11/06/63	2,035,000	W	38.66	52,638
60051	2550	12/11/24	24/11/64	1,993,000	10/63	38.96	51,155
60052	2551	29/11/24	22/01/66	2,021,000	9/63	38.83	52,047
60053	2552	11/12/24	27/05/63	1,964,000	W	38.47	51,053
60054	2553	31/12/24	28/06/64	1,863,000	W	39.50	47,165
60055	2554	31/12/24	04/09/61	2,023,000	W	37.68	53,689
60056	2555	07/02/25	13/05/63	1,896,000	W	38.27	49,543
60057	2556	18/02/25	28/10/63	2,141,000	9/63	38.62	55,438
60058	2557	28/02/25	19/06/63	1,829,000	W	38.31	47,742
60059	2558	25/03/25	17/12/62	2,524,000	W	37.71	66,932
60060	2559	28/03/25	23/09/63	1,992,000	W	38.48	51,767
60061	2560	17/04/25	08/09/63	2,019,000	W	38.40	52,578
60062	2561	30/05/25	26/12/64	2,029,000	W	37.58	53,991
60063	2562	27/06/25	28/06/64	1,947,000	W	39.00	49,923
60064	2563	09/07/24	04/09/61	2,014,000	W	37.16	54,198
60065	2564	14/07/24	28/06/64	2,235,000	W	39.95	55,945
60066	2565	16/07/24	08/09/63	1,896,000	W	39.14	48,441
60067	2566	14/08/24	29/12/62	1,904,000	W	38.37	49,622
60068	2567	14/08/24	01/09/62	1,823,000	W	38.04	47,923
60069	2568	19/09/24	01/10/62	2,200,000	W	38.04	57,834
60070	2569	24/09/24	04/05/64	2,200,000	W	39.60	55,556
60071	2570	27/09/24	12/10/64	2,268,000	10/63	38.25	59,294
60072	2571	30/09/24	22/10/62	2,242,000	W	38.08	58,876
60073	2572	03/10/24	19/08/63	2,382,000	W	38.88	61,265
60074	2573	08/10/24	08/04/63	2,171,000	W	38.58	56,273
60075	2574	11/10/24	13/01/64	2,174,000	10/63	38.96	55,801
60076	2575	14/10/24	29/10/62	2,141,000	W	38.04	56,283
60077	2576	19/10/24	13/07/64	2,142,000	16/6/63	38.65	55,420
60078	2577	24/10/24	22/10/62	2,233,000	W	37.99	58,779
60079	2578	29/10/24	16/09/61	1,948,000	W	36.92	52,763
60080	2579	03/11/24	12/10/64	2,123,000	10/63	39.00	54,436
60081	2580	09/11/24	01/10/62	2,052,000	W	37.92	54,114
60082	2581	30/11/24	02/09/63	2,194,000	W	38.76	56,605
60083	2582	06/12/24	18/05/64	2,109,000	10/63	38.91	54,202
60084	2595	22/02/30	23/11/64	1,929,000	W	34.75	55,511
60085	2596	22/02/30	12/10/64	1,820,000	10/63	33.68	54,038
60086	2597	07/04/30	18/11/63	1,794,000	10/63	33.48	53,584
60087	2598	14/06/30	28/10/63	1,963,000	12/62	32.54	60,326
60088	2599	12/07/30	14/10/63	1,969,000	W	33.63	58,549
60089	2743	22/08/28	14/10/63	1,846,000	12/62	34.36	53,725
60090	2744	23/08/28	28/10/63	1,917,000	12/62	34.36	55,792
60091	2745	08/09/28	12/10/64	1,562,000	10/63	35.14	44,451
60092	2746	26/10/28	12/10/64	1,839,000	10/63	35.01	52,528
60093	2747	24/11/28	28/04/62	1,695,000	W	33.42	50,718
60094	2748	20/12/28	24/02/64	1,677,000	12/62	34.02	49,295
60095	2749	26/01/29	15/04/61	1,516,000	W	32.21	47,066
60096	2750	23/02/29	09/09/63	2,037,000	12/62	34.54	58,975
60097	2751	07/03/29	24/08/63	1,920,000	W	34.46	55,717
60098	2752	20/04/29	28/10/63	1,719,000	W	34.52	49,797
60099	2795	19/04/30	28/10/63	2,042,000	12/62	32.61	62,619
60100	2796	17/05/30	19/06/65	1,927,000	12/62	32.61	59,092
60101	2797	04/06/30	11/04/63	1,815,000	12/62	32.54	55,778
60102	4471	10/07/22	11/11/61	1,905,000	W	39.01	48,834
60103	4472	24/02/23	15/01/63	2,075,000	W	39.86	52,057
60104	4473	17/03/23	07/12/59	1,874,000	W	36.75	50,993
60105	4474	24/03/23	16/06/63	2,223,000	W	40.23	55,257
60106	4475	28/04/23	26/12/64	2,643,000	W	41.67	63,427
60107	4476	26/05/23	01/09/63	2,252,000	7/63	40.16	56,076
60108	4477	16/06/23	19/10/63	2,079,000	W	40.35	51,524
60109	4478	30/06/23	29/12/62	2,076,000	W	39.50	52,557
60110	4479	25/07/23	23/05/63	2,149,000	W	39.83	53,954
60111	4480	17/08/23	29/12/62	1,937,000	W	39.37	49,200
60112	4481	08/09/23	26/12/64	1,962,000	W	41.31	47,495
60113	4470	11/04/22	19/11/1962	2,078,700	W		
60113	4470	11/04/22	01/05/45	1,212,346	Rebuilt	23.04	52,615
60113	4470	25/09/45	19/11/1962	866,354	W	17.17	50,457

W='At Withdrawal'

extent of repairs required. It was always claimed that general overhaul returned the locomotive to a pristine condition, but clearly this was not literally possible, for not only wear but fatigue had to be anticipated. The loco would be stripped, and the major components would go to the shops dealing with, say boilers, wheels, copper work and so on. Doncaster, as a policy, kept a number of spare components and as the A3 was cleaned, repaired and reassembled, different components could be used. If the boiler had required repairs and been lifted, when ready the next available suitable boiler would be put on the loco. Likewise wheels, etc. Even the frames might well be altered if there was any cracking. I remember visiting Doncaster in the early 1950s when someone, exultant, had seen a set of frames marked up '60057' at one end, only to discover that the other end, the cab sides and other parts nearby were those of one of our local A3s! So in fact an A3 was an assembly of parts, no more. The very visible change in the last decade was the fitting of a double Kylchap, and a few years later for most of the class, trough smoke deflectors. The livery was GN apple green until the early 1940s when it was replaced by wartime black. Post-war, apple green returned, but on nationalisation, after a number had been painted in an experimental purple, BR blue (based on the Caledonian Railway livery) became the passenger livery. This did not wear well, and yielded to a dark green which was strangely reminiscent of 1925.

W.B. Yeadon's *Register* shows that almost every general overhaul saw an A3 emerge from Doncaster with a different boiler and tender. The FLYING FOX of my 1964 trip had a boiler off FLYING SCOTSMAN, the tender off SIR FREDERICK BANBURY, axleboxes repaired or new, motion off another A3, various parts either new or off other A3s and a GN tender originally built for SCEPTRE. A distinctly unromantic view, but true.

So what does a mileage figure represent? It represents the ability of the depot and works to run that set of A3 components for so many thousands of miles over a period. At general overhaul, they will have needed to be changed. One-offs such as GREAT NORTHERN or the W1 might have needed a little longer because not all components were interchangeable and the overhaul period might have been longer, depending upon what repairs were required. As the transition to diesel and electric traction progressed, the budget for the cost of repairs was reduced, increasing the likelihood of withdrawal of an engine on the grounds – as with SOLARIO – that it would cost too much to repair. The financial processes of the railway were a dark art, but once one understood how to work the system, it was surprising what could be done. Financial dexterity was

casting of front numberplates involved a rogue 6 (or 9) for some years, with a curly tail. Then the numberplates of about a dozen A3s seemed to have exchanged position with the handrail. Even St.SIMON's unique cab migrated to MERRY HAMPTON.

A comparison of mileages from the steam age is interesting. However, first of all one needs to realise that a locomotive is a number and a name, and little more. When an A3 went into Doncaster, as it was dismantled there would be agreement on the nature and

LOCOMOTIVES IN ANNUAL MILEAGE ORDER

BR No.	RECORDED MILEAGE	MILEAGE LIFE*	AVERAGE ANNUAL MILEAGE
60059	2,524,000	37.75	66,861
60106	2,643,000	41.67	63,427
60099	2,042,000	32.69	62,466
60073	2,382,000	38.88	61,265
60087	1,963,000	32.54	60,326
60097	2,057,000	34.46	59,692
60035	1,617,000	27.17	59,514
60088	1,969,000	33.25	59,218
60100	1,927,000	32.61	59,092
60096	2,037,000	34.54	58,975
60072	2,242,000	38.06	58,907
60078	2,233,000	37.99	58,779
60071	2,268,000	39.09	58,020
60069	2,200,000	38.02	57,864
60037	1,695,000	29.44	57,575
60082	2,194,000	38.76	56,605
60076	2,141,000	38.04	56,283
60074	2,171,000	38.58	56,273
60107	2,252,000	40.16	56,076
60065	2,235,000	39.95	55,945
60038	1,637,000	29.27	55,928
60075	2,174,000	38.96	55,801
60090	1,917,000	34.36	55,792
60101	1,815,000	32.57	55,726
60043	1,552,000	27.90	55,627
60070	2,200,000	39.61	55,542
60084	1,929,000	34.75	55,511
60057	2,141,000	38.62	55,438
60077	2,142,000	38.65	55,420
60039	1,577,000	28.52	55,295
60105	2,223,000	40.23	55,257
60055	2,023,000	36.68	55,153
60080	2,123,000	39.00	54,436
60041	1,577,000	29.04	54,304
60083	2,109,000	38.91	54,202
60064	2,014,000	37.17	54,183
60081	2,052,000	37.90	54,142
60047	2,089,000	38.60	54,119
60085	1,820,000	33.68	54,038
60110	2,149,000	39.82	53,968
60089	1,846,000	34.36	53,725
60086	1,794,000	33.48	53,584
60042	1,509,000	28.36	53,209
60040	1,535,000	29.00	52,931
60079	1,948,000	36.89	52,806
60050	2,035,000	38.66	52,638
60113(A1)	1,212,000	23.04	52,604
60062	2,029,000	38.58	52,592
60061	2,019,000	38.40	52,578
60109	2,076,000	39.50	52,557
60092	1,839,000	35.01	52,528
60046	2,039,000	38.86	52,470
60049	2,005,000	38.25	52,418
60036	1,535,000	29.31	52,371
60052	2,021,000	38.83	52,047
60103	2,075,000	39.89	52,018
60060	1,992,000	38.48	51,767
60113(all)	2,078,000	40.20	51,692
60108	2,079,000	40.35	51,524
60051	1,993,000	38.96	51,155
60044	1,992,000	38.96	51,129
60053	1,964,000	38.47	51,053
60104	1,874,000	36.73	51,021
60093	1,695,000	33.44	50,688
60113(A1/1)	866,000	17.16	50,466
60063	1,947,000	39.00	49,923
60098	1,719,000	34.52	49,797
60067	1,904,000	38.38	49,609
60056	1,896,000	38.27	49,543
60094	1,677,000	34.04	49,266
60111	1,937,000	39.36	49,212
60048	1,907,000	39.03	48,860
60102	1,905,000	39.01	48,834
60045	1,907,000	39.27	48,561
60066	1,896,000	39.14	48,441
60068	1,823,000	38.05	47,911
60058	1,829,000	38.31	47,742
60112	1,962,000	41.31	47,495
60054	1,863,000	39.50	47,165
60095	1,516,000	32.29	46,950
60091	1,562,000	35.14	44,451

*Life of the loco (in years) over which the total mileage has been logged.

TOTAL MILEAGE, IN DESCENDING ORDER

BR No.	Total Mileage
60106	2,643,000
60059	2,524,000
60073	2,382,000
60071	2,268,000
60107	2,252,000
60072	2,242,000
60065	2,235,000
60078	2,233,000
60105	2,223,000
60069	2,200,000
60070	2,200,000
60082	2,194,000
60075	2,174,000
60074	2,171,000
60110	2,149,000
60077	2,142,000
60076	2,141,000
60057	2,141,000
60080	2,123,000
60083	2,109,000
60047	2,089,000
60108	2,079,000
60113	2,078,700
60109	2,076,000
60103	2,075,000
60081	2,052,000
60099	2,042,000
60046	2,039,000
60096	2,037,000
60050	2,035,000
60062	2,029,000
60055	2,023,000
60052	2,021,000
60061	2,015,000
60064	2,014,000
60049	2,005,000
60051	1,993,000
60060	1,992,000
60044	1,992,000
60088	1,969,000
60053	1,964,000
60087	1,963,000
60112	1,962,000
60079	1,948,000
60063	1,947,000
60111	1,931,000
60084	1,929,000
60100	1,927,000
60097	1,920,000
60090	1,917,000
60045	1,907,000
60048	1,907,000
60102	1,905,000
60067	1,904,000
60056	1,896,000
60066	1,896,000
60104	1,874,000
60054	1,863,000
60089	1,846,000
60092	1,839,000
60058	1,829,000
60068	1,823,000
60085	1,820,000
60101	1,815,000
60086	1,794,000
60098	1,719,000
60093	1,695,000
60037	1,695,000
60094	1,677,000
60038	1,637,000
60035	1,617,000
60039	1,569,000
60041	1,577,000
60091	1,562,000
60043	1,552,000
60036	1,535,000
60040	1,535,000
60095	1,513,000
60042	1,509,000

one of the unintended blessings of the Good Doctor's regime, and it was a pity that it came so late.

Mileage figures should not be taken too literally, for their means of compilation lacked the precision suggested by being quoted to the last mile – I have rounded to the nearest 1,000. They have at times been prey to typing mistakes in the past, and different mileages have been quoted in 1961 and 1962. For example, GLADIATEUR has been quoted officially as having achieved a life mileage of 1,501,468, a figure which is at least half a million miles less than the average life mileage of her sisters in the north east. A different estimate quoted 1,347,000 miles. Comparison with her Darlington stablemate, GALOPIN confirms this view. An estimate of 1.9 million miles has been quoted, but the annual mileage rates of the NB-built A1s in the NE area suggests to me that 2.2 million might be nearer what was achieved. It may simply be that the figure 1 should be 2 in the quoted mileage, but we shall never know now.

What is still more interesting is the approximate annual mileage figure, reached by dividing the total mileage by the locomotive life to withdrawal. Obviously this assumes that the stoppage time over the long life of the A3s evens out between individual engines. The average annual mileage shows how well the A3 was utilised – for example the figure for most of the Haymarket fleet is about 50% higher than Carlisle, where the quartet there took far longer to reach their shopping mileage. The two Southern area A3s achieved 66,700 (TRACERY) and 65,400 (FLYING FOX) miles per annum, a remarkably good figure for A3s in the Southern area. In reality, this was maintained over nearly four decades. Certainly the two were among that group of ever-present locomotives on the southern end of the main line, though both had periods at Leicester on the GC section in the 1950s. What the annual figures show is that Haymarket made best use of its Pacifics, with the NE not too far behind. It also shows the Carlisle engines quite clearly as underused by comparison, which is hardly surprising when one considers their more limited radius of action. If we compare mileages, naturally the oldest locomotives tend towards the higher figures, although the North British-built A1s of the north east stand out.

The annual mileage figure is of course an average, which does not take account of stoppages for intermediate or general overhauls, and in some years the annual figure for a particular year would have been still higher. For at least half their lifetime A3s were secondary express locomotives, deferring to the A4s from 1935 and the newer Peppercorn A1s from 1949, and limited post-war to 7P status, which suggests that in the first fifteen years the Gresley A1s and A3s were running very good mileages. With the large number of Pacifics at the southern end of the East Coast main line, actual annual mileages tended to be in the 55-65,000 range post-war.

After the two remarkable Southern Area A3s comes not one of the Tyneside fleet but CALL BOY, one of the 1930 build of A3s, the first to come to Haymarket. She was the first A3 as built to reach two million miles, by the end of 1962. Haymarket's use of the A3s was outstanding. Six out of the ten highest annual mileages were by Haymarket A3s, and although some of the duties were slower or more lightly laden, the incidence of stops and sharp gradients was more onerous. By the early 1960s some of the Scottish Pacifics had been stored over varying periods.

The records in general use are not complete, but show the broad picture. Nevertheless, scrutiny of the records at the NRM reveals an occasional snippet. Brian Bailey's studies revealed, for example, that as early as January 1960 Doncaster had been directed to send the nameplates of PAPYRUS to the National Collection, a message repeated in March 1961. By 18/4/63 the A3 had been taken out of service, and according to the Record Card, at Doncaster it was found to have a 'split' in the frame behind the left-hand bogie wheel. Unsurprisingly, she was condemned on 9/9/63, and Yeadon records her sale to Arnott Young at Carmyle in June 1964. Reference to the *Railway Observer* however reveals that PAPYRUS was at Cowlairs in August and September of that year, and then stored at Parkhead before being hauled to Arnott Young with five other Haymarket A3s.

Remembering PAPYRUS, whilst the embryo NRM was based at Triangle Place in the 1960s, the unwanted dynamometer rolls were sold off at 10s each. There were a number of fascinating rolls to examine, and most were bought by the Gresley Society subsequently. John Aylard and I were browsing, and John found a roll marked '2750'. Knowing that the various test runs had not involved PAPYRUS, there was a chance that it was the record of the 108mph run. On examination, we found that it was indeed the famous run, and John hastily paid his ten bob for the roll. It is now safely in the ownership of the Stephenson Locomotive Society.

So there is still interesting research to occupy us in the future, but it is essential to cross check information. The decline of steam was not always faithfully recorded as attention was focused on new traction, and withdrawn steam locos were just so much scrap metal.

GREAT NORTHERN just about to leave Kings Cross on March 3rd 1923 with an express. The engine was still not a year old, and was photographed by W Beckerlegge, one of the famous photographers of the GNR. The boiler and tender are of course the originals. An interesting sight in the background is an Ivatt N1 0-6-2T: so often we see their larger sister N2s at Kings Cross, and the work of the N1s was less often photographed in the London area.

WINDSOR LAD

Built	10/7/34
Works No	1790
LNER Nos.	2500, 570 (7/4/46), 35 (15/6/46)
Wartime black livery	18/4/42
LNER livery	3/9/47
BR No.	60035 (25/11/48)
BR blue livery	13/1/50
BR dark green livery	16/8/51
Double Kylchap fitted	21/9/59
Withdrawn	4/9/61

Allocation	
To Haymarket	10/7/34
To Ferryhill	28/3/37
To Haymarket	4/4/37
To Carlisle Canal	23/4/61
To Haymarket	28/6/61

WINDSOR LAD was the first of batch of nine new A3s with a new boiler, Diagram 94A, in which the main steam delivery pipe had been enlarged from 5 to 7ins in diameter. Both the Superheater Co. and later André Chapelon, had drawn Gresley's attention to the throttling effect of inadequate steam passages, and the loss of power resulting. The new boiler had a banjo shaped steam collector with a very characteristic cladding. WINDSOR LAD immediately became a firm favourite, and was the regular engine of one of the senior top link, Bill Stevenson, before his partnership with MERLIN post-war.

A strange incident during that time, related by Norman McKillop, occurred to WINDSOR LAD while at Haymarket. The run to Edinburgh from Newcastle had been uneventful, until the engine reacted to an irregularity in the road. The reason became apparent at Haymarket, since one of the coupled wheels had shed a tyre. It was said that the tyre had broken in one place, but that seems unlikely.

The arrival of A4s at Haymarket to power the Coronation streamliner, did not displace the A3s completely and even with the arrival of five Peppercorn A1s the A3s were still working the principal expresses post-war. Haymarket lent WINDSOR LAD to Ferryhill and, near the end, to Carlisle Canal, probably as a replacement for FLAMINGO, just withdrawn. It was just over a year since the A3 had been overhauled, and if she went to Canal, she soon went on to Doncaster Works for attention. It is doubtful whether she ever returned to Haymarket as she stayed at Doncaster, and it was decided to withdraw her, probably due to the anticipated cost of repairs.

Otherwise Haymarket kept a firm hold of one of their best A3s. One of the most infrequent visitors to the south, I would say that the sum of her appearances there could be counted on one hand. WINDSOR LAD, sadly, was one of the earliest withdrawals.

Haymarket's old favourite, WINDSOR LAD, pulls away from north Newcastle with a train of oil tanks, in early 1954. Here is an excellent example of the 'Rogue 6'. Comments on the train hauled by BROWN JACK (page 58) apply also here. The engine has a Diagram 94A boiler and a GN tender (5567). (Jim Smith)

A down Glasgow express gets under way through Princes Street Gardens behind WINDSOR LAD in May 1959. The A3, now fitted with AWS, has a Diagram 94A boiler No.27058 and an A3 non-corridor tender No.5567. Numberplate now has the correct '6'.

COLOMBO

Built	9/7/34
Works No.	1791
LNER Nos.	2501, 36 (1/12/46)
Wartime black livery	16/7/42
LNER livery	12/4/47
BR No.	60036 (23/7/48)
BR experimental purple livery	23/7/48
BR blue livery	22/7/49
BR dark green livery	18/12/51
Double Kylchap fitted	14/11/58
Trough deflectors fitted	19/7/62
Withdrawn	23/11/64

Allocation

To Gateshead	9/7/34
To York	9/12/39
To Heaton	28/3/43
To Gateshead	3/11/45
To Kings Cross	1/8/47
To Gateshead	9/9/47
To Neville Hill	6/2/49
To Copley Hill	11/6/61
To Ardsley	10/9/61
To Gateshead	16/6/63
To Darlington	15/12/63

Although the second of the batch, COLOMBO was completed ahead of WINDSOR LAD, and actually entered traffic first. Gateshead had five new A3s already, but COLOMBO was the first A3 of the third batch to go there, built with a Diagram 94A boiler. Of the nine, five went to Haymarket and four to Gateshead. Gateshead's A3s hauled the down mid-day Anglo-Scottish service, 13.20 or so from Kings Cross, and the excellent running of COLOMBO and her sisters was often noted in C.J. Allen's monthly articles 'Locomotive Practice and Performance' in the *Railway Magazine*. While Haymarket's A3s seldom strayed, Gateshead provided pilots at Darlington and York, and there was a frequent exchange with Heaton, across the Tyne. COLOMBO, however, moved south to Kings Cross before going to Neville Hill for over 12 years. The Neville Hill stud of five A3s, as far as those in the south were concerned, disappeared off the planet, rarely making a visit, even when running-in. They worked north on the North Briton and the Queen of Scots Pullman to Newcastle and, for a spell, through to Edinburgh.

In late 1958 the driver of COLOMBO entered a bay platform at York with more than usual vigour, overrode the buffer stop and damaged a platform kiosk. As a result of the impact her coupled wheels were bent beyond belief. In June 1961 she was moved across Leeds to Copley Hill, from where she was once again seen in the south. She was quite a frequent visitor to London at the time, but with the arrival of diesel traction, she eventually returned to the north east, and withdrawal.

It was one of the final quartet of NE A3s in November 1964.

A magnificent shot of Gateshead's COLOMBO going well with an up Anglo-Scottish express when fairly new on June 4th 1937. First thoughts are that it is south of Barkston, though the bridge could be the one at Markham Moor, now demolished. Note the semaphore about to be replaced by a colour light. The A3 has a Diagram 94A boiler No.8777 and an A3 non-corridor tender No.5568. (Rev. A C Cawston, courtesy Brian Bailey)

COLOMBO, piloted by unrebuilt B16/1 4-6-0 61473, with a cross country express in 1953 at Monkton Moor, between Northallerton and Harrogate. Double headed Pacifics were not an uncommon sight in the NE area. The A3 has a Diagram 94A boiler (27064 or 59) and a GN tender (5227).

An up express rolls into York on April 18th 1960 behind COLOMBO, now a double Kylchap engine but within a fortnight of general overhaul. The unusual vehicles in the distance are the York District Engineer's tunnel inspection vehicles. The double Kylchap A3 has a Diagram 94A boiler 27057 and a GN tender (5227).

HYPERION

Built	25/7/34
Works No.	1792
LNER Nos.	2502, 37 (25/8/46)
Wartime black livery	30/1/43
LNER livery	12/7/47
BR No.	60037 (25/10/48)
BR blue livery	22/6/50
BR dark green livery	19/3/52
Double Kylchap fitted	8/10/58
Trough deflectors fitted	19/5/62
Withdrawn	12/12/63

Allocation	
To Haymarket	25/7/34
To St.Margarets	6/3/38
To Haymarket	15/3/39
To Carlisle Canal	7/2/54
To Haymarket	8/3/54
To St.Margarets	6/11/61

HYPERION was a long term resident at Edinburgh, for nearly 27 years, only leaving for a year at St.Margarets and a month at Canal. At the beginning she had a poor reputation, but some determined work on valve setting suggested by Norman McKillop cured any shortcomings. A hardworking stalwart over the years, she was almost unknown down south. With the conversion to double Kylchap exhaust the Haymarket A3s worked turn and turn about with the A1s, A2s and A4s, their smooth riding and fast running being an advantage on the lighter services.

One late summer evening in the mid-1950s, however, I was about to leave the lineside at milepost 7 when a gleaming loco appeared in the distance on the Dringhouses goods in place of the usual York V2. The light was fading fast, and I was down to 1/60th with a wide open lens. This was no York V2, and as the A3 drew nearer, her identity became clear - HYPERION. The photograph was poor: hand held at 1/60th was asking too much. On a visit to Doncaster in 1962 it was good to see that HYPERION had been overhauled, and a few months later, she relieved QUICKSILVER at Newcastle on the 11.00 from Kings Cross.

The 10.30 departure pulls out of Edinburgh Waverley behind HYPERION on August 29th 1953 as confirmed by the clock on the North British Hotel. The frame-mounted guard irons are still in place. She has a Diagram 94A boiler No.27072 and a GN tender No.5285. (J Robertson, transporttreasury.co.uk).

HYPERION of Haymarket in 1947-8 apple green with LNER numbering and ownership. The A3 is a sight for sore eyes, and John Robertson's beautiful photograph does her justice. The works plate details can even be picked out. The A3 has Diagram 94HP boiler 8720 and GN tender No.5261.

HYPERION makes a strong start from Waverley through the Mound Tunnel in Princes Street Gardens with a Perth express. It looks as though the driver is keen to get the fruits of the fireman's labours burning through. The date is not known, and the A3 may still be in blue livery. She has a Diagram 94A boiler No.27072 and a GN tender No.5285. (J Robertson, transporttreasury.co.uk).

FIRDAUSSI

Originally intended to be APRIL THE FIFTH

Built	11/8/34
Works No.	1793
LNER Nos.	2503, 38 (27/10/46)
Wartime black livery	2/4/42
LNER livery	13/3/47
BR No.	60038 (10/6/48)
BR blue livery	20/1/50
BR dark green livery	6/9/51
Double Kylchap fitted	30/9/59
Trough deflectors not fitted	
Withdrawn	18/11/63

Allocation

To Gateshead	11/8/34
To Heaton	30/9/39
To Gateshead	10/11/39
To Heaton	4/1/43
To Gateshead	3/5/43
To Darlington	22/2/53
To Gateshead	30/8/53
To Darlington	19/8/56
To Gateshead	24/2/57
To Holbeck	21/2/60
To Neville Hill	16/6/63

It is a subjective judgment of course, but FIRDAUSSI seems to have been one of the most elusive of the A3s, at least photographically. The Gateshead A3s were regular visitors to Kings Cross before the 1939-45 war on such diagrams as that involving the 13.20 to Edinburgh as mentioned earlier. On 4/11/35, FIRDAUSSI worked the southbound Silver Jubilee, in order to test the feasibility of using a 'green engine' as Gresley called them. There were only two A4s in existence at the time, and testing an A3 was a sensible precaution. 2510 QUICKSILVER worked the return trip. A fortnight later, on 19/11/35, QUICKSILVER remained at Newcastle while FIRDAUSSI worked the round trip to assess coal consumption. Somewhat embarrassingly, the A3 used fractionally less than the A4, 36.15lbs/mile compared with 36.7. So much for the hypothetical saving from streamlining, but two different firemen on two different runs were unlikely to return identical figures. On 23/1/36 FIRDAUSSI again worked the Silver Jubilee, replacing SILVER KING.

There were regular exchanges between Gateshead and Darlington to provide pilot engines, but with the alteration of regional boundaries in 1957 and the advent of diesel traction, allocations that had lasted for two decades and more began to change. FIRDAUSSI became a frequent sight on the Leeds-Carlisle route, and was seen in unusual places on the old LMSR system such as the old GSWR main line and at Stirling. With more diesels introduced, the end was near, and a short move to Neville Hill was followed by withdrawal.

FIRDAUSSI heads the 15.50 departure at Kings Cross in summer 1962. Now with AWS; front frames worksplate removed. The Gateshead A3 has been sent to a place called Holbeck in Leeds, unthinkable in the A3's prime. The growing fleet of A3s in the West Riding were popular with crews, but usually lacked a cleaner's touch as in this case. The electrification warning flashes have not been fixed in the usual position on the frames (as on SANDWICH on page 51 top for instance). The A3 has Diagram 107 boiler 27960 and A3 non-corridor tender No.5583. (P J Coster)

FIRDAUSSI at Haymarket in unusually splendid external condition in the early 1950s. Peppercorn A2 SAYAJIRAO is in the background. The A3 has a Diagram 94A boiler and A3 non-corridor tender.

One of Gateshead's more coy A3s, FIRDAUSSI, arrives at Haymarket shed in May 1959. The worksplates on the front frames are still in position. These duplicated the original brass plates on the smokebox. Boiler: Diagram 94A No.27018, A3 non-corridor tender No.5583.

SANDWICH

Originally intended to be FIRDAUSSI

Built	9/9/34
Works No.	1794
LNER Nos.	2504, 39 (8/7/46)
Wartime black livery	25/9/42
LNER livery	7/9/46
BR No.	60039 (9/7/48)
BR blue livery	31/3/50
BR dark green livery	26/10/51
Double Kylchap fitted	31/7/59
Trough deflectors fitted	2/6/61
Withdrawn	14/3/63

Allocation

To Gateshead	9/9/34
To Doncaster	30/11/35
To Kings Cross	6/3/39
To Grantham	9/12/41
To Kings Cross	4/6/50
To Grantham	9/9/51
To Leicester Central	7/10/56
To Kings Cross	7/4/57

SANDWICH was one of the four A3s in the 1934 batch which were sent to Gateshead, but when it was decided to move SILVER KING to there from Kings Cross, she was sent to Doncaster, curiously, as compensation. She was the first Pacific with a Diagram 94A boiler in the Southern Area, and had a good reputation as a result. For much of the time SANDWICH was a Grantham engine, but after a winter at Leicester GC, she came to Top Shed. Like many A3s, SANDWICH was a regular sight on the main line, hard at work, but nothing of note comes to mind. At Kings Cross, once the trainloads were reduced and the A3s more widely employed, she was used on Leeds and Newcastle duties. With double Kylchap exhaust she was a regular performer on the Yorkshire Pullman and Talisman services. SANDWICH was unusual in that she kept the same non-corridor high sided tender throughout her life, No.5573.

The down Talisman at speed through the new station at Hadley Wood on September 16th 1959. It is hauled not by an A4 or A1, but by newly fitted double Kylchap A3, SANDWICH. The A3 is in typically immaculate Top Shed condition, probably working hard but with a relatively clear exhaust. An excellent shot of an A3 in as fine a condition as they ever were, albeit in the evening of their time. How Sir Nigel, who once lived at Hadley Wood, would have enjoyed the sight and sound of one of his 'green engines' running so well! (Rev. A C Cawston, courtesy Brian Bailey)

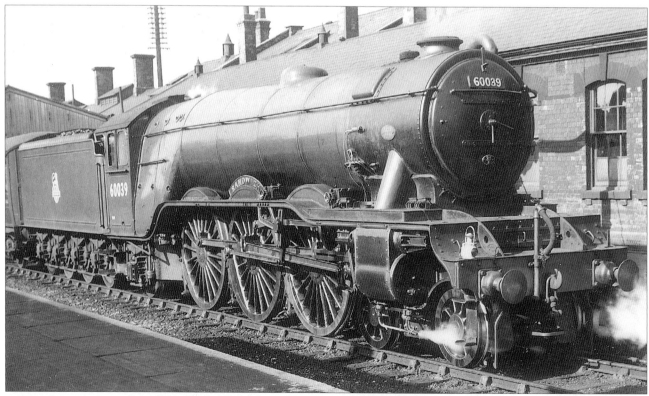

SANDWICH stands at Grantham, about to couple on or come off an up express. The date is March 22nd 1952. She has Diagram 94HP boiler 27060 and her long term companion, A3 non-corridor tender 5573.

SANDWICH runs slowly through Doncaster station on the up through line. The year is 1961, when trough deflectors were being fitted. The Class C freight is easier to identify: No.273up, the 00.30 from Inverkeithing, which was worked south of York by the engine off the previous day's 16.15 Kings Cross-Dringhouses freight. She has Diagram 107 boiler 27968 and her long term A3 non-corridor tender 5573. A minor detail – the frame mounted electrification warning flashes were moved to the curved footplate section on some A3s see page 48 and 144 for instance, among others.

SANDWICH makes a gentle start from Kings Cross platform 6 with the down Yorkshire Pullman in summer 1961. The train is formed of new roller-bearing Metro-Cammell Pullman cars with an old second class brake at each end. No brakes were built with the 1961 batch, a miserly touch by the Department of Transport. SANDWICH has new Diagram 94A boiler 27968 and her familiar A3 non-corridor tender 5573. (Derek A Potton, transporttreasury.co.uk)

CAMERONIAN

Originally intended to be SANDWICH
Built	27/10/34
Works No.	1795
LNER Nos.	2505, 575 (17/3/46), 40 (19/5/46)
Wartime black livery	29/11/42
LNER livery	22/3/47
BR No.	60040 (31/8/48)
BR blue livery	1/12/49
BR dark green livery	23/5/52
Double Kylchap fitted	16/10/59
Trough deflectors fitted	24/3/62
Withdrawn	6/7/64

Allocation
To Haymarket	27/10/34
To Gateshead	16/11/36
To York	2/12/39
To Gateshead	9/12/39
To Heaton	28/3/43
To Gateshead	3/11/45
To Darlington	20/9/53
To Gateshead	21/3/54
To Darlington	7/8/55
To Gateshead	12/2/56
To Darlington	3/11/57
To Gateshead	4/5/58
To Darlington	6/12/59
To Gateshead	19/6/60
To Gateshead	16/6/63
To Darlington	24/6/62
To Darlington	9/12/62
To Gateshead	16/6/63

Originally sent to Haymarket, CAMERONIAN went to Gateshead in late 1936, compensating for the loss of SANDWICH a year earlier. Gateshead played ping-pong with Darlington and Heaton in post-war years with their A3s, some more than others as can be seen. CAMERONIAN appeared to work north much of the time, being a rare sight in single blast days down south. She worked with her sisters on the heavy 13.20 Kings Cross-Edinburgh in the 1930s, amongst other duties. In the post-war years CAMERONIAN was a very infrequent visitor to the south, until the resumption of through working between London and Newcastle and the conversion to double Kylchap.

A down relief express for Edinburgh heads through Warkworth on August 4th 1951, headed by 60040 CAMERONIAN in blue.
I suspect that by the look of the stock and the NE reporting number, the relief has not come a long way, no farther than York.
The A3 has a Diagram 94A boiler (27026) and a GN tender (5253). (Rev. A C Cawston, courtesy Brian Bailey)

The Gateshead A3s from the last batch seemed to work north and were not frequent visitors to London except perhaps SINGAPORE. Here CAMERONIAN heads north of Wood Green Tunnel with an evening Newcastle service in 1961. The A3 has a Diagram 94A boiler (27018) and a GN tender (5253). (P J Coster)

A filthy CAMERONIAN stands, dead, at Doncaster shed in August 1959 with coach now reduced to departmental status for company. She will have been towed from the shed across to the works later, and given a general overhaul during which her existing Diagram 94A boiler No.27079 will have been removed for heavy repairs and renovated boiler No.27012 substituted.

SALMON TROUT

Originally intended to be CAMERONIAN

Built	19/12/34
Works No.	1797
LNER Nos.	2506, 41 (7/7/46)
Wartime black livery	9/5/42
LNER livery	7/5/47
BR No.	60041 (26/11/48)
BR blue livery	7/7/50
BR dark green livery	13/2/52
Double Kylchap fitted	31/7/59
Trough deflectors fitted	17/1/63
Withdrawn	4/12/65

Allocation
To Haymarket	19/12/34
To St Margarets	13/7/60

SALMON TROUT seems to have been well regarded at Haymarket when new. She was coupled to corridor tender No.5325 from October 1935 to December 1936 but there is no record of her having been used in 1936. In the event she was a reserve for sister A3 BROWN JACK. No more of note is known about her, and with the arrival of A4s and then post-war the A2s and A1s, the A3s were rather less prominent, but were still used on the principal services to Newcastle and in Scotland. Late in the steam era SALMON TROUT paid a visit or two to London working from Doncaster after general overhaul. She was one of the final three A3s on BR, earning a brief period of fame before withdrawal.

Below. SALMON TROUT runs into Waverley station to take up a southbound express on August 15th 1959. The A3 had only recently returned from Doncaster Works with a double Kylchap. Here is an example of the handrail and numberplate transposed. She has a Diagram 94A boiler No.27049 and a GN tender No.5272. (J Robertson, transporttreasury.co.uk).

SALMON TROUT in April 1957, cleaned and prepared for an important top link turn, The Queen of Scots Pullman from Edinburgh to Newcastle, returning with the down service. She has a Diagram 94A boiler No.27082 and a GN tender No.5272. It looks as though her driver is in deep discussion with a Loco Inspector on the left.

SALMON TROUT standing at Eastfield shed in 1936. Although she is attached to A3 corridor tender No.5325, SALMON TROUT was never more than a standby, sister engine BROWN JACK dominating the Non-stop in that year. The Diagram 94A boiler is No.8782. It is noticeable that the banjo dome had its shape simplified over the years. Here is one in original condition.

SINGAPORE

Originally intended to be SALMON TROUT

Built	1/12/34
Works No.	1798
LNER Nos.	2507, 42 (10/11/46)
Wartime black livery	25/8/43
LNER livery	4/1/47
BR No.	60042 (9/4/48)
BR blue livery	16/12/49
BR dark green livery	18/12/52
Double Kylchap fitted	5/9/58
Trough deflectors fitted	5/9/62
Withdrawn	13/7/64

Allocation	
To Gateshead	1/12/34
To Neville Hill	27/9/45
To Gateshead	6/5/46
To Darlington	22/3/53
To Gateshead	20/9/53
To Darlington	7/3/54
To Gateshead	5/9/54
To Darlington	11/11/56
To Gateshead	5/5/57
To Heaton	9/9/62
To Ferryhill	7/4/63
To St.Margarets	27/10/63

SINGAPORE was the newest of Gateshead's A3s, and as part of her duties was standing as pilot for the southbound Coronation on March 24th 1939. It proved to be a memorable night in railway history. 4493 WOODCOCK had been working the Coronation as far as Tweedmouth and had been replaced by C7 4-4-2 2205 after running hot. Driver Nash of Kings Cross had no doubt been alerted to take over SINGAPORE as replacement for the Atlantic. Two days earlier he had to take another A3 pilot in similar circumstances (see TRIGO).

In the no doubt urgent business of changing engines, coupling the A3 to her train by other than the heater pipe was overlooked, as became clear when SINGAPORE set off. As a result, 8 mins more were lost in coupling correctly *and* renewing the heater pipe, and Driver Nash set off 34½ mins late. The crew made one of the fastest, if not the fastest time between Newcastle and Kings Cross, 228½ mins gross, arriving 26 mins late. The train had the winter loading of 290 tons and two TSRs (Temporary Speed Restrictions) were in force, making calculation of the net time somewhat subjective. The usual figure is 222½ mins, but it depended on the rate of acceleration and braking, and 221 might be nearer.

Bear in mind we are considering the railway of 1939; this amazing run was completed mainly in darkness, oil-lit signals, no AWS, with long sections necessarily at high speed, a magnificent example of the professional skill of such as Driver Nash. The two runs by Driver Nash, together with that of PAPYRUS, demonstrated that the A3, driven hard, was not a great deal inferior to the A4. A thousand pities that nobody recorded the run.

SINGAPORE followed the usual Gateshead pattern with a number of six monthly spells as Darlington pilot, but it was preceded by six months at Neville Hill. At the end of steam she moved first to Heaton, and then for a brief spell at Ferryhill, the only time an A3 had been allocated there post-war. SINGAPORE was one of the more common visitors down south, especially after fitting with a double Kylchap.

The up Flying Scotsman was usually worked from Edinburgh by Gateshead post-war. Blue livery 60042 SINGAPORE heads the up service on August 4th 1950 at Warkworth. The train consists of thirteen Thompson or 'Newton' all-steel coaches, splendid vehicles for their time, pressure-ventilated and running on Gresley heavy duty bogies. They were covered with teak-painted panels in accordance with LNER carriage livery. (Rev. A C Cawston, courtesy Brian Bailey)

SINGAPORE, which made probably the fastest run between Newcastle and Kings Cross in 1939, has fallen on neglected times externally. Filthy, she waits at York on November 10th 1957 with the 9.40 Newcastle-Liverpool express. Even if the Gateshead A4s on the Talisman were cleaned, it is clear that so far as the rest were concerned, old habits died hard. The boiler is Diagram 94A No.27083 and the GN tender is No.5260. (M Mitchell)

BROWN JACK

Originally intended to be named CALIGULA

Built	9/2/35
Works No.	1800
LNER Nos.	2508, 43 (23/8/46)
Wartime black livery	8/6/42
LNER livery	8/6/47
BR No.	60043 (11/8/48)
BR blue livery	21/4/50
BR dark green livery	24/8/51
Double Kylchap fitted	21/2/59
Trough deflectors fitted	3/2/62
Withdrawn	14/5/64

Allocation
To Haymarket	9/2/35
To St Margarets	6/11/61

BROWN JACK, the last A3 to be built in 1935, was coupled to corridor tender no.5330 from April 1935 to February 1937 and she was used in both the 1935 and 1936 seasons on the non-stop Flying Scotsman before the A4s took over the duty in 1937. It had been proposed to fit the last A3 of the batch with rotary cam poppet valves, but it was decided in August 1934 to conduct the experiment on the hapless COCK O'THE NORTH instead. BROWN JACK had always been one of Haymarket's most popular and reliable engines. Her 29 years were free of incident and she was a regular sight on the principal East Coast services. Visits to the south were as rare as with the other Scottish A3s but I do remember that, in the midst of the summer Saturday morning expresses from Yorkshire, she was borrowed by Doncaster for a little extra running-in on an up Hull express.

Below. At one time oil traffic ran between Nottinghamshire and Scotland, and as part of this service, a train of oil tanks gets under way north of Newcastle. The loco is one of Haymarket's more famous A3s from pre-war Non-stop days, BROWN JACK. Oil tanks needed to be separated from steam traction by a pair of barrier wagons to offset any fire risk with low flashpoint oils. In order to provide through braking, the barrier wagons needed to be piped if not fitted, but those in the picture give little promise. The A3 is running as a Class E which required a minimum of four braked vehicles or a limited load: I presume the latter case applies here. The location is not far from Newcastle, in the Benton-Forest Hall area, as witness the third rail of the one-time NE DC suburban electrification. No date is given, but from the early totem, the transposed numberplate/handrail, the frame-mounted guard irons removed and elderly tank wagons, I would guess at 1954. The engine has a Diagram 94A boiler and a GN tender (5256). (Jim Smith)

One can only envy John Robertson's good fortune in being able to photograph a magnificent train, headed by an immaculate A3, in the wonderful theatre of Waverley station. The date is May 10th 1952 and the weather looks as though it was no help to the photographer. A superb picture. The boiler is Diagram 94A No.27055 and the GN tender No.5255. (J Robertson, transporttreasury.co.uk)

BROWN JACK gets under way from Newcastle past Damdykes in February 1956 with the 10.5 express from Kings Cross to Glasgow in distinctly cold weather. The A3 is in splendid external condition, despite the weather, in which the dust and dirt of the road combine with slush to coat the locomotives and stock. The reversed headboard is for either the North Briton or the Queen of Scots Pullman. Boiler: Diagram 94A No.27075, tender: No.5256. (Jim Smith)

MELTON

Built	28/6/24
Works No.	1598
Long travel valves fitted	29/12/30
LNER Nos.	2543, 44 (1/9/46)
Wartime black livery	9/12/42
Rebuilt as an A3 with LNER green livery	18/9/47
BR No.	60044 (11/8/49)
BR blue livery	11/8/49
BR dark green livery	4/12/52
Double Kylchap fitted	10/6/59
Trough deflectors fitted	30/8/61
Withdrawn	16/6/63

Allocation (A1)	
To Grantham	28/6/24
To Doncaster	21/8/24
To Gorton	1/9/24
To Doncaster	8/9/24
To Kings Cross	4/3/27
To Doncaster	20/3/27
To Grantham	19/1/30
To Doncaster	12/6/30
To Kings Cross	11/3/30
To New England	12/3/44
To Kings Cross	24/9/44
To Copley Hill	6/12/44
To New England	22/1/45
(A3)	
To Grantham	9/11/47
To Copley Hill	23/4/50
To Doncaster	9/9/51
To Leicester GC	15/11/53
To Neasden	27/3/55
To Kings Cross	25/3/56
To Grantham	16/9/56
To Kings Cross	7/4/57

MELTON was a southern area engine as both A1 and A3, and could have been seen at some time at every main line depot in the old Eastern Region - apart from the GE of course. Although no notable historical event occurred during her existence, she was one of those ever-present locos on the main line on one turn or another. MELTON was one of those A3s of which there is no shortage of illustrations.

At one time she was very run down with a high mileage, perhaps at the time of my run with her, and Shedmaster Peter Townend proposed her for general overhaul. However, the Shopping Bureau at Doncaster Works, which controlled the admission of the halt and the lame, rejected her on the grounds that she had not reached a shopping mileage, despite Peter's declared intention to take MELTON out of service. When there was a failure to agree, the Bureau's Inspector adjudicated, and in this case he maintained that the A3 was fit to work 'suitable duties'. The problem was that Top Shed had no 'suitable duties'. Peter, a protégé of the famous L.P. Parker, had learnt a trick or two over the years, and one was to mark the loco as 'Waiting Works' on his Availability Return, knowing that it would sting the Shopping Bureau into action. It was a matter of pride at the Bureau that waiting time was kept to a minimum. As a result of the ensuing confrontation, MELTON was rostered as Shed Pilot for a few days, after which she was called to Doncaster. In fact she remained out of steam since the driver, reluctant to shunt the shed with an A3, used the usual small tank engine, which was temporarily renumbered 60044 on his Driver's Ticket!

Once fitted with a double Kylchap, MELTON was one of Top Shed's regular A3s on the principal services out of London, rarely less than well turned out, working through to Newcastle as of old.

MELTON starts away from old platform 8 at Kings Cross on July 1ˢᵗ 1960. A Darlington-built A1 is in old platform 6, coupled to one of New England's trusty Green Arrows, 60924. The A3 has Diagram 94HP boiler 27072 and GN tender No.5274. (B. Wilson, transport treasury.co.uk)

Now modified with a double chimney and trough deflectors, with a GN tender again, 60044 MELTON heads a down express north of Oakleigh Park station in October 1961. The A3 is an example of the works plates having been transferred to the cab sides. In the background, in the modest up yard, crated Vauxhall car components were staged forward from Luton to the London docks, the trains being hauled by J52 0-6-0Ts and later J50 0-6-0Ts. How things have changed! Boiler: 94A (27072) Tender: GN (5274). (John F Aylard)

MELTON at speed with the down Tees-Thames north of Hitchin in December 1959. When photographing an express moving fast, it was essential to catch the steam locomotive with the coupling rods at or near top dead centre, revealing the full expanse of the driving wheels as in John Aylard's shot of this engine. It was largely a matter of luck of course since one had only one twentieth of a second or less at speed. The result of failure is here, and with the coupling rods at bottom dead centre, any impression of speed is lost, but I can assure the reader that MELTON was indeed going very fast. The A3 has Diagram 94A boiler 27035 and GN tender No.5274. (P J Coster)

LEMBERG

Built	26/7/24
Works No.	1600
LNER Nos.	2544, 45 (3/11/46).
Rebuilt as A3/2 long travel valves	3/12/27
Fitted with 19ins cylinders	16/4/32
Wartime black livery	20/5/42
LNER livery	18/6/47
BR No.	60045 (5/6/48)
BR experimental purple livery	5/6/48
BR blue livery	8/11/50
BR dark green livery	18/4/52
Double Kylchap fitted	17/10/59
Trough deflectors fitted	1/11/62
Withdrawn	23/11/64

Allocation (A1)	
To Gorton	26/7/24
To Doncaster	27/8/24
(A3)	
To Gateshead	6/1/37
To Heaton	17/5/38
To Gateshead	22/1/40
To Darlington	28/2/54
To Gateshead	7/3/54
To Darlington	21/3/54
To Gateshead	26/10/54
To Darlington	13/11/55
To Gateshead	27/5/56
To Darlington	4/5/58
To Gateshead	16/11/58
To Heaton	9/9/62
To Darlington	9/12/62
To Gateshead	16/6/63
To Heaton	2/6/63
To Gateshead	16/6/63
To Darlington	15/12/63

LEMBERG was one of the two A1s selected for fitting with the new Diagram 94HP 220psi boiler in 1927. The experiment in higher pressure was undertaken as a result of the 1925 Exchange with the GWR. She was fitted with longer travel valves at the same time. LEMBERG had her cylinders lined down to 18¼ins to achieve parity of tractive effort with the A1, while the other A1, ENTERPRISE, retained her 20ins cylinders. Subsequent testing was in comparison with sister Doncaster shed standard A1, 4473 SOLARIO, but not with ENTERPRISE as well. As one might expect from two very similar locomotives, the results were virtually identical. LEMBERG was, however, noticeably faster despite smaller cylinders. In her ten years at Doncaster, she gained a very good reputation, especially for speed in the hands of her usual driver, Charlie Molson. The A3/2 designation was scrapped in 12/38, LEMBERG becoming an A3.

Experience with LEMBERG led Gresley to base the A3 design on the new boiler and 19ins cylinders, midway between the 20ins of the A1s and LEMBERG. In due course she became a standard A3. The conversion to A3 was really no more than reboiling and presumably lining the existing cylinders down from 20 to 19ins. The arrangement and size of steam pipes should have been improved at this stage but they were not, and the limited and contorted A1 arrangement was perpetuated.

With the arrival of the A4s, a number of A1s and A3s went north from the southern area, one of them LEMBERG. Like the other Gateshead A3s, she spent several periods as the Darlington pilot. This task usually required a low mileage A3, though it was only the Tees-Tyne Pullman or Night Scotsman which was likely to bring a Darlington pilot up to London. With the increased through working restored in 1956-57, LEMBERG was an occasional visitor with the overnight services, hitherto dominated by Peppercorn A1s.

Gateshead's **LEMBERG** brings an up train in towards Newcastle, past Damdykes on December 29th 1954. The A3 is running easily with a fairly light load that includes a fair number of parcels vans. Although she had only been at Gateshead two months, the external condition of LEMBERG is quite appalling, and although there may be some valid reason such as a lack of space and staff, Gateshead's record of cleanliness was as bad as any main line shed on the East Coast main line and worse than most. The signals by the A3 are good examples of the pre-war LNER single aspect colour light design, with the truncated semaphore arm serving as a mechanically operated filter in front of the powerful Adlake single lamp. Boiler: Diagram 94A No.27063 and GN tender No.5228. (Jim Smith)

LEMBERG pounds up to Potters Bar past Greenwood with a heavy train, the 16.00 from Kings Cross, in June 1929. She has a Diagram 94HP boiler No.8028 and a GN tender No.5228. The rebuilt A1 retains right-hand drive. One of the GN O2s (or one of the then O1s) is on the down goods, waiting for the road through the bottleneck. The down home somersault signal has a sighting board behind the arm.

Doncaster's 2544 LEMBERG was either a replacement for failure, or has been borrowed by Kings Cross during the 1931 winter timetable. It is seen here working the up Flying Scotsman, pulling away from Grantham. She has boiler No.8027 from the 1931 general overhaul, with GN tender No.5228. (Rev. A C Cawston, courtesy Brian Bailey)

DIAMOND JUBILEE

Built	9/8/24
Works No.	1601
Long travel valves fitted	29/5/31
Rebuilt as an A3	23/8/41
Wartime black livery	14/3/43
LNER Nos.	2545, 46 (13/7/46)
LNER green livery	13/11/47
BR No.	60046 (5/8/49)
BR blue livery	5/8/49
BR dark green livery	29/10/52
Double Kylchap fitted	8/8/58
Trough deflectors fitted	7/12/61
Withdrawn	16/6/63

Allocation (A1)	
To Gorton	9/8/24
To Kings Cross	3/9/24
To Grantham	7/6/28
(A3)	
To Copley Hill	30/9/43
To Kings Cross	8/12/44
To Copley Hill	30/5/48
To Doncaster	9/9/51
To Grantham	14/6/59
To New England	9/9/62
To Grantham	21/4/63

DIAMOND JUBILEE, as a single blast Pacific, never conveyed the impression post-war that she was one of the better A3s. She was not one that was seen regularly on top duties at busy times. She was selected from the Kings Cross fleet to replace FLYING FOX as the LNER representative in the 1925 exchanges on the LNER main line, but ran badly and there was trouble with the sanding gear. It was also unfortunate that her driver, Ben Glasgow, like many of his contemporaries, had learnt his skills on old slide valve engines, and drove on the regulator with a long cut-off, hardly the best way to handle a Gresley Pacific even with short travel valves. However, having been modified with a double Kylchap near the end of her life, a rejuvenated DIAMOND JUBILEE became a much more common sight on the main line from Doncaster and Grantham.

Below. **DIAMOND JUBILEE, a Doncaster engine complete with White Rose headboard, standing at Grantham facing north on May 11th 1953. The White Rose didn't stop there in the down direction as it was non-stop to Doncaster, but the up train did, and its engine, DIAMOND JUBILEE, would have been replaced by a Kings Cross engine, in this case, 60800 GREEN ARROW. So DIAMOND JUBILEE has been turned ready to return north (in which case the headboard should have been taken off). The engine has a Diagram 94A boiler (27047) and the A4 non-corridor tender (5644) which she retained from rebuilding. (R E Vincent, transporttreasury.co.uk)**

DIAMOND JUBILEE in old platform 7 at Kings Cross with a down express on July 7th 1962. From my experience, this A3 was transformed by fitting a double Kylchap, and became a regular sight on the main line. The engine has a Diagram 94A boiler (27086) and an A4 non-corridor tender (5644).

As DIAMOND JUBILEE drifts into Peterborough with a down freight, an Ivatt 4MT 2-6-0 sets out with a local freight. By this time the large fleet of Ivatt Senior and Gresley's J6 0-6-0s had almost disappeared, and the 2-6-0s of Ivatt Junior were left to cope with the dwindling freight service. New England had lost a great deal of its vast allocation by 1963, and all sorts of strangers were used on the main line, even some ex-LMSR types. I would imagine that 60046 was within a few weeks of withdrawal. The engine has a Diagram 94A boiler (27086) and an A4 non-corridor tender (5644). (B Richardson, transporttreasury.co.uk)

DONOVAN

Built	30/8/24
Works No.	1602
Long travel valves fitted	23/12/27
Wartime black livery	18/12/42
LNER Nos.	2546, 47 (17/9/46)
Rebuilt to A3 with LNER green livery	9/1/48
BR No.	60047 (8/5/48)
BR blue livery	16/6/49
BR dark green livery	20/2/52
Double Kylchap fitted	2/7/59
Trough deflectors fitted	7/61
Withdrawn	8/4/63

Allocation (A1)	
To Kings Cross	30/8/24
To Grantham	1/6/28
To Kings Cross	7/6/28
To Neasden	30/6/39
To Gorton	23/2/41
To Kings Cross	18/12/42
To Gorton	26/7/44
To Kings Cross	29/10/44
To Copley Hill	17/12/44
To Doncaster	22/1/45
To Grantham	28/10/45
To Kings Cross	19/5/46
(A3)	
To Doncaster	4/6/50
To Kings Cross	7/1/51
To Grantham	9/9/51
To Kings Cross	20/6/54
To Grantham	17/10/54
To New England	9/9/62

DONOVAN, in LNER apple green livery and BR numbering and ownership, roars through Hadley Wood with a down Edinburgh express in the period mid-1948 to mid-1949. A constant presence on the GN over the years, mostly a long-term Grantham engine, she has a heavy train, and by the look of the exhaust, both fireman and A3 are working hard. One of the last conversions to A3 at the beginning of 1948, she has a Diagram 94A boiler (8778) and a GN tender No.5284. She is still right-hand drive.

DONOVAN had been a Kings Cross engine for several years when on May 1st 1928 the very first non-stop Flying Scotsman ran between Kings Cross and Edinburgh Waverley. FLYING SCOTSMAN ran hot on the first down train, although the overheating was contained by use of the slacker pipe. She was repaired at Haymarket and returned on May 2nd, while at Kings Cross DONOVAN was hastily got ready as a replacement.

Why, one may ask, when the A1s with corridor tenders, DONCASTER and ROYAL LANCER should have been available? FLYING FOX was due for overhaul, but DONCASTER and ROYAL LANCER had recently undergone general overhauls and attachment to a corridor tender. In passing, general overhauls in the 1920s seemed to take about three months. Indeed, the corridor tender no.5327 attached to DONCASTER on April 26th at Doncaster was removed at Kings Cross on May 2nd and attached to DONOVAN.

This happened at a time when it had been decided that the locomotive number would be moved from the tender side to the cab. DONOVAN had the number on the tender, and the new corridor tender no.5327 bore only the LNER characters, therefore she was anonymous numerically. After a successful return trip, the tenders were exchanged back again, DONOVAN recovering her original GN tender. By the end of the 1930s, the arrival of 35 A4s had resulted in the displacement of the older Pacifics to the GC and lesser sheds on the main line such as York and Neville Hill; DONOVAN moved first to Neasden and then to Gorton.

One of the last A1s, now A10s since the rebuilding of GREAT NORTHERN in 1945, DONOVAN emerged rebuilt in the first days of BR. Most of her time was divided between Kings Cross and Grantham, mainly the latter, and she was one of the regular A3s there when the principal services were worked by Peppercorn A1s, occasionally deputising for the top link. In the 1950s when Grantham lost its A1s, the remaining turns were taken over by the A3s, which were being fitted with double Kylchaps. At first the loss of the A1s was felt keenly, but when it was realised how well the rejuvenated A3s would run, crews took to them happily, DONOVAN being one of the more regular visitors to London.

The down Queen of Scots Pullman passing through the old Hadley Wood station, hauled by DONOVAN. The leading brake has been replaced by a BG. The period is probably 1948-49. The A3 is in apple green livery, is still right-hand drive, and has a Diagram 94A boiler (8778) and a GN tender No.5284.

LNER 2546, before naming as DONOVAN, with a down express north of New Southgate in 1925. The train hardly looks inviting, but no doubt the construction of new Gresley stock would soon start to make an improvement. The A1 has Diagram 94 boiler 7764 and a GN tender No.5256.

DONCASTER

Built	30/8/24
Works No.	1603
Long travel valves fitted	25/2/28
Wartime black livery	19/9/42
LNER Nos.	2547, 48 (16/5/46)
Rebuilt to A3	16/5/46
LNER green livery	23/6/47
BR No.	60048 (11/11/48)
BR blue livery	15/9/50
BR dark green livery	19/9/52
Double Kylchap fitted	29/5/59
Small deflectors fitted	26/11/59
Trough deflectors fitted	15/12/61
Withdrawn	8/9/63

Allocation (A1)	
To Grantham	30/8/24
To Kings Cross	11/3/27
To Grantham	27/3/27
To Kings Cross	26/4/28
To Doncaster	31/10/35
(A3)	
To Leicester GC	6/2/49
To Doncaster	15/11/53
To Kings Cross	8/6/58
To Doncaster	25/1/59
To Grantham	8/2/59
To New England	9/9/62
To Grantham	21/4/63

DONCASTER, despite the name, had been running for 11 years before going there. In 1928 she was sent to Kings Cross after general overhaul, complete with a new corridor tender for duty on the non-stop Flying Scotsman. She retained this until June 1933, and in 1935 went north to her namesake shed, displaced by the first A4s. She had nearly five years on the GC post-war before returning to Doncaster, followed by spells at Kings Cross, Grantham and New England. With the fitting of the double Kylchap, DONCASTER was one of the four selected for the trial fitting of small deflectors, which proved unsuccessful.

DONCASTER at Doncaster shed soon after general overhaul, in 1954 or 1956. The A3 has a Diagram 94A boiler, and her usual GN tender No.5283.

DONCASTER, one of the pre-war Kings Cross Non-stop A1s, at speed through the old Hadley Wood station with an up Grimsby express. The A3 is still in LNER numbering and livery, which would suggest summer 1948. In fact there was only one train until the 1950s when a second was added, reaching Kings Cross at about 13.15. In March 1950, Pacifics and V2s gave way to B1s from Immingham. The old signalbox, by then a ground frame, is still in place with its connection to the then defunct goods yard. The A3 is still right-hand drive, and has Diagram 94HP boiler 9573 and an A3 non-corridor tender No.5566.

DONCASTER, in truly appalling external condition, enters Peterborough on August 6th 1960. She was one of the four A3s fitted with the small chimneyside deflectors to avoid drifting exhaust with the double Kylchap. These were ineffective and were replaced by trough deflectors. The boiler is a Diagram 94A boiler 27039 and the GN tender No.5283. (Frank Hornby)

GALTEE MORE

Built	27/9/24
Works No.	1604
Long travel valves fitted	18/10/28
Wartime black livery	26/3/42
Rebuilt to A3	13/10/45
LNER Nos.	2548, 517 (25/4/46), 49 (14/7/46)
LNER green livery	28/12/46
BR No.	60049 (24/6/48)
BR blue livery	31/8/50
BR dark green livery	25/7/52
Double Kylchap fitted	4/3/59
Trough deflectors fitted	21/10/60
Withdrawn	29/12/62

Allocation (A1)	
To Grantham	27/9/24
To Doncaster	5/7/30
To Grantham	17/8/30
To New England	5/1/42
To Grantham	10/7/42
To New England	11/10/42
To Grantham	8/5/43
To Doncaster	13/10/43
To Grantham	12/10/44
To Doncaster	6/12/44
(A3)	
To Leicester GC	6/2/49
To Kings Cross	26/6/55
To Grantham	15/9/57

GALTEE MORE was one of the group of A1s at Grantham that performed yeoman service in the 1920-30 period, before war intervened. A long spell at Leicester followed before returning to Grantham. GALTEE MORE was notable as the prototype for trough type deflectors in October 1960. After Grantham's Peppercorn A1s had moved to Kings Cross and Doncaster, the newly double blast A3s took over, and for a few years before the end, ran very well. GALTEE MORE was one of this group.

2548 GALTEE MORE leaving Grantham on 7.25 a.m. Kings Cross to Leeds & York on 'Grand National' Friday, March 1932. (Rev. A C Cawston, courtesy Brian Bailey)

GALTEE MORE was the first A3 to be fitted with trough deflectors as an experiment in October 1960, based on the German design. This shows the A3 with the 14.00 from Kings Cross in early 1961 when grime ('BR Grey') had become the universal livery. The A3 has Diagram 94A boiler 27005 and a GN tender No.5232. (P J Coster).

PERSIMMON

Built	25/10/24
Works No.	1605
Long travel valves fitted	23/7/27
Wartime black livery	14/3/42
Rebuilt to A3	15/12/43
LNER Nos.	2549, 518 (18/3/46), 50 (8/7/46)
LNER green livery	3/4/47
BR No.	E50 (3/2/48), 60050 (18/8/48)
BR blue livery	27/7/49
BR dark green livery	26/9/52
Double Kylchap fitted	20/4/59
Trough deflectors fitted	19/10/61
Withdrawn	11/6/63

Allocation (A1)	
To Doncaster	25/10/24
To Grantham	16/7/27
To New England	5/1/42
To Grantham	10/7/42
To New England	11/10/42
To Grantham	7/5/43
(A3)	
To Kings Cross	27/10/46
To Grantham	30/5/48
To Kings Cross	16/6/48
To Neasden	3/2/49
To Kings Cross	3/7/55
To Neasden	9/10/55
To Kings Cross	24/6/56
To Grantham	16/9/56
To New England	17/6/62

PERSIMMON was one of those locomotives that seemed, from the lineside and on the main line, to be fairly anonymous post-war. She was one of the Grantham fleet that was renowned in the 1920-30s as the Peppercorn A1s post-war. By April 1940, when the LNER was operating a heavily reduced passenger service, individual trainloads had rocketed. The up morning Newcastle was hauled by PERSIMMON, and by the time the train had arrived at Peterborough the load had grown to roughly 850 tons. The A1 was relieved by brand new V2 4800 for the run to Kings Cross. After the war PERSIMMON was passed around before spending seven years on the GC section at Neasden. Neasden's Pacifics seemed to spend more time out of service, no doubt waiting for repaired components, and she was a frequent sight standing behind the shed. Once fitted with a double Kylchap she was a more familiar sight on the main line. My last memories of PERSIMMON are of an A3 that could hardly be blacker; apart, that is, for the compulsory unemptied smokebox and burnt door, double heading a failed Type 4 into Kings Cross.

60050 PERSIMMON at Neasden shed in May 1957. The A3 has Diagram 94HP boiler 27084 and a GN tender No.5259. (P J Coster).

LNER 2549 PERSIMMON of Grantham in the Kings Cross milk dock sidings, probably off an up service. The A1 is in forward gear but no doubt when the road is clear will back into the loco yard and turntable. The year is 1933, the Diagram 94 boiler 7790 (built for SCEPTRE) and GN tender No.5264.

BLINK BONNY

Built	12/11/24
Works No.	1606
Long travel valves fitted	8/11/27
Wartime black livery	14/3/42
LNER Nos.	2550, 51 (24/8/46)
Rebuilt to A3	17/11/45
LNER green livery	17/5/47
BR No.	60051 (25/9/48)
BR blue livery	23/11/50
BR dark green livery	4/12/52
Double Kylchap fitted	8/8/59
Trough deflectors fitted	29/3/62
Withdrawn	23/11/64

Allocation (A1)	
To Gorton	12/11/24
To Grantham	9/2/25
To New England	5/1/42
To Grantham	2/5/43
To New England	11/6/44
To Gorton	14/7/44
To Kings Cross	29/10/44
To Grantham	11/11/44
(A3)	
To Kings Cross	27/10/46
To Neasden	3/2/49
To Grantham	15/11/53
To Copley Hill	2/5/54
To Heaton	15/9/57
To Gateshead	5/1/58
To Darlington	8/6/58
To Gateshead	7/12/58
To Darlington	19/6/60
To Gateshead	18/12/60
To Heaton	9/9/62
To Gateshead	15/12/63
To Darlington	2/6/63

BLINK BONNY was one of the Grantham stud for nearly two decades before the transfer merry-go-round of the 1939-45 war. After the war there were spells at several depots, notably Copley Hill. Some drivers there were happy to take BLINK BONNY on London turns, notably Driver Nicholls. Copley Hill had a small number of A3s along with their 10-12 Peppercorn A1s, but if an A3 appeared, it was usually BLINK BONNY. I have mentioned elsewhere her occasional appearances on the down 'Bradford Flyer', the lusty roar of the single blast A3 accelerating her train out of London contrasting with the quieter rasping sound of a Peppercorn A1. She was a regular sight on the main line post-war, and was still a frequent visitor when she was moved to Tyneside. With changes to the Regional boundary in 1957, the four A3s then at Copley Hill were sent to Heaton and Gateshead, where they spent several spells as Darlington pilot.

BLINK BONNY on a down express in 1925-28. The location is a puzzle since the lineside and signalling has changed so much in eight decades. I would plump for the approach to the old Stevenage station, where a long straight led south to Langley troughs, with a girder overbridge and a three-arch bridge at the troughs. Stevenage South signalbox is in the right background – I think. The Diagram 94 boiler is 7768, and the GN tender is No.5260.

Grantham's BLINK BONNY pounds up the last yards to the summit at Potters Bar on August 15th 1939 with a down express. The A1 has Diagram 94 boiler 7696 and GN tender No.5260.

A poor print, but suited to the times; BLINK BONNY in wartime black with the wartime NE on the tender. The date would be prior to May 1947 when apple green was restored. The location is the long curve from Brookmans Park towards Welham Green, better known to GNR aficionados as Marshmoor. The A3 has Diagram 94HP boiler 8081 and a GN tender No.5260.

75

PRINCE PALATINE

Built	29/11/24
Works No.	1607
Long travel valves fitted	23/11/29
Rebuilt to A3	8/8/41
Wartime black livery	22/4/43
LNER Nos.	2551, 520 (5/4/46), 52 (11/5/46)
LNER green livery	24/6/47
BR No.	60052 (7/10/48)
BR blue livery	18/5/49
BR dark green livery	9/4/52
Double Kylchap fitted	20/11/58
Trough deflectors fitted	12/10/62
Withdrawn	17/1/66

Allocation (A1)

To Gorton	29/11/24
To Grantham	9/2/25

(A3)

To Copley Hill	28/9/43
To New England	29/5/44
To Doncaster	12/12/48
To Leicester	22/5/49
To Neasden	4/7/54
To Leicester	5/12/54
To Copley Hill	28/8/55
To Heaton	15/9/57
To Gateshead	5/1/58
To Darlington	19/6/60
To Gateshead	18/12/60
To Heaton	9/9/62
To Darlington	9/12/62
To Heaton	2/6/63
To Gateshead	16/6/63
To St.Margarets	25/8/63

After most of her pre-war years at Grantham, PRINCE PALATINE had a lengthy spell on the GC. Two years at Copley Hill brought her occasionally down the main line to London, but in 1957 the Leeds quartet was sent to Heaton and Gateshead. Hitherto she had been at sheds that were not involved in London-Newcastle through working. In single blast condition PRINCE PALATINE had led a relatively anonymous existence and conveyed the impression that she was not one of the better performers in the class. She was not one of the more frequent A3 visitors on the main line, but with conversion to double Kylchap, like most of the class, the number scarcely mattered. At Newcastle she worked overnight services to Kings Cross, quite possibly for the first time in her existence. It was ironic that she should have survived to be the last A3 in service.

PRINCE PALATINE cruises through Manors with a Scottish Locomotive Preservation Society railtour on June 5th 1965. The A3 has Diagram 107 boiler 29294 and a GN tender No.5288. (I S Carr)

PRINCE PALATINE, the last A3 to remain in service, at Haymarket, 1959-61. She was one of the last of the old GN Pacifics to proceed north displaced, first by A4s, then Peppercorn A1s, and lastly, diesels. The A3 has Diagram 94A boiler 27012 and a GN tender No.5288.

In 1955 after six years on the GC section, 60052 PRINCE PALATINE was sent to Copley Hill, from where she appeared on the Ardsley diagram for the 13.18 from Kings Cross to Leeds in 1956. The stock was that of the 7.28 from Leeds, which remained in platform and formed the 13.18. This made for a long wait for the relief crew, sitting on the incoming Kings Cross A4 on the buffer stops for nearly two hours. The A3 has Diagram 94A boiler 27058 and a GN tender No.5288.

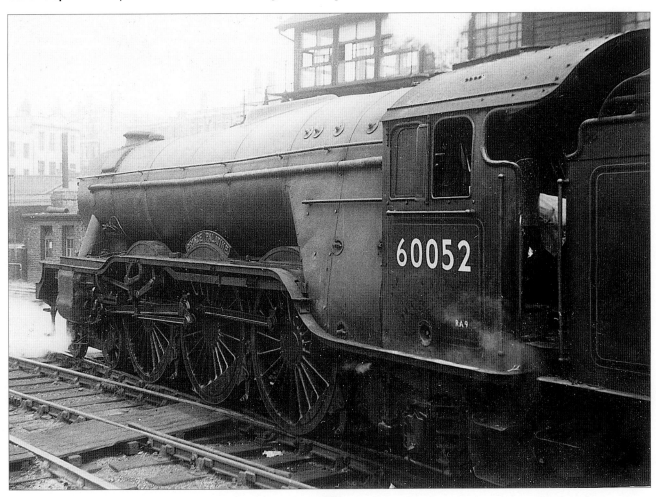

SANSOVINO

Built	11/12/24
Works No.	1608
Long travel valves fitted	25/2/28
Rebuilt to A3 with black livery	2/9/43
LNER Nos.	2552, 521 (16/3/46), 53 (30/11/46)
LNER green livery	17/10/47
BR No.	60053 (5/2/49)
BR blue livery	12/5/52
Double Kylchap fitted	12/11/58
Trough deflectors not fitted	
Withdrawn	27/5/63

Allocation: (A1)
To Kings Cross	11/12/24
To Neasden	14/6/39
To Kings Cross	21/11/42
To Copley Hill	15/2/43
(A3)	
To New England	26/12/44
To Leicester	7/2/49
To Doncaster	22/5/49
To Grantham	31/5/49
To Copley Hill	2/5/54
To Gateshead	15/9/57
To Darlington	7/12/58
To Gateshead	7/6/59
To Darlington	18/6/61
To Gateshead	17/12/61
To Heaton	9/9/62
To St.Margarets	21/4/63

SANSOVINO was one of the Kings Cross favourites, over nearly 15 years. In June 1928 she was coupled to corridor tender no.5329 but despite having been modified with long travel valves, she was only used twice in 1928. Post-war she had spells at Grantham and Copley Hill before migrating north to Tyneside. A very common sight on the GN main line, SANSOVINO was curiously evasive when cameras were about.

The Queen of Scots was given over to 4-6-2 haulage south of Leeds in September 1936, when A1s 2553 PRINCE OF WALES and 2555 CENTENARY were transferred to Copley Hill to replace the aging Ivatt C1 4-4-2s that had monopolised the duty (together with D11 4-4-0s for a short period 1930-32). In August 1938 it is 2553 that is captured for posterity by Arthur Cawston descending Stoke bank near Saltersford crossing with the down train. The dating is confirmed by the class A1 painted on the buffer beam; this practice was only introduced in April 1938 and the replacement A3 2744 GRAND PARADE and the later A4s were the first to receive this addition on their fronts.

'Is that where the key goes?' The driver of SANSOVINO on the 14.00 Newcastle is more concerned to see the Guard's green flag. The train is in old platform 10 at Kings Cross. The A3 now has a double Kylchap and the BR speedometer, and has been moved to Gateshead. The date would be May-June 1961. She has a Diagram 94A boiler 27013, and her usual A3 non-corridor tender No.5570. (P J Coster)

PRINCE OF WALES (MANNA)

Built	31/12/24
Works No.	1609
Renamed	11/11/26
Long travel valves fitted	21/12/29
Rebuilt to A3 with black livery	28/7/43
LNER Nos.	2553, 522 (17/3/46), 54 (23/9/46)
LNER green livery	2/11/46
BR No.	60054 (9/4/48)
BR blue livery	20/4/50
BR dark green livery	14/11/51
Double Kylchap fitted	29/8/58
Trough deflectors fitted	10/5/62
Withdrawn	28/6/64

Allocation (A1)

To Gorton	31/12/24
To Kings Cross	28/1/25
To Doncaster	11/5/28
To Copley Hill	28/10/36
To Doncaster	27/5/40
To Grantham	18/3/40
To New England	11/10/42
(A3)	
To Leicester	7/2/49
To Kings Cross	10/6/56
To Grantham	16/6/57
To Doncaster	8/9/63
To New England	20/10/63

PRINCE OF WALES was one of the two A1s sent from Doncaster to Copley Hill in 1936. This transfer was partly to replace the Ivatt Atlantics on the Queen of Scots Pullman and partly to be a standby in case the Kings Cross A4 was unfit to work back to London with the West Riding Limited streamliner, introduced in autumn 1937. She was one of the occasional substitutes; on 7/7/38 for example. Access over the Calder Viaduct at Wakefield had been restricted until the early 1930s, and although A1s and A3s worked into Leeds, none was allocated there. After the 1939-45 war, there were long spells on the GC at Leicester and at Grantham. PRINCE OF WALES had a good reputation at Grantham and while at Kings Cross she took part in trials to assess any problems arising with the use of A3s to Newcastle on lodging turns. Many of the returning Leicester A3s impressed with their reliability, and one got the impression that maintenance there was of a high standard.

Note the shape of the banjo dome – more properly now described as 'streamlined'.

PRINCE OF WALES leaving Doncaster for the south. The engine has a double Kylchap and a Diagram 107 boiler, which sets the date after September 1958. She is just ex-works, so either that or March 1960 are the probable dates. The boiler number is 29308 or 17, and the GN tender No.5264. Note the shape of the banjo dome – more properly now described as 'streamlined'. (transporttreasury.co.uk)

PRINCE OF WALES, a Top Shed A3, is a magnificent sight starting away from Kings Cross with the 12.18 Northumbrian on May 18th 1957. The A3 has been overhauled two months earlier, and is in immaculate external condition. The boiler is Diagram 94A No.27024 and the GN tender is No.5264. The author of the smoke behind the signalbox would be in trouble as a result of the Clean Air Act if caught! (J Robertson, transporttreasury.co.uk)

PRINCE OF WALES at the head of a heavy down express, passing Wood Green Tunnel signalbox. As the number is on the cab side, the date must be after 1928, but as the class is not displayed on the buffer beam it must be before March 1938. There is little else to focus it more precisely. The A1 Pacific has a Diagram 94 boiler and a GN tender, but which one depends on the actual date.

WOOLWINDER

Built	31/12/24
Works No.	1610
Long travel valves fitted	14/6/30
Rebuilt to A3 with black livery	3/6/42
LNER Nos.	2554 then 55 (28/9/46)
LNER green livery	14/11/47
BR No.	60055 (4/6/48)
BR blue livery	4/8/50
BR dark green livery	28/11/51
Double Kylchap fitted	17/6/58
Small deflectors fitted	28/10/59
Trough deflectors not fitted	
Withdrawn	4/9/61

Allocation (A1)	
To Doncaster	31/12/24
To Grantham	29/4/27
To Kings Cross	15/7/29
To Grantham	6/10/29
To Doncaster	10/10/29
To Grantham	16/10/29
To Gorton	18/8/39
(A3)	
To Grantham	22/11/42
To Copley Hill	2/10/43
To Kings Cross	16/12/44
To Doncaster	4/6/50
To Kings Cross	10/6/56

WOOLWINDER was at Grantham pre-war for a long spell, and at Doncaster post-war, where she was a regular sight on such as the 9.15 York and Hull to Kings Cross. When she came to Kings Cross, she was well spoken of, being used on tests with PRINCE OF WALES as mentioned above. She was the first A3 to be fitted post-war with a double Kylchap. Later she was fitted with small deflectors which were of little use. Sadly, she was one of the three early withdrawals in 1961, when her condition was judged to be beyond economic repair.

WOOLWINDER at Kings Cross shed in her first years. The engine has her original Diagram 94 boiler (7772) and GN tender (5264). Early A1 hydrostatic lubricator feeds alongside the boiler.

The 15.50 Kings Cross-Leeds express passes through the bottleneck that was Peterborough North on June 23rd 1954, via the down slow, hauled by Doncaster's 60055 WOOLWINDER. The A3 had a low mileage, having been overhauled some months before, and at that time she was a regular sight on the 9.15 from York and Hull to Kings Cross and the 15.50 return. (R E Vincent, transporttreasury.co.uk)

CENTENARY

Built	7/2/25
Works No.	1611
Long travel valves fitted	25/3/27
Wartime black livery	24/10/42
Rebuilt to A3	16/8/44
LNER Nos.	2555 then 56 (10/7/46)
LNER green livery	5/9/47
BR No.	60056 (18/5/49)
BR blue livery	18/5/49
BR dark green livery	13/5/52
Double Kylchap fitted	15/7/59
Trough deflectors fitted	18/8/61
Withdrawn	13/5/63

Allocation (A1)	
To Doncaster	7/2/25
To Gorton	9/2/25
To Doncaster	24/2/25
To Grantham	5/10/29
To Doncaster	17/10/29
To Grantham	13/12/35
To New England	1/1/36
To Kings Cross	5/2/36
To New England	19/2/36
To Grantham	23/10/36
To Copley Hill	29/10/36
To Doncaster	26/2/40
To Grantham	18/3/40
To Doncaster	11/12/41
(A3)	
To Grantham	6/12/44
To Kings Cross	27/10/46
To Copley Hill	30/5/48
To Doncaster	9/9/51
To Grantham	7/10/51
To Doncaster	25/5/52
To Kings Cross	22/6/52
To Grantham	15/2/53

CENTENARY was the first A1 built in 1925 and was named to commemorate the Centenary celebrations of 1925. She was the first A1 to be fitted experimentally with the 1926 revised valve gear with a longer valve travel. Subsequent testing established the extent of CENTENARY's superiority in coal and water consumption, although the pivotal moment came when Gresley himself rode on her from Doncaster to Kings Cross. Previously unconvinced of the need to spend what would have been a considerable sum on almost new locomotives, Gresley promptly authorised the modification on arrival at Kings Cross. CENTENARY moved around the main line depots, principally Doncaster, before joining PRINCE OF WALES at Copley Hill in 1936. After the 1939-1945 war she was at Grantham for most of the time, where she was one of the A3s often used in place of the Peppercorn A1s.

In 1952 a series of test runs took place to establish section times for timetabling, and CENTENARY was nominated for the tests as a typically high mileage A3 by L.P. Parker, the Regional Motive Power Superintendent. Ted Hailstone was the driver, and CENTENARY was driven hard, so hard that his superb fireman, Jim Wilson, said that if this was the future, he was leaving the railway! On one descent from Stoke, Peter Townend, in charge of testing, prompted Ted that the speed was less than 90mph and he should go a little faster. 88mph was not 90mph in LP's judgment! As the cut-off was lengthened, Peter noticed that the Flaman recorder needles were fouling, and on adjusting them, the speed shot up to 96mph! She was one of Grantham's regular deputies for their Peppercorn A1s, and over time worked most of their top duties.

CENTENARY gathering speed with a very heavy train at Harringay. The date is later than 1928 but no details are given. I would assume the period to be mid-1930s. She is right-hand drive, and has Diagram 94 boiler and a GN tender No.5264.

CENTENARY, passing Tollerton with an express. The date must lie between April 1957 and early 1959, but the problem with the Plain of York, unless one knows it closely, is that it is difficult to distinguish between down and up. The shadows point to an up express. The Diagram 94A boiler is probably 27017 and the GN tender No.5257.

ORMONDE

Built	18/2/25
Works No.	1612
Long travel valves fitted	6/11/30
Wartime black livery	12/12/41
Rebuilt to A3 with LNER green livery	11/1/47
LNER Nos.	2556 then 57 (8/9/46)
BR No.	60057 (16/8/48)
BR blue livery	28/7/49
BR dark green livery	10/10/52
Double Kylchap fitted	19/9/58
Trough deflectors fitted	21/9/61
Withdrawn	28/10/63

Allocation (A1)	
To Grantham	18/2/25
To Kings Cross	1/6/28
To Grantham	7/6/28
To Doncaster	15/9/38
To Haymarket	9/3/39
To St.Margarets	15/3/39
To Eastfield	2/2/40
To Haymarket	4/12/40
To Tay Bridge	7/3/43
To Haymarket	24/4/43
(A3)	
To Carlisle Canal	23/4/61
To Haymarket	15/5/61
To St.Margarets	13/12/61

ORMONDE was another of the Grantham fleet that was a familiar sight over the years, but with the arrival of more A4s in the south, two A1s moved north to Tyneside, and one, ORMONDE, went to Haymarket. While at Grantham, ORMONDE was transferred to Kings Cross in 1928 and coupled to corridor tender no.5329. Within a fortnight the tender was attached to SANSOVINO since ORMONDE had short travel valves and as such was unsuitable for through running. Ironically, having returned to Grantham immediately and received long travel valves, she was called on to relieve FLYING SCOTSMAN at Grantham with the last down Non-stop. With both Gateshead crews on board, she worked through, regaining all lost time, and ran in three minutes before time!

The Scottish A1s tended to move around to where they were needed most, and ORMONDE was no exception. Once a daily sight, she was no longer seen down south, and I have only one recollection of her, running-in after overhaul. In summer 1950 two Kings Cross and two Doncaster A3s were exchanged for four Haymarket former A1s, followed by another Kings Cross A3 early in 1951 without any balancing transfer from Scotland. SIR VISTO was widely hoped for, but in vain. At the same time the only visit that I can recall by ORMONDE occurred, prompting wild speculation at school that this sad gap in our notebooks could be filled. Alas it was not to be. ORMONDE was worked hard at Haymarket, as witness her better mileage than her sisters down south.

ORMONDE was one of the earliest emigrants from the GN, displaced by new A4 Pacifics. At Haymarket she remained one of the rarest visitors to the GN section, although it was hoped that she might be a quid pro quo for FELSTEAD in early 1951. As she is in BR blue, the date must be between August 1949 and late 1952. The A3 has Diagram 94HP boiler 8083 (renumbered 27019) and a GN tender No.5284 or 5281.

ORMONDE, fresh from overhaul at Doncaster Works, where she was fitted with trough deflectors, in late 1961. The A3 is working empty stock at Haymarket East Junction, apparently heading for Slateford. The ECS may be in connection with a rugby match at nearby Murrayfield, but it appears largely to be suburban non-corridor stock. Note inspection plate at front left open... She has just been equipped with a Diagram 107 boiler (29323) off an A4, and has GN tender No.5281. (N E Preedy)

Once one of Grantham's immaculate fleet pre-war, a thoroughly disreputable ORMONDE stands in Waverley as super-power for the 15.43 slow service to Berwick-on-Tweed. The date is July 27th 1961, and the A3 was to receive trough deflectors at Doncaster Works in September 1961. She has a Diagram 107 boiler No.29290 and a GN tender No.5281 (J Robertson, transporttreasury.co.uk).

BLAIR ATHOL

Built	28/2/25
Works No.	1613
Long travel valves fitted	4/5/31
Wartime black livery	12/12/41
Rebuilt to A3	8/12/45
LNER green livery	20/4/47
LNER Nos.	2557 then 58 (7/12/46)
BR No.	60058 (10/3/49)
BR blue livery	14/2/51
BR dark green livery	30/3/53
Double Kylchap fitted	3/10/58
Trough deflectors not fitted	
Withdrawn	19/6/63

Allocation (A1)	
To Gorton	28/2/25
To Grantham	25/3/25
To Kings Cross	21/11/42
To Copley Hill	15/2/43
To Doncaster	29/9/43
(A3)	
To Kings Cross	1/10/50
To Doncaster	29/10/50
To Copley Hill	13/6/54
To Gateshead	15/9/57
To Darlington	16/11/58
To Gateshead	7/6/59
To Darlington	17/12/61
To Gateshead	24/6/62
To Heaton	9/9/62

BLAIR ATHOL was another Grantham stalwart before the war; afterwards, she worked from a number of sheds principally Doncaster and Copley Hill. BLAIR ATHOL was one of the Copley Hill quartet that moved to Tyneside in 1957. She was a fairly common but unremarkable sight on the main line over the years, especially from Copley Hill.

BLAIR ATHOL approaches Grantham from the south with a parcels or ECS train on May 11th 1953. It is, maybe, 812dn, the 11.15 to York, a Doncaster turn for years. The smokebox numberplate is below the handrail, an anomaly that a dozen of the class had over the years. She has a Diagram 94A boiler (27029) and a GN tender No.5271. (R E Vincent, transporttreasury.co.uk)

At the old station at Hatfield there were several splendid vantage points to photograph the down expresses. One such was at the south end of the down platform, as the train leaned to the curve, limited post-war to 70mph in the steam era. This is a superb picture of an A3 at speed, and one can almost hear her from looking at the shot. Here BLAIR ATHOL, from Doncaster and recently ex-works, approaches with the 15.50 Leeds express on June 29th 1953. She has a Diagram 94A boiler (27069) and a GN tender No.5289. Here, Brian Green has caught the valve gear of the A3 raised, and the picture conveys a far greater impression of speed than your author's humble efforts at Hitchin with MELTON and HERMIT. Boiler, Diagram 94A No.27029, tender, GN No.5271. (B K B Green, Initial Photographics)

Gateshead's new acquisition, still recognisably green, BLAIR ATHOL surmounts the sharp rise to Wood Green flyover with the Sunday 11.30 Glasgow. With engineering work at Hadley Wood, all main line services were diverted via the New Line through Hertford North on many weekends in winter 1958-59. She has a Diagram 94A boiler (27051) and an A4 non-corridor tender No.5643. (Peter J Coster)

TRACERY

Built	25/3/25
Works No.	1614
Long travel valves fitted	17/11/28
Rebuilt to A3 with wartime black livery	25/7/42
LNER green livery	14/12/46
LNER Nos.	2558 then 59 (26/10/46)
BR No.	60059 (8/7/48)
BR blue livery	18/8/49
BR dark green livery	8/8/52
Double Kylchap fitted	17/7/58
Trough deflectors fitted	29/9/61
Withdrawn	17/12/62

Allocation (A1)	
To Gorton	25/3/25
To Grantham	17/4/25
To Gorton	19/9/38
(A3)To Kings Cross	29/12/42
To New England	16/4/44
To Kings Cross	24/9/44
To Leicester	18/3/51
To Kings Cross	7/4/57

TRACERY was another A1 that performed similar work to her sisters in the Doncaster A1 build, but she was particularly consistent and reliable. Indeed TRACERY achieved the second highest mileage for the A3 class, over 2.5 million miles; moreover the average annual mileage was the highest of the class, just under 67,000 over a life of nearly 38 years. Her inevitable presence drew many a youthful groan from the lineside. Post-war she spent a long spell at Leicester GC, and on her return to Kings Cross, was used on turns to York and Newcastle. In due course she was fitted with a double Kylchap, at a time when mileage since overhaul was, at a guess, about 40,000. The new exhaust made such a difference to the steaming and free running that the driver of the 14.00 from Kings Cross was convinced that TRACERY had just had a general overhaul! She was often on the hardest turns at Kings Cross, and was one of the best of the class.

An up express approaches Muskham troughs, hauled by TRACERY, in 1958. One of the early Kylchap conversions not carried out at general overhaul but during a casual at Doncaster, TRACERY was the A3 with the second highest mileage, and was usually hard at work on the main line somewhere. The A3 has Diagram 94A boiler No.27078 and GN tender No.5284. (A H Lucas, transporttreasury.co.uk)

The southbound Tees-Tyne Pullman races over Werrington troughs behind TRACERY. While in the early 1950s it might have been a substitution, the A3s returned to through workings to Newcastle once loads were reduced generally in 1957, performing well even before conversion to double Kylchap. TRACERY was one of the more frequently used A3s on the lodging turns to Leeds and Newcastle. The A3 has Diagram 94HP boiler 27073 or 78 and GN tender No.5284. (P Ransome-Wallis)

LNER 2558 TRACERY seen from Grantham North signalbox, leaving Grantham having taken over a down Newcastle express. The period is summer 1932, and the A1 has a Diagram 94 boiler (7777) and her original GN type tender No.5268. The provision of tall signals with co-acting sky arms seems unnecessary with so many trains calling there, but it may well date from the famous accident in September 1906 to ensure no repetition. A D2 4-4-0 waits in the down bay with a stopping service, while another is in the yard, and a C1 Atlantic is either entering or leaving the yard. (Rev. A C Cawston, courtesy Brian Bailey)

THE TETRARCH

Built	28/3/25
Works No.	1615
Long travel valves fitted	7/6/30
Rebuilt to A3 with wartime black livery	16/1/42
LNER green livery	12/4/47
LNER Nos.	2559, 528 (13/4/46), 60 (22/6/46)
BR No.	60060 (1/10/48)
BR blue livery	4/1/50
BR dark green livery	15/8/51
Double Kylchap fitted	14/3/59
Trough deflectors not fitted	
Withdrawn	23/9/63

Allocation (A1)	
To Gorton	28/3/25
To Kings Cross	28/4/25
To Doncaster	30/4/27
To Grantham	14/10/33
To Doncaster	4/7/34
To Grantham	9/3/38
To Gateshead	9/3/39
(A3)	
To Darlington	27/1/52
To Gateshead	17/8/52
To Darlington	8/5/55
To Gateshead	13/11/55
To Darlington	26/5/57
To Gateshead	1/12/57
To Darlington	18/12/60
To Gateshead	18/6/61
To Heaton	9/9/62
To Gateshead	16/6/63

THE TETRARCH was a Southern Area Pacific that moved among the main line sheds, before joining LEMBERG on Tyneside in 1939. Not a common sight down south post-war, she had four spells as Darlington pilot. In general, like many of the class, THE TETRARCH had an average and unremarkable history. In the mid-1950s she was tested for through running to Kings Cross with ST GATIEN.

THE TETRARCH, now the Darlington pilot, is coaled and watered ready for emergency action. The date is May 17th 1952, and the magnificent external condition belies the fact that it is nine months since the Pacific was last repainted. The A3 has a Diagram 94A boiler (27054) and an A3 non-corridor tender No.5482. (R E Vincent, transporttreasury.co.uk)

A very clean A3, **THE TETRARCH**, surely not long ex-works, pulls out of Newcastle Central with a parcels or ECS train bound for the north. This is a splendid view of one of the most intricate track layouts in the country. The task of relaying all or part of that S&C, let alone keeping it maintained and tight, didn't bear thinking about! The A3 has a Diagram 94A boiler and an A3 non-corridor tender No.5482.

One of the more camera shy A1s in later years down south, **THE TETRARCH**, in a well-known shot, is working hard with a down express just north of New Southgate in 1938. Up to this point she was mainly a Doncaster A1, but in 1938 was displaced northwards by the new A4s. By now the A1 has gained an A3 non-corridor tender, No.5566. The first coach is a magnificent beast, 12 wheels and a clerestory roof, from the earlier days of the East Coast main line. The A1 has a Diagram 94 boiler No.7769.

PRETTY POLLY

Built	17/4/25
Works No.	1616
Long travel valves fitted	25/1/30
Wartime black livery	23/8/42
Rebuilt to A3	6/5/44
LNER green livery	27/4/47
LNER Nos.	2560, then 61 (18/11/46)
BR No.	60061 (20/11/48)
BR blue livery	2/11/50
BR dark green livery	26/8/52
Double Kylchap fitted	23/10/58
Small deflectors fitted	7/11/59
Trough deflectors fitted	3/2/62
Withdrawn	8/9/63

Allocation (A1)	
To Gorton	17/4/25
To Kings Cross	23/5/25
To Grantham	25/11/28
To New England	10/10/42
(A3)	
To Leicester	6/2/49
To Doncaster	4/6/50
To Copley Hill	26/11/50
To Kings Cross	18/2/51
To Neasden	15/7/51
To Grantham	22/2/53
To Kings Cross	29/8/54
To Grantham	17/10/54
To Doncaster	8/2/59
To Kings Cross	5/4/59
To New England	13/9/59
To Kings Cross	8/11/59
To Grantham	16/6/63

PRETTY POLLY was another well travelled A1 which was often about on the main line, usually working from Grantham. One wonders at the sense of choosing such a name for an express locomotive, even if the racehorse's owner was possibly a friend of an influential member of the LNER management. She was one of four A3s fitted with small deflectors in an attempt to clear drifting exhaust, later superseded by trough deflectors. She was always somewhere, hard at work. I remember seeing her on the up White Rose from Grantham consistently in the early 1950s, despite being a year and a half from her last overhaul, audibly so!

PRETTY POLLY in 1925-28 with an up train at Greenwood. It is described as an excursion, which used to be an excuse for ransacking the nether roads of the carriage sidings for anything that would move! One hesitates to use the word 'express' when looking at the train, comprised as it appears to be of many 6-wheelers of considerable antiquity, no doubt the engineers' mess vans of the future. The A1 has a Diagram 94 boiler No.7778 and a GN tender No.5270.

PRETTY POLLY starts away from a packed Platform 10 at Kings Cross with the 13.00 Edinburgh in mid-late May 1948. The end of platform 10 was always busy in steam days. The reason for the crowd is in platform 6, the statuesque Great Western 6018 KING HENRY VI with the 13.10 to Leeds, as part of the hugely entertaining but pointless Locomotive Exchanges. The King is on a familiarisation run, complete with GWR lamps prominently displayed. The A3 has Diagram 94A boiler 8781 and GN tender No.5290.

An up Leeds express waits at Peterborough North behind PRETTY POLLY in 1962. This unfortunately named A3 was one of the GN stalwarts, a common sight in the south. The top lamp bracket has been lowered, requiring the handrail to be split. This change was made to improve safety for crews, with the onset of electrification. The A3 has a Diagram 94A boiler (27026) and a GN tender (5290). (L Perrin, Gresley Society Trust)

MINORU

Built	30/2/25
Works No.	1617
Long travel valves fitted	30/11/29
Wartime black livery	26/9/42
Rebuilt to A3	24/6/44
LNER green livery	5/11/47
LNER Nos.	2561, then 62 (18/10/46)
BR No.	E62 (4/3/48), 60062 (6/7/49)
BR blue livery	6/7/49
BR dark green livery	9/10/52
Double Kylchap fitted	4/2/59
Trough deflectors fitted	11/7/61
Withdrawn	26/12/64

Allocation (A1)	
To Gorton	30/5/25
To Doncaster	20/6/25
To Grantham	19/4/26
To Kings Cross	27/3/27
To New England	25/6/40
(A3)	
To Gorton	7/7/44
To Kings Cross	26/11/44
To Haymarket	11/4/45
To Kings Cross	22/5/45
To Copley Hill	30/5/48
To Doncaster	9/9/51
To Grantham	15/2/53
To Kings Cross	25/10/53
To New England	10/9/61
To Grantham	16/6/63
To Doncaster	8/9/63
To New England	2/10/63

MINORU was predominantly a London engine, spending 24 of her more than 39 years at Top Shed. The wartime loan for a month to Haymarket as a quid pro quo for LORD PRESIDENT must have delighted those local enthusiasts that saw MINORU in action. Post-war, at one time Kings Cross had few A3s (only one for a period) standing in for A4s on Grantham and Peterborough turns, sometimes further afield. MINORU was one of these. The drivers were happy with her and her running was not significantly different from the A4 that she was replacing. Once, in the 1950s, O.S. Nock was travelling on the up Flying Scotsman and after Peppercorn A1s had hauled him south to Grantham, he was surprised to see an A3 couple on, MINORU. As he said at the time, the rasping, hissing exhaust of the A1s was replaced by the full-blooded Gresley roar, as Driver Alf Smith got her away to Stoke. Alf was without his beloved MALLARD, and had the A3 in her place. I saw him flying in past Finsbury Park, the smokebox door looking somewhat burnt. No wonder there was a roar from MINORU - the regulator could not be opened fully, and the cut-off had to be lengthened to keep time.

Once modified with a double Kylchap, with the lighter loads from 1957, the A3s were revived, and their work was excellent, and often indistinguishable from the A4s. On a down run mentioned earlier with 400 tons, MINORU got into her stride quickly, and the start was quite unlike that of the usual A3 - much more reminiscent, instead, of the recently retired Bill Hoole. The highlight was the down Yorkshire Pullman, with its gleaming A3, striding effortlessly north. MINORU had no specific event or modification in her history, but was an excellent and reliable locomotive.

MINORU waits with the Tees-Thames at old platform 6 at Kings Cross on a rainy 29th December 1959. She was in magnificent condition, and the driver made a rapid start, passing Potters Bar in 7mins 31secs, a very fast time. The running, described in the text, was well up to A4 standard. The A3 has a Diagram 94A boiler (27021) and a GN tender (5289). (P J Coster)

MINORU runs through Grantham up platform, without doubt to take up position in the up loco spur to await an up express. The old Kings Cross favourite has a Diagram 94A boiler 27021 and GN tender No.5289.

ISINGLASS

Built	27/6/25
Works No.	1618
'E' type superheater fitted at building	27/6/25
Long travel valves fitted and	
'E' type superheater removed	4/9/30
Wartime black livery	7/7/43
Rebuilt to A3	6/4/46
LNER green livery	15/5/47
LNER Nos.	2562, 531 (6/4/46), 63 (3/7/46)
BR No.	60063 (21/1/49)
BR blue livery	2/3/51
BR dark green livery	13/11/52
Double Kylchap fitted	6/2/59
Trough deflectors fitted	10/8/61
Withdrawn	28/6/64

Allocation (A1)	
To Doncaster	27/6/25
To Gateshead	7/12/25
To Doncaster	26/9/26
To Grantham	14/10/28
To Kings Cross	0/4/38
To Leicester	24/8/39
To Neasden	3/12/39
To Gorton	23/2/41
To Kings Cross	22/11/42
To Gorton	9/7/44
To Copley Hill	3/8/44
To Doncaster	22/1/45
(A3)	
To Kings Cross	4/6/50
To Grantham	9/9/51
To Neasden	22/2/53
To Kings Cross	13/3/55
To Neasden	25/3/56
To Kings Cross	24/6/56
To Grantham	16/9/56
To Kings Cross	30/10/60
To Grantham	16/6/63
To Doncaster	8/9/63
To New England	20/10/63

ISINGLASS was the last A1 built at Doncaster and equipped experimentally with an E type double superheater, in response to a suggestion by the Superheater Co. to improve the steaming capacity and superheated steam temperature of the A1s. The E type had double the heating area of the normal A1 superheater. ISINGLASS was tested in comparison with TRANQUIL, working from Gateshead. The superheater temperature forecast was not achieved, and it was replaced at the same time as the longer travel valves were fitted. For most of her career this locomotive moved around between the main line and the GC, more so post-war. On the main line she was usually hard at work, and in the Indian Summer of steam, she worked either from Grantham or Kings Cross.

ISINGLASS, in as deplorable an external condition as I have ever seen, pulls away from York with an up express. From the look of the stock it is one of the principal services, too. The A3 certainly looks run-down, although appearances could be deceptive, and it was an increasingly common sight. I would guess at late 1960, when she had just moved to Top Shed. No doubt she would be sorted out and cleaned there. The new shedplate has escaped incineration on a badly burnt smokebox door – no doubt caused by the box not being cleared for some while. The A3 has a Diagram 107 boiler 29295, and her usual GN tender No.5231. (transporttreasury.co.uk)

ISINGLASS coasts downhill through Greenwood with an up Leeds and Harrogate express on 5 June 1950. A Doncaster engine since rebuilding in 1946, she had just been transferred to Kings Cross. Still in apple green livery, the A3 has a new Diagram 94A boiler and GN tender No.5231. (Rev. A C Cawston, courtesy Brian Bailey)

Barry Richardson's photograph of ISINGLASS has no details, and it is taken at the unknown location that he often used, frustratingly. Having mentally pounded the length of the GN main line, I am fairly sure that it is not on the main line although those that know the Gamston area offer it as a possibility. The curve is too sharp in my view, and I have concluded that it was a Sunday diversion via Spalding, taken just north of Werrington Junction, which would explain why the driver has shut the regulator. Boiler: Diagram 107 No.29328, tender: GN No.5231. (B Richardson, transporttreasury.co.uk)

TAGALIE (WILLIAM WHITELAW)

Built	9/7/24
North British Loco Co Works No.	23101
Long travel valves fitted	27/4/28
Renamed TAGALIE	2/8/41
Rebuilt to A3 and wartime black livery	13/11/42
LNER green livery	11/2/47
LNER Nos.	2563, 64 (20/10/46)
BR No.	E64 (30/1/48), 60064 (9/7/48)
BR blue livery	9/7/49
BR dark green livery	6/2/53
Double Kylchap fitted	2/6/59
Trough deflectors not fitted	
Withdrawn	4/9/61

Allocation (A1)	
To Haymarket	9/7/24
To Ferryhill	27/4/35
To Eastfield	27/11/37
To St.Margarets	19/7/38
To Tay Bridge	12/1/40
To Eastfield	11/10/40
To Haymarket	4/12/40
(A3)	
To Doncaster	2/7/50
To Grantham	14/6/59

WILLIAM WHITELAW was the first A1 to be built to contract by the North British Loco Co at Glasgow, and was named after the LNER Chairman. She was also the first Pacific to be allocated to Haymarket, where main line work hitherto had been largely provided for by the NER at Newcastle. On March 20th 1927 she worked a 400 tons test train from Edinburgh to Carlisle, but the driver was unfamiliar with the A1 and the coal taken on at Canal was poor, leading to a disappointing run.

When the Flying Scotsman started to run non-stop from Kings Cross to Waverley, Haymarket was allocated 2573 HARVESTER and 2580 SHOTOVER, both coupled to corridor tenders and fitted with new 220psi 94HP boilers, while Haymarket's 2563 and 2564 were coupled to corridor tenders. Apart from a month in 1930, 2563 had a corridor tender from May 1928 until April 1935, when it was attached to BROWN JACK. She was used in the first season on the Non-stop, and again in 1929, 1930 and 1932, after which newer A3s displaced the A1s. No doubt her name ensured special attention at Haymarket. On arrival of the A3s in 1930, the five A1s circulated between the sheds at Aberdeen, Dundee, Glasgow, and across the city at St.Margarets for a while until war broke out.

In 1941 A4 4462 GREAT SNIPE was renamed WILLIAM WHITELAW to mark the latter's retirement a few years earlier, and 2563 was given the name TAGALIE. After the war, the four Haymarket Pacifics were sent south in exchange for four of the 1928 batch of A3s in mid-1950. While it deprived the southern area of some fine A3s, the vision of A3s, unseen hitherto down south was a great and pleasant surprise for those still in short trousers! I can remember still my astonishment at seeing the 17.35 Newcastle, not with its usual Heaton Pacific, but with a travel stained A3 with the legend HAYMARKET on her buffer beam - TAGALIE. She remained a Doncaster A3 for nine years before moving to Grantham. In the gathering gloom for steam, it was judged too expensive to overhaul her, and she was condemned.

The first Scottish A1, then WILLIAM WHITELAW, in works grey for its official photograph at North British Loco Co. The engine has a Diagram 94 boiler (7785) and a GN tender No.5273. She was coupled to a corridor tender in 1928. The NB A1s differed in slight details such as the firebox and main steam pipe cladding, the long cranked reversing rod, and the distinctive NB works plate.

TAGALIE, in her last few years, seemed to be perpetually in a filthy state. Here she heads an up express at Red Hall, south of Hatfield. The driver has closed the regulator, presumably because Marshmoor's distant is at caution. The date is August 8ᵗʰ 1959. She has a Diagram 94A boiler 27043 and A3 non-corridor tender No.5584.

For a short period in 1948, while such vital issues as engine livery and numbering were under discussion (like the Grouping more than two decades earlier) some engines had a character appended to the number indicating their origin. At Haymarket TAGALIE was ex-works at the end of January 1948 in apple green livery and numbered E64. The A3 has a Diagram 94A boiler 9122, and her usual A3 non-corridor tender No.5584.

KNIGHT OF THISTLE
(KNIGHT OF THE THISTLE)

Built	14/7/24
North British Loco Co Works No.	23102
Long travel valves fitted	19/6/28
Renamed KNIGHT OF THISTLE	28/12/32
Wartime black livery	4/3/44
Rebuilt to A3 and LNER green livery	23/3/47
LNER Nos.	2564, 65 (25/10/46)
BR No.	60065 (23/7/48)
BR blue livery	18/11/49
BR dark green livery	24/12/52
Double Kylchap fitted	31/10/58
Trough deflectors fitted	25/11/61
Withdrawn	28/6/64

Allocation (A1)	
To Haymarket	14/7/24
To Eastfield	15/2/37
To Carlisle Canal	20/11/40
To Haymarket	1/12/41
(A3)	
To Kings Cross	2/7/50
To Grantham	9/9/51
To New England	17/6/62
To Grantham	16/6/63
To Doncaster	8/9/63
To New England	20/10/63

KNIGHT OF THE THISTLE was very much a sister locomotive to TAGALIE in her history. Having moved south she was a constant sight on the main line, wherever she was working from. One of Haymarket's stalwarts on the Non-stop, she was coupled to a corridor tender no.5325 from July 1928 until October 1935. She was used in 1929, and was a reserve in other years. 2564 was the only Scottish A1 not to be fitted with a tablet catching apparatus for working to Aberdeen. She emerged at the end of 1932 with a new nameplate, with the indefinite article missing, strangely. It was a mistake which was never corrected. It always struck me as more than a coincidence that it happened in Christmas week!

Before the 1939-45 war, when the use of excursions were far more common in support of football, rugby and hockey events, usually at Wembley, long distance operating was far more commonplace. The newspapers were scanned for details of competing teams, and a north country presence was always welcome. Schoolboys were regaled by older enthusiasts with stories of those days, of Raven Pacifics and Atlantics working through to Kings Cross. When England were playing Scotland, early risers were rewarded with the sight of Scottish A1s and A3s. On one occasion a late friend saw CAPTAIN CUTTLE, borrowed by Haymarket from Carlisle, LADAS from Dundee and a couple of Haymarket's Pacifics working enthusiast specials, a prospect that belonged to the realms of dreamland for my generation.

KNIGHT OF THISTLE at Doncaster shed. The date given is October 1958, but at that time 60065 was across the way in the Plant for a general overhaul, during which she would be fitted with a double Kylchap and repainted. Clearly she has already been fitted, but has not been repainted, which suggests that either she is waiting to go to shops and has already been fitted with the Kylchap, possibly on Grantham shed, or more likely that the date is wrong. It is possible that it is October 1960, when the engine had a light/casual repair. The A3 has Diagram 94A boiler 27027 and GN tender No.5285.

A light engine coming off Welwyn Viaduct on September 9th 1953. Most pictures are of down trains, and there was a very useful home signal just north of the viaduct which afforded such a view. There was also an advance starter at the south end, which gave a good view of the viaduct and southbound traffic, although it would be coasting here. At this time there was a rather wasteful diagram requiring a Pacific to run light, or haul a Friday relief from Lincoln or West Yorkshire, between Grantham to Kings Cross, then work north to York with the heavy 'Aberdonian' service, before returning to Grantham on an overnight parcels service. The A3 is KNIGHT OF THISTLE, a Grantham engine. On that day, she headed the 'Aberdonian' and the A3 has the necessary headboard reversed. Oddly she carries open lights instead of a light engine headcode. The top link A1 was often stopped for washout on Wednesdays – BONGRACE on this occasion I believe – and an A3 often deputised. The A3 has a Diagram 94A boiler (27037) and a GN tender No.5285.

KNIGHT OF THISTLE with the up overnight parcels service from York south of Hatfield, early in 1954. The A3 has Diagram 94HP boiler 27037 and GN tender No.5276. This boiler was the one fitted to GAINSBOROUGH when new in 1930.

MERRY HAMPTON

Built	16/7/24
North British Loco Co Works No.	23103
Long travel valves fitted	4/4/28
Wartime black livery	14/12/41
Rebuilt to A3	9/12/45
LNER Nos.	2565, 66 (7/746)
BR No.	60066 (17/3/48)
LNER green livery	21/12/46
BR blue livery	6/10/49
BR dark green livery	14/1/53
Double Kylchap fitted	15/10/58
Trough deflectors fitted	13/10/61
Withdrawn	8/9/63

Allocation (A1)	
To Haymarket	14/7/24
To Gateshead	5/5/28
To Haymarket	5/7/28
To Tay Bridge	6/10/30
To Haymarket	17/8/31
To Tay Bridge	1/12/31
To Ferryhill	10/8/35
To Eastfield	4/5/36
To Ferryhill	9/6/36
To Eastfield	28/3/37
To Carlisle Canal	19/11/40
To Haymarket	12/2/41
(A3)	
To Doncaster	6/8/50
To Kings Cross	1/10/50
To Doncaster	29/10/50
To Kings Cross	10/6/56
To Doncaster	5/8/56
To Kings Cross	16/6/57
To Doncaster	2/11/58
To Kings Cross	5/4/59
To New England	13/9/59
To Kings Cross	1/11/59
To Grantham	16/6/63

MERRY HAMPTON seems to have been the member of the Haymarket A1 quintet that was used in the 1930s as a spare by all the main sheds. MERRY HAMPTON was coupled to corridor tender no.5330 for over three months early in 1929 before it was transferred to sister A3 LADAS for the first up run of the 1929 season. The Flying Scotsman called at Newcastle during the summer timetables outside the period of non-stop running, and the engines worked through between London and Edinburgh. It is possible that she may have worked through before or after non-stop running started.

When fairly new in 1926, while hauling the up Flying Scotsman on May 10th, she was derailed at Cramlington by striking miners, although the driver had reduced speed to walking pace in anticipation. Strangely, the same locomotive, hauling the same train, on the same Berwick-Newcastle section, came to a similar but far more serious end 21 years later on Sunday October 26th. The driver, distracted by an unofficial footplate passenger failed to react to signals warning of an engineering diversion, and had eleven of his fifteen coaches on the floor. Sadly, 28 lives were lost. As a result, at overhaul she was given the unique cab off ST SIMON, in shops at the same time.

On moving south, MERRY HAMPTON was the subject of a tug-of-war between Doncaster and Kings Cross, the former winning at first, but Top Shed seems to have taken a liking to her. On June 17th 1957, Driver Fred Dines, temporarily denied his regular A4 WALTER K WHIGHAM, was offered MERRY HAMPTON to work the down Tees-Tyne Pullman. I would imagine that there would have been some diffidence on Fred's part, since the Pullman was the top job, and he would be returning the following day with the new Morning Talisman. On returning, he told Peter Townend that he was satisfied and would keep her until WALTER was available again.

Later *The Railway Magazine* published the run of the up Morning Talisman, and all became clear. Fred, a quiet man but a splendid driver, had cut the Darlington-Kings Cross timing by 14½ minutes, averaging 90.5 between Northallerton and York, and reaching 96 down Stoke. His net time equalled that of the Silver Jubilee with a trainload some 40 tons heavier. MERRY HAMPTON's turn of speed had impressed me in 1953, when she relieved GOLDEN PLOVER at Doncaster on the Elizabethan. With Bill Hoole in charge, the A3 was almost on time passing Wood Green, but she was going considerably faster than the CCE would have liked!

A down Aberdeen express descends the sharp curve off the Tay Bridge headed by Ferryhill's 2565 MERRY HAMPTON in August 1936. The A1 has a Diagram 94 boiler (7785) and a GN tender No.5276. (Rev. A C Cawston, courtesy Brian Bailey)

MERRY HAMPTON with the up Norseman approaching Retford on August 2nd 1958. The A3 has yet to receive AWS, and has the familiar bogie dust shields of earlier days together with the high ventilator cab off ST.SIMON. Although she is only two months off general overhaul, the A3 looks in good condition generally. In the distance an ex-GCR N5 0-6-2T waits on pilot duty. Diagram 107 boiler, No.29322, and GN tender No.5223. (R J Buckley, Initial Photographics)

MERRY HAMPTON, having paused for the platform end signal, ambles away to Top Shed via down main one. The time must lay between the fitting of the double Kylchap in October 1958 and the same month in 1961 when trough deflectors were fitted. The A3 has a Diagram 107 boiler, and the GN tender is No.5223. (D Potton, transporttreasury.co.uk

LADAS

Built	14/8/24
North British Loco Co Works No.	23104
Long travel valves fitted	13/7/28
Rebuilt to A3	4/11/39
Wartime black livery	16/5/42
LNER Nos.	2566, 67 (13/10/46)
BR No.	60067 (30/7/48)
LNER green livery	19/4/47
BR blue livery	16/2/50
BR dark green livery	27/9/51
Double Kylchap fitted	10/4/59
Trough deflectors fitted	26/4/61
Withdrawn	29/12/62

Allocation (A1)	
To Haymarket	14/7/24
To Tay Bridge	18/8/30
To Eastfield	7/2/37
(A3)	
To St.Margarets	2/2/40
To Haymarket	26/11/40
To Kings Cross	2/7/50
To Grantham	9/9/51
To Doncaster	18/5/52
To Kings Cross	22/6/52
To Doncaster	18/10/53
To Grantham	14/6/59
To New England	13/9/59
To Kings Cross	1/11/59

LADAS was the last A1 to be named, in February 1926. She followed the usual pattern of the Scottish A1s, moving about after the arrival of more powerful A3s and then A4s at Haymarket. So far as I can ascertain, she was only used on the non-stop Flying Scotsman in 1929, although 1930 was a possibility for a few weeks. Otherwise she may have simply worked through, as in the case of MERRY HAMPTON. In 1939 it was decided to convert the A1s into A3s, and the first was LADAS. Conversion to A3 appeared to be little more than reboiling with Diagram 94A or in a few cases 94HP boilers, and either replacing or lining the cylinders to 19ins.

Moving south, LADAS was the last of the Scottish quartet at Haymarket to take her place on the GN main line, and on one her first few duties, she suffered a failure at Yaxley with either side rods or valve gear. Much of her time was spent at Doncaster or Kings Cross, where she was regularly used. With a double Kylchap, she was a frequent sight on the top turns, but was one of the many favourites lost in the great cull of December 29th 1962.

LADAS on April 17th 1957 at Kings Cross with the 15.52 down Leeds express. Note cranked reversing lever, prominent in this view of an NB-built A1/A3. The A3 has a Diagram 94HP boiler No.27059 and the A3 non-corridor tender is No.5479. (Brian Bailey)

Early morning at Peterborough North. A down service hauled by LADAS pauses on the down main, while York's 60522 STRAIGHT DEAL approaches with an up express. The connection in the up line is a tandem, one lead within another, difficult to maintain and normally not allowed on main lines today. The date must be after mid-1961. The A3 has a Diagram 107 boiler No.29277, and the A3 non-corridor tender is No.5479. (B Richardson, transporttreasury.co.uk)

SIR VISTO

Built	14/8/24
North British Loco Co Works No.	23105
Long travel valves fitted	4/4/28
Wartime black livery	2/4/43
LNER Nos.	2567, 68 (25/8/46)
BR No.	60068 (19/9/48)
Rebuilt to A3	10/12/48
LNER green livery	20/3/47
BR blue livery	25/10/50
BR dark green livery	12/8/52
Double Kylchap fitted	9/4/59
Trough deflectors not fitted	
Withdrawn	27/8/62

Allocation (A1)

To Haymarket	14/8/24
To Tay Bridge	3/7/30
To Eastfield	7/2/37
To St.Margarets	20/11/38
To Eastfield	2/2/40
To Carlisle Canal	20/11/40
(A3)	
At Carlisle Canal until withdrawal	

SIR VISTO was one of the fabled beasts in the A3 class that was rarely seen south of Doncaster, and many were the trainspotting prayers that graced the Wailing Walls of the lineside fencing, with SIR VISTO prominent among them. The last of the Scottish A1s, she led a very similar existence but for one exception. She never had a corridor tender at all, and was always a rare visitor down south. She was shedded at Tay Bridge from 1930 to 1937. Moving then to Eastfield, 2567 was used on duties that took it through to Leeds on the Queen of Scots Pullman or the North Briton. For three years or so, the remaining seventeen A1s were reclassified A10, since the new A1 was the rebuilt GREAT NORTHERN. The last A10 to be converted to A3 was SIR VISTO. Like the other A3s at Carlisle, BAYARDO, CORONACH and FLAMINGO, SIR VISTO stayed put until the LM Region decided in 1961, with hordes of diesel and electric locomotives arriving, that the four 'non-standard' Pacifics would be early withdrawals. Confined almost entirely to the Waverley route, only occasionally reaching Newcastle, she was often to be seen at Edinburgh, and was almost a daily sight somewhere on the Waverley route. Late in her history, she appeared, running-in, on the down Dringhouses freight, much to friend John Aylard's astonishment: his excellent photograph is in the first *Book of the A3 Pacifics*.

SIR VISTO at Edinburgh Waverley with an westbound service in August 1938. The A1 was an Eastfield engine at the time. The receiver of the Strowger-Hudd experimental predecessor to AWS is visible beneath the buffer beam. Her Diagram 94 boiler is 7798, and her A4 non-corridor tender is No.5637. (Rev. A C Cawston, courtesy Brian Bailey)

SIR VISTO was the last of the original A1s, first reclassified A10 before being modified as an A3 in December 1948, and from 1950 was the oldest Scottish Pacific. The cabside hole for the token catcher can be seen, when she worked over the Usan-Montrose single line section on the Aberdeen main line. The Carlisle Canal A3s worked almost entirely in Scotland, whatever the various shedcodes applying at the time, though the shed itself of course was in England. So she 'resided' in the later but very largely worked in the former. The name was an abiding presence on any wish list down south, and her visits to the Metropolis over the years could be counted on one hand. Here she is at Haymarket on May 13th 1959. Scottish Director THE LADY OF THE LAKE is on the left, with the preserved MAUDE on the right, together with Ferryhill's BAHRAM, another reclusive locomotive. She has a Diagram 94A boiler No.27036 and a GN tender No.5224. (W Hermiston, transporttreasury.co.uk).

SCEPTRE

Built	19/9/24
North British Loco Co Works No.	23106
Long travel valves	9/12/27
Rebuilt to A3 in wartime black livery	31/5/43
LNER Nos.	2568, 537 (23/4/46), 69 (26/5/46)
LNER livery	18/1/47
BR No.	60069 (8/7/48)
BR blue livery	19/1/51
BR dark green livery	17/7/52
Double Kylchap fitted	4/9/59
Trough deflectors not fitted	
Withdrawn	1/10/62

Allocation (A1)	
To Gateshead	19/9/24
To York	11/12/36
(A3)	
To Heaton	28/3/43
To Tweedmouth	14/9/58
To Copley Hill	12/6/60
To Holbeck	20/11/60
To Copley Hill	11/6/61
To Ardsley	10/9/61

SCEPTRE was the first A1 to be allocated permanently to the North East. ST. SIMON spent a few months on test at Gateshead in 1923-24, but SCEPTRE was the first of fifteen new North British-built A1s destined for the two Newcastle sheds. She spent most of her time in long spells at Gateshead, then Heaton, but with the withdrawal of the Raven Pacifics from York, SCEPTRE was moved to York. She returned to Heaton for a long spell, before a tour of the sheds at Leeds, having been displaced from Tyneside by new diesels. Heaton had jobs to Grantham, Peterborough, and for a while Kings Cross, but SCEPTRE was not one of the commonest visitors. She was used for a while successfully on the Leeds-Carlisle route along with other ex-Tyneside A3s.

The first Gresley Pacific to go to the North Eastern Area, SCEPTRE and one of the more retiring members of the class so far as photographers were concerned, accelerates away from York with an up express. As the A3 is left-hand drive and single chimney, the date must fall between June 1954 and September 1959: the extent of carmine and cream stock would suggest earlier rather than later. The A3 probably has Diagram 94A boiler 27020 or 2537 and GN tender No.5258.

Copley Hill's 60069 SCEPTRE at Hadley Wood on August 20th 1960, heading towards New Barnet and Kings Cross with an early morning Leeds area summer extra, non-stop from Doncaster. The A3 has Diagram 94HP boiler 27040 and GN tender No.5258. (Brian Bailey)

GLADIATEUR

Built	24/9/24
North British Loco Co Works No.	23107
Long travel valves	22/3/28
Wartime black livery	6/3/43
LNER Nos.	2569, 538 (17/3/46), 70 (2/6/46)
Rebuilt to A3 with LNER green livery	18/1/47
BR No.	60070 (27/8/48)
BR blue livery not applied	
BR dark green livery	15/2/52
Double Kylchap fitted	25/4/59
Trough deflectors fitted	13/9/61
Withdrawn	4/5/64

Allocation (A1)	
To Gateshead	24/9/24
To York	18/4/38
To Gateshead	6/5/46
(A3)	
To Darlington	12/12/48
To Gateshead	27/1/52
To Darlington	30/8/53
To Gateshead	28/2/54
To Darlington	5/5/57
To Gateshead	3/11/57
To Darlington	7/6/59
To Gateshead	6/12/59
To Copley Hill	12/6/60
To Holbeck	20/11/60
To Copley Hill	11/6/61
To Ardsley	10/9/61
To Neville Hill	16/6/63
To Gateshead	8/12/63

After some initial coolness on Tyneside, the Gresley A1s gained approval from the footplate crews. GLADIATEUR became a favourite at Gateshead, to the extent that in 1928, when she was one of three Tyneside Pacifics selected to work the non-stop Flying Scotsman, there was more than a little procrastination and her departure was delayed. Attached to a corridor tender, she was sent to Haymarket on Gresley's orders, but ran hot en route. A change of policy resulted in the preparation of two Haymarket A1s, and GLADIATEUR surrendered her corridor tender to WILLIAM WHITELAW. As a result GLADIATEUR, a Westinghouse engine, returned to Gateshead with a vacuum braked tender off WILLIAM, which limited her use in the north east temporarily. Her original tender was restored a month later.

After the war, A3s were used as main line pilots at Darlington, and GLADIATEUR was transferred there in 1948 with GALOPIN. It was three years before they returned to Gateshead, still in apple green livery. By that time the express passenger livery had changed to GWR dark green, which suited the A3s better than the previous dark blue livery, but not as well as apple green. Once or twice, the up Tees-Tyne Pullman appeared with one of Darlington's apple green apparitions, reminding us of what we had lost with the uniformity and standardisation of BR. GLADIATEUR had three more spells as Darlington pilot, before many of the Tyneside favourites were dispersed to the Leeds area.

Below. In a striking image, Gateshead's **GLADIATEUR** leaves Grantham with the down Flying Scotsman in February 1930. Gateshead and Kings Cross shared the working of the Flying Scotsman, the former working up MWFO and down the following day. The A1 has Diagram 94 boiler No.7796 and GN tender No.5279. (Rev. A C Cawston, courtesy Brian Bailey)

Gateshead's favourite A1, GLADIATEUR, calls at Grantham with the up Flying Scotsman in the early 1930s. The Westinghouse pump was originally fitted for working NER stock. Still with Darlington-style painting – 4.6.2. on buffer beam for instance, low cabside numbers. The A1 has Diagram 94 boiler No.7796 and GN tender No.5279. (Rev. A C Cawston, courtesy Brian Bailey)

The former favourite at Gateshead, GLADIATEUR, stands as pilot at Darlington. GLADIATEUR and GALOPIN were at Darlington for just over three years between 1948 and 1952, and with the low rate of mileage accrual they remained apple green until 1952, by which time the BR blue livery had come and gone. GLADIATEUR went to directly to BR dark green after a general overhaul in early 1952. After then the Darlington pilot was usually a Gateshead A3 just returned from general overhaul, exchanged after about six months for another A3. She returned to Darlington after general overhaul at Doncaster Works in August 1953, having been converted to left-hand drive and painted in dark green. Inspection plate open. The date of the photo must be soon after since the A3 did not return until 1957, when the second BR totem was in use. Diagram 94A boiler 27009, A3 non-corridor tender No.5477. (R S Carpenter)

TRANQUIL

Built	27/9/24
North British Loco Co Works No.	23108
Long travel valves	20/12/27
Wartime black livery	16/1/43
Rebuilt to A3	28/10/44
LNER livery	9/10/47
LNER Nos.	2570, 71 (27/10/46)
BR No.	60071 (18/5/48)
BR experimental purple livery	18/5/48
BR blue livery	20/7/50
BR dark green livery	1//11/51
Double Kylchap fitted	4/7/58
Trough deflectors fitted	4/11/61
Withdrawn	12/10/64

Allocation (A1)	
To Gateshead	27/9/24
To York	11/11/36
(A3)	
To Neville Hill	29/9/45
To Gateshead	6/5/46
To Darlington	27/1/52
To Gateshead	16/3/52
To Darlington	5/9/54
To Gateshead	13/2/55
To Darlington	27/5/56
To Gateshead	11/11/56
To Darlington	24/2/57
To Gateshead	26/5/57
To Darlington	6/12/59
To Gateshead	19/6/60
To Heaton	9/9/62
To Gateshead	16/6/63

TRANQUIL was one of the hardworking A1s in the north east, one moreover that was a frequent visitor to southern climes. The diffidence with which the first A1s were regarded gave way to appreciation, and the fifteen NE A1s aggregated more than 30 million miles over the years. TRANQUIL was one of the seven A3s painted in the experimental BR purple livery in 1948, before wiser counsels prevailed; well, a bit wiser! TRANQUIL was one of the A3s that had several sessions as Darlington pilot. She was well regarded at Gateshead, one of their best, a regular visitor to the capital on the main duties, especially when fitted with a double Kylchap.

TRANQUIL draws slowly to a halt in old platform 8 at Kings Cross, with the 8.10 from Newcastle. It is late summer 1958, and the A3 has Diagram 94A boiler 27065 and GN tender No.5291. (P J Coster)

TRANQUIL at Doncaster Works after general overhaul, probably in November 1961, in her final condition. Boiler: Diagram 107 No.29290, GN tender No.5291. Colourrail.co.uk

SUNSTAR

Built	30/9/24
North British Loco Co Works No.	23109
Long travel valves	9/3/28
Rebuilt to A3	12/7/41
Wartime black livery	17/2/43
LNER Nos.	2571, 72 (27/7/46)
LNER livery	5/3/48
BR No.	E72 (5/3/48), 60072 (19/8/48)
BR blue livery	17/8/49
BR dark green livery	5/6/52
Double Kylchap fitted	18/7/59
Trough deflectors not fitted	
Withdrawn	22/10/62

Allocation (A1)	
To Gateshead	30/9/24
(A3)	
To Heaton	28/3/43
To Tweedmouth	14/9/58
To Copley Hill	12/6/60
To Holbeck	20/11/60
To Heaton	9/9/62

SUNSTAR must have been a popular engine, as both Gateshead and Heaton seemed reluctant to part with her. In the post-war years, when Heaton Pacifics worked through to London, SUNSTAR, then in blue livery, was one of the commonest, on the 17.35 Kings Cross-Newcastle. The Heaton Pacifics were as well cleaned as any on the East Coast main line at the time, and the sight of a gleaming A3 roaring north, with the added *frisson* that it was from the north east, was an evening treat after school. SUNSTAR worked alternately with her sisters or one of the new Peppercorn A1s on this duty. After September 1951 when the policy of engine changing was introduced, Pacifics from Newcastle, other than the roller bearing A1s, were far less often to be found in London. SUNSTAR, having been a frequent visitor, now became one of the rarest. She was another NE engine that worked over the Leeds-Carlisle road in the last few years.

One of the happier sights of post-war years was the cleanliness of the Heaton Pacifics working through to London on the Tees-Tyne Pullman and the 7.53 from Sunderland. When Heaton worked the Pullman we saw such sights as this – an immaculate SUNSTAR accelerating the Pullman away from York, under Holgate bridge. The duty passed to Top Shed with the summer book in 1949, so by implication the date is between September 1948 and May 1949. The A3 has Diagram 94A boiler No.8780, and her A3 non-corridor tender is No.5476.

SUNSTAR, not long out of Doncaster Works, at Haymarket after June 1952. Note the revised smokebox handrail and numberplate. The A3 has a Diagram 94A boiler, and the A3 non-corridor tender is No.5476.

SUNSTAR was a long term Heaton A3, and she is seen here near Beningbrough with a down express. She looks very scruffy for a Heaton A3, but shows little sign of effort as she works the train up to speed. The date must be prior to December 1953 as she hasn't been altered to left-hand drive, and is probably 1951. The A3 has Diagram 94A boiler 27042 or 79, and her A3 non-corridor tender is No.5476.

ST GATIEN

Built	3/10/24
North British Loco Co Works No.	23110
Long travel valves	31/12/27
Wartime black livery	10/10/42
Rebuilt to A3	10/11/45
LNER Nos.	2572, 73 (27/10/46)
LNER livery	16/4/47
BR No.	60073 (31/3/49)
BR blue livery	21/12/50
BR dark green livery	17/6/52
Double Kylchap fitted	15/8/58
Trough deflectors fitted	30/7/61
Withdrawn	19/8/63

Allocation (A1)
To Gateshead	3/10/24
To York	28/3/43
(A3)	
To Heaton	6/5/46
To Gateshead	16/6/63

ST GATIEN was another locomotive that spent almost her entire life at the two Newcastle sheds, 36 out of 39 years. ST GATIEN was frequently to be found down south, and she was no stranger at Haymarket either. Withdrawn just short of her fortieth year, little of note bears mentioning about her, other than that she must have been a popular engine. Insofar as one can rely on official mileages, ST GATIEN had the highest of the NE A3s, and her average annual mileage was the best of the NE Pacifics.

ST.GATIEN, fresh from overhaul, repainting and redraughting, arrived light in platform 14 among the N2s one evening in the middle of the rush hour – such as it was. This beautiful gleaming locomotive was definitely a change for the rush-hour commuters from the 0-6-2Ts. It had come to East Goods Yard and for some reason could not get into Top Shed via the Goods Lines for servicing, hence its unconventional route to the depot. The date is July-August 1958. The A3 has Diagram 94A boiler 27050, and her GN tender is No.5278. (Peter J Coster)

ST. GATIEN was, I believe, the patron saint of fertility in some traditions. The A3 achieved the highest mileage of the fifteen hard working Pacifics at Gateshead and Heaton; no small feat. She has a good head of steam as she passes under the Wood Green flyover with the 17.35 Newcastle. I would guess at summer 1951, when the A3 was in BR blue livery and right-hand drive. The A3 has Diagram 94A boiler 27020, and her GN tender is No.5212. (Gresley Society Trust)

ST.GATIEN and CORONACH wait between duties at the east end of Haymarket shed on August 26th 1960. The boilers, respectively, are 27006 and 74 (94A) and the GN tenders are 5278 and 87. (Brian Bailey)

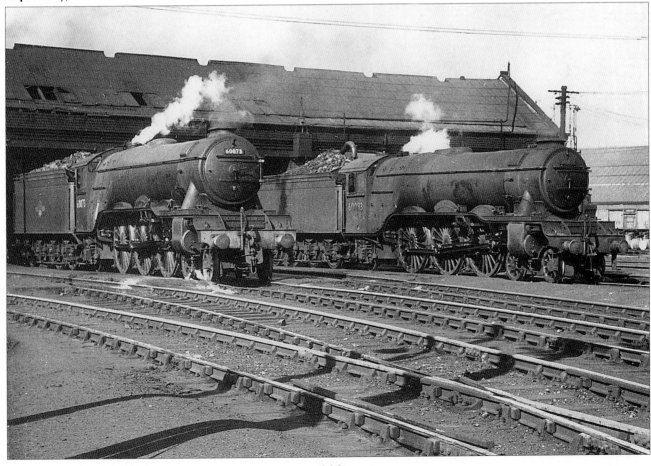

119

HARVESTER

Built	8/10/24
North British Loco Co Works No.	23111
Rebuilt to A3/1 (with long travel valves)	17/4/28
Wartime black livery	14/7/42
LNER Nos.	2573, 542 (7/4/46), 74 (30/6/46)
LNER livery	2/8/47
BR No.	60074 (19/5/48)
BR experimental purple livery	22/5/48
BR blue livery	17/11/50
BR dark green livery	6/11/52
Double Kylchap fitted	20/3/59
Trough deflectors not fitted	
Withdrawn	8/4/63

Allocation (A1)	
To Gateshead	27/9/24
(A3)	
To Haymarket	18/4/28
To Gateshead	5/7/28
To Haymarket	12/4/37
To Gateshead	21/2/38
To Neville Hill	2/12/39
To York	28/2/40
To Heaton	28/3/43
To Gateshead	3/11/45
To Neville Hill	6/2/49
To York	27/11/50
To Neville Hill	17/12/50

HARVESTER, by contrast, was a locomotive with an eventful history. She was reboilered in 1928 as part of the development of the A3 from the A1 design, with long travel valves but retaining 20in cylinders. With the intention to commence non-stop running between Kings Cross and Waverley, two of the reboilered Pacifics, HARVESTER from Gateshead and SHOTOVER from Heaton were sent to Haymarket. Although, subsequently, it was decided to use two of Haymarket's A1s, HARVESTER completed five round trips in the 1928 season. Whilst at Haymarket she was route tested as far as Montrose, opening the way to a wider use of the A1s and the arrival of new A3s. It is surprising that one of the Scottish A1s had not been route tested earlier, which suggests that their main purpose was to work from Edinburgh to Newcastle or Glasgow.

In late 1939 three A3s were sent to Neville Hill, HARVESTER being one. The experiment was a short one, but it was revived in 1949, the three returning together with two more A3s. Their sphere of work lay to the north, and they rarely appeared in the south. An exception was HARVESTER. The International Harvester company had a special train annually, and no doubt an enthusiast in the company knew of the A3's name, and she was sent south to haul the special. The Neville Hill A3s worked the Queen of Scots Pullman and the North Briton services together with lesser services between Newcastle, Leeds and York. At one time they worked to Edinburgh, and Glasgow before 1939.

In 1961 five Type 4 diesels D345-D349 were allocated to Neville Hill, but BR was engulfed in teething troubles with diesel traction in many areas, and the Neville Hill A3s had to replace the diesels on their long diagrams until reliability had been achieved. Only the Newcastle-Edinburgh section was worked by fresh locomotives. Neville Hill A3s, for the first time, worked into Kings Cross on an overnight sleeper, and returned north on the Queen of Scots.

HARVESTER, a Neville Hill engine and unusually clean, stands at Gateshead between duties. She was used to haul the annual special for International Harvester, the agricultural equipment company, which may explain her unconventional appearance, although the tender has yet to be dealt with. By now the original cranked reversing lever has been replaced by a straight one. Gateshead's TEHRAN stands behind, presumably with her shedmate HYCILLA, by the look of the short nameplate. The year is 1953, so the boiler is Diagram 94HP No.27040 and the GN tender is No.5268. (C J B Sanderson, J W Armstrong Trust)

The up Flying Scotsman hauled by HARVESTER, taking water at Langley Troughs. The period is probably 1930-31, and as the Gateshead A3 is in charge, it must be the winter timetable. From summer 1932 the headboard was carried all year round. The A3 has Diagram 94HP boiler No.8030 or 8252 and her GN tender was No.5283.

A well-known photograph of HARVESTER on July 1st 1928, near Montrose, probably between there and Kinnaber. The route from Kinnaber Junction into Aberdeen was owned by the LMSR, and it was necessary to establish what strengthening and clearance works were required for the LNER to operate the bigger locomotives. The opportunity had been taken to use a reboilered A1 with corridor tender to ascertain whether Pacifics could work into Aberdeen. Lead fingers (touch posts) were fitted to monitor actual overhead clearances, although clearly the dimensions of the Pacific would have been checked against the rolling stock gauging records for the route beforehand. The clearances through tunnels and longer overbridges would be important.

ST. FRUSQUIN

Built	11/10/24
North British Loco Co Works No.	23112
Long travel valves	14/12/28
Rebuilt to A3 with wartime black livery	26/6/42
LNER Nos.	2574, 75 (27/10/46).
LNER livery	17/10/47
BR No.	60075 (28/5/48)
BR experimental purple livery	28/5/48
BR blue livery	5/12/50
BR dark green livery	13/6/52
Double Kylchap fitted	14/8/59
Trough deflectors not fitted	
Withdrawn	13/1/64

Allocation (A1)
To Gateshead	11/10/24

(A3)
To Darlington	17/8/52
To Gateshead	22/2/53
To Darlington	31/10/54
To Gateshead	8/5/55
To Darlington	18/6/61
To Gateshead	17/12/61
To Darlington	24/6/62
To Heaton	9/12/62
To Darlington	2/6/63
To Gateshead	15/12/63

ST FRUSQUIN was another very long term resident at Gateshead, but with a rather anonymous history in terms of detail. The one occurrence of note, really, was in 1959 when, newly fitted with a double Kylchap, ST FRUSQUIN took over the down Flying Scotsman at Newcastle. Starting 24 mins late, she ran from Newcastle to Edinburgh with 420 tons in 113 mins, 17 mins less than the schedule and almost certainly the fastest time on record by an A3. ST. FRUSQUIN was a curious omission from the number of A3s fitted with trough deflectors, a result of a clerical error. They were never fitted subsequently.

ST. FRUSQUIN stands pilot at Darlington on August 15th 1962. Three years earlier the A3, just ex-works with a double Kylchap, took over the 420 tons Flying Scotsman at Newcastle from Type 4 D208, and ran to Edinburgh in a net time of 113 minutes, a record time for an A3. With a load a third heavier than the Coronation, the A3 had cut seven minutes off the schedule. The BRB engineers at the time maintained that double chimneys made no difference to performance, demonstrating the old engineering adage that facts are useless against prejudice! The A3 has Diagram 107 boiler No.29324 and her GN tender was No.5287. (Jack Hodgkinson)

An unusual photograph in a familiar location. ST. FRUSQUIN coasts past Copenhagen Junction with an up express in the early 1960s. The south portal of Copenhagen Tunnel is where the mayhem in *The Ladykillers* took place. The remnants of the Necropolis station are on the extreme right. The A3 has a Diagram 107 boiler 29324 and GN tender No.5257. (D I D Loveday, The Gresley Society Trust)

GALOPIN

Built	14/10/24
North British Loco Co Works No.	23113
Long travel valves	27/6/28
Rebuilt to A3	27/6/41
Wartime black livery	7/10/42
LNER Nos.	2575, 76 (15/9/46)
LNER green livery	25/1/47
BR No	60076 (2/9/48)
BR blue livery not applied	
BR dark green livery	11/3/52
Double Kylchap fitted	30/6/59
Trough deflectors not fitted	
Withdrawn	29/10/62

Allocation (A1)
To Gateshead	24/9/24

(A3)
To Darlington	19/12/48
To Gateshead	27/1/52
To Darlington	16/3/52
To Gateshead	14/9/52
To Darlington	12/2/56
To Gateshead	19/8/56
To Darlington	1/12/57
To Gateshead	8/6/58
To Darlington	18/12/60
To Gateshead	18/6/61
To Heaton	9/9/62

GALOPIN followed the normal pattern for A3s at Gateshead and, with GLADIATEUR went to Darlington as pilot for over three years. Over this time, some 3½ years between general overhaul, she retained the LNER livery until March 1952. GALOPIN returned as pilot four more times. She was a somewhat reclusive engine as far as photographers were concerned, and despite an average annual mileage of 56,000, had an unremarkable history.

A down train of empty stock between the tunnels at Welwyn. The A3 is GALOPIN, just fresh from Doncaster Works, running-in. The visible part of the train is outer suburban non corridor stock, a likely service being 812 down, the 11.15 ECS train from Holloway Sidings to York, which often comprised vehicles for repair or scrap. It was usually a Doncaster turn, often used for running-in. The A3 has Diagram 94A boiler No.27034 and her GN tender was No.5232. (R Wilson, transporttreasury.co.uk)

GALOPIN, fresh from general overhaul, in July 1959 at Doncaster Works. On the adjacent road, a BR Class 5 4-6-0 appears to have run into trouble. The A3 has a Diagram 94A boiler No.27046 and a GN tender No.5232.

A relief to the 11.00 down Edinburgh express approaches New Southgate on August 5th 1961. The wall on the right is the boundary of the famous Colney Hatch mental hospital, and one can see where coal was once delivered by turntable off the down siding. The A3 has a Diagram 94A boiler No.27067 and a GN tender No.5262. (Brian Bailey)

THE WHITE KNIGHT

Built	19/10/24
North British Loco Co Works No.	23114
Long travel valves	15/6/28
Rebuilt to A3 with wartime black livery	10/7/43
LNER Nos.	2576, 545 (24/3/46),77 (30/6/46)
LNER green livery	23/11/46
BR No.	60077 (17/11/48)
BR blue livery	28/9/50
BR dark green livery	4/3/52
Double Kylchap fitted	1/4/59
Trough deflectors fitted	7/7/61
Withdrawn	13/7/64

Allocation (A1)	
To Gateshead	19/10/24
To York	17/11/36
To Gateshead	11/12/36
To York	28/3/43
(A3)	
To Heaton	6/5/46
To Holbeck	21/2/60
To Ardsley	10/9/61
To St.Margarets	16/6/63

THE WHITE KNIGHT was one of the four Gateshead Pacifics which migrated post-war to Heaton for a similarly long period. In 1929 THE WHITE KNIGHT was selected for an experiment with an ACFI feedwater heater and pump fitted to the Diagram 94 180psi boiler. The equipment, although designed aesthetically, disfigured the handsome lines of the A1. This would not have mattered if the equipment had proved effective and economical, but it did not, partly due to the tendency to scale up, and partly from a lack of interest at the depot. It was removed during the December 1938 general overhaul. As mentioned with SUNSTAR, THE WHITE KNIGHT was another regular visitor to Kings Cross, returning with the 17.35 Newcastle. In the last years she moved to Leeds and became one of the group of ex-Tyneside A3s working over the Leeds-Carlisle route. The Midland men took to the double Kylchap A3s, and some went as far as to claim that they were the best engines that had worked on the line. Before long, however, the diesels took over, and steam was finished. THE WHITE KNIGHT eventually went to St.Margarets, from where she was withdrawn.

THE WHITE KNIGHT gathers speed through Harringay in summer 1961 with a down express. The view is an unusual one with the station in the distance. The A3 has Diagram 94A boiler No.27046 and A3 non-corridor tender was No.5581. (D I D Loveday, Gresley Society Trust)

THE WHITE KNIGHT, specially cleaned, stands out from the general murk and grime at Holbeck in May 1961. There is a headboard up – for the Thames-Clyde or The Waverley over the Settle and Carlisle. Formerly a Tyneside engine, as a consequence of the administrative changes in 1957 she went to Holbeck in 1960. Boiler 94A (27046) Tender A3 non-corridor (5581). (Peter J Coster)

NIGHT HAWK

Built	24/10/24
North British Loco Co Works No.	23115
Long travel valves	27/4/28
Wartime black livery	28/2/42
Rebuilt to A3	15/1/44
LNER Nos.	2577, 78 (10/11/46)
LNER green livery	22/2/47
BR No.	60078 (10/4/48)
BR blue livery	7/10/50
BR dark green livery	6/5/52
Double Kylchap fitted	27/2/59
Trough deflectors fitted	8/3/62
Withdrawn	22/10/62

Allocation (A1)	
To Gateshead	24/10/24
To York	7/1/37
(A3)	
To Neville Hill	29/9/45
To Gateshead	6/5/46
To Darlington	13/2/55
To Gateshead	7/8/55
To Heaton	9/9/62

NIGHT HAWK was the Pacific longest resident at Gateshead, with roughly 28 out of 38 years spent there. To judge from her recorded mileage and the length of time at Gateshead, she was a popular engine. She was one of the small group of Pacifics that were transferred to York, displaced by the new A4s. Again, there are few events in the history of NIGHT HAWK to relate. She could never be described as a common sight in the south.

York's new acquisition, NIGHT HAWK starts a down express vigorously away from her new home station in summer 1938. The A1 has Diagram 94 boiler 7775 and her original GN tender No.5287. (Rev. A C Cawston, courtesy Brian Bailey)

Leaving Grantham on a Saturday in spring 1932 behind Gateshead's NIGHT HAWK. The A1 has Diagram 94 boiler No.7766 and GN tender No.5287. (Rev. A C Cawston, courtesy Brian Bailey)

BAYARDO

Built	29/10/24
North British Loco Co Works No.	23116
Rebuilt to A3/1 (with long travel valves)	22/5/28
Wartime black livery	16/1/42
LNER Nos.	2578, 79 (7/11/46)
LNER livery	29/3/47
BR No.	60079 (18/3/48)
BR blue livery	19/5/50
BR dark green livery	31/1/52
Double Kylchap fitted	1/1/60
Trough deflectors not fitted	
Withdrawn	11/9/61

Allocation (A1)	
To Heaton	29/10/24
(A3)	
To Doncaster	28/3/37
To Haymarket	11/9/37
To Heaton	31/1/38
To Gateshead	22/1/40
To Heaton	6/1/45
To Gateshead	28/5/45
To Carlisle Canal	30/5/48

Of the batch of five new Diagram 94HP 220psi boilers, two were fitted to LEMBERG and ENTERPRISE, experimental conversions to develop the A3 design. Three other A1s at Newcastle received the remaining three 94HP boilers in 1928 - HARVESTER at Gateshead, BAYARDO and SHOTOVER at Heaton. There had been occasional problems over Cockburnspath Bank with the heaviest loads, and the choice of the three NE Pacifics was intended to see whether the greater tractive effort would eliminate loss of speed or even stalling on the 1 in 96 gradient. The greater tractive effort compromised the locomotives' adhesive factor and would have required more careful handling when pulling hard.

BAYARDO was a frequent sight until 1948, when a number of A3s and A4s were painted in the experimental purple livery. One selected, strangely, was CAPTAIN CUTTLE of Carlisle Canal, but when it was realised that she would be seen by few on the windswept moors of the Waverley route, she was sent to Gateshead, and BAYARDO went into purdah at Carlisle Canal in its stead. Quite why to Gateshead, since six A3s there already had the purple livery, is puzzling. Also puzzling, is why Canal needed four A3s to run the handful of services, when either the stronger and smaller-wheeled V2s would have been better, or Haymarket could have covered the few expresses with ease. As with the other three, with the number of diesels now available and far better suited to the Waverley, when BAYARDO needed general overhaul, she was condemned. Whereas SIR VISTO and FLAMINGO came south but once or twice post-war, their sisters BAYARDO and CORONACH did so several times when running-in from Doncaster. BAYARDO'S life mileage was about half a million greater than the other long-term Carlisle residents, demonstrating the extent of the work done at Heaton prior to transfer.

BAYARDO at Haymarket, soon after transfer from Heaton to Carlisle Canal. Although she was overhauled and painted in apple green in March 1948 using the 12ins numerals of the time, the Canal shed painter has altered the allocation on the buffer beam, using titled instead of upper case. The worksplate is mounted on the central splasher, an NB feature. The NBL cranked reversing shaft is well illustrated. Boiler: Diagram 94HP No.8247, GN tender No.5277.

BAYARDO with an up Waverley line freight at Portobello, passing Ivatt 2MT 2-6-0 46462 on August 29th 1960. Boiler: 94A(27070) Tender: GN (5277). (Brian Bailey)

DICK TURPIN

Built	3/11/24
North British Loco Co Works No.	23117
Long travel valves	16/1/29
Rebuilt to A3 and wartime black livery	26/11/42
LNER Nos.	2579, 80 (2/11/46)
LNER livery	9/8/47
BR No.	60080 (18/3/49)
BR blue livery	20/10/50
BR dark green livery	5/2/52
Double Kylchap fitted	13/10/59
Trough deflectors fitted	3/11/61
Withdrawn	12/10/64

Allocation (A1)	
To Heaton	3/11/24
(A3)	
To Gateshead	31/8/44
To Heaton	3/11/45
To Holbeck	8/5/60
To Ardsley	11/6/61
To Neville Hill	16/6/63
To Gateshead	8/12/63

DICK TURPIN is a name that is entirely in accord with the horse racing theme of the A1 and A3 names but of course, as has been pointed out many times, the name is that of the rider and not the horse, Black Bess. A long-term Heaton resident, DICK TURPIN was a frequent sight in apple green in the late 1940s, having been one of later changes to BR dark blue. One of my boyhood memories is of a gleaming apple green DICK TURPIN on the down Flying Scotsman, varnished teak and all, the carriage roofboards bearing the names of faraway places like Edinburgh and Aberdeen. She was usually about in any journey north, and when moved to Leeds worked over a wider variety of routes from those depots.

A photograph that anyone would be proud to produce. One would need to use 1/500th shutter speed to 'stop' an express pin-sharp at this angle. DICK TURPIN was in full flight on the 7.50 Sunderland-Kings Cross, a heavy southbound express on June 16th 1951. The A3 is in BR blue livery, and the location is between Shaftholme Junction and Moss. The A3 would have worked through to London and returned on the 17.35 down service to Newcastle. She is still right-hand drive, and has Diagram 94HP boiler 27003 and a GN tender No.5288. (R E Vincent, transporttreasury.co.uk)

On Sunday July 11th 1954, DICK TURPIN pulls away from Waverley station with the 11.30 departure for Kings Cross. The A3 is in splendid external condition, ten months after general overhaul. She has been converted to left-hand drive, and has Diagram 94A boiler 27002 and a GN tender No.5229. (J Robertson, transporttreasury.co.uk).

SHOTOVER

Built	9/11/24
North British Loco Co Works No.	23118
Rebuilt to A3/1 (with long travel valves)	16/2/28
Wartime black livery	25/9/43
LNER Nos.	2580, 81 (1/12/46)
LNER livery	12/10/46
BR No.	60081 (3/6/48)
BR blue livery	17/11/50
BR dark green livery	12/2/53
Double Kylchap fitted	31/10/58
Trough deflectors not fitted	
Withdrawn	1/10/62

Allocation (A1)

To Heaton	9/11/24

(A3)

To Haymarket	18/4/28
To Gateshead	29/9/28
To Heaton	5/3/30
To Neville Hill	2/12/39
To York	28/2/40
To Heaton	28/3/43
To Gateshead	3/11/45
To Neville Hill	6/2/49

SHOTOVER was the shortest-lived of the A1s, having been rebuilt only 3½ years after completion at North British Loco Co. She was one of the three reboilered A1s, now A3s, two of which were nominated for the non-stop Flying Scotsman, coupled to corridor tenders and loaned to Haymarket. SHOTOVER worked the inaugural up train, and ten more return trips in the 1928 season. Earlier in 1928, SHOTOVER had worked a second test train over the Waverley route successfully, unlike the earlier attempt with 2563.

In 1929 SHOTOVER, with THE WHITE KNIGHT, was selected for an experiment with an ACFI feedwater heater and pump fitted, in this case, to the Diagram 94HP 220psi boiler. It was removed during the February 1939 general overhaul. (See THE WHITE KNIGHT)

Just before the 1939-45 war, SHOTOVER was one of a few Pacifics transferred to Neville Hill, and although she soon returned to the main line, in 1949 she returned to Neville Hill with four other Pacifics. The comments on work at Neville Hill regarding COLOMBO, HARVESTER, TRIGO and GAINSBOROUGH, apply equally to SHOTOVER.

SHOTOVER in her Neville Hill days with the Queen of Scots Pullman at Headingley on August 8th 1959. It is not stated whether it is the down or up service, but my distant memories suggest that it is the up. The Diagram 94A boiler is No.27054, with GN tender No.5273. (M Joyce, Gresley Society Trust)

The Pacific that worked the first up non-stop Flying Scotsman in 1928 at Kings Cross after completing the journey. SHOTOVER was fitted with a 220 psi Diagram 94HP boiler, and the Heaton Pacific was then loaned to Haymarket for the Non-stop. Later, when Haymarket's A1s were equipped with corridor tenders, they took the duty over. The rebuild was later classified A3, but Darlington Works continued the NE practice of painting CLASS 4.6.2. on the buffer beam after a general overhaul see GLADIATEUR for instance. The tinplate headboard was a novelty at the time, enthusiastically adopted by the LNER for the other named trains. The Westinghouse pump remained in position although not used during the loan. Boiler: Diagram 94HP No.8029, A3 corridor tender No.5326.

135

NEIL GOW

Built	30/11/24
North British Loco Co Works No.	23119
Long travel valves	4/1/29
Rebuilt to A3 and wartime black livery	15/1/43
LNER Nos.	2581, 82 (20/6/46)
LNER livery	29/5/48
BR No.	60082 (26/5/48)
BR blue livery	24/9/49
BR dark green livery	28/3/52
Double Kylchap fitted	18/9/59
Trough deflectors fitted	25/8/61
Withdrawn	2/9/63

Allocation(A1)
(A3)

To Heaton	3/11/24
To Gateshead	13/6/48
To Darlington	14/9/52
To Gateshead	22/3/53
To Heaton	6/5/56
To Holbeck	8/5/60
To Heaton	16/7/61
To Gateshead	25/3/62
To Heaton	9/9/62
To Gateshead	16/6/63

NEIL GOW was another of Heaton's A1s which stayed in the Newcastle area for much of the time. Her history is quite uneventful; she spent some years post-war moving between Heaton and Gateshead to supplement their Pacific fleets.

NEIL GOW starts explosively from platform 2, her coupled wheels no doubt spinning, with the 10.45 relief to Newcastle from Kings Cross on April 25th 1962. By that time the omnipresent Brush Type 2 diesels had ousted the once familiar N2 0-6-2Ts on ECS duties as well as passenger work. The Diagram 107 boiler is No.29310, with GN tender No.5226. (R F Orpwood, Gresley Society Trust)

NEIL GOW gathers speed north of Finsbury Park with a down express at a time between 1928-34. The boiler is a Diagram 94, and the GN tender is 5291

NEIL GOW standing on shed. Converted to left-hand drive, she has the first of the Diagram 94HP boilers authorised in May 1944 by Edward Thompson (27000). This sets the date around 1954/55. The A3 has GN tender No.5226. (P Ransome-Wallis)

SIR HUGO

Built	6/12/24
North British Loco Co Works No.	23120
Long travel valves	19/2/30
Rebuilt to A3 and wartime black livery	17/12/41
LNER Nos.	2582, 83 (20/6/46)
LNER livery	17/8/46
BR No.	60083 (27/5/49)
BR blue livery	28/5/49
BR dark green livery	2/9/52
Double Kylchap fitted	2/9/59
Trough deflectors fitted	18/5/64
Withdrawn	8/2/62

Allocation (A1)	
To Heaton	6/12/24
To Gateshead	17/6/40
To Heaton	26/10/40
(A3)	
To Gateshead	16/6/63

SIR HUGO was the last A1 built by North British. It took Doncaster a year to build twenty A1s, whereas North British took five months. SIR HUGO was unusual in that she spent some 38 years at Heaton, separated midway in wartime with four months at Gateshead. That she was retained in preference to other A1/A3s suggests that she was highly regarded there. She was one of the few A3s restored to apple green livery while still with its original number, 2582.

The only information available for this superb photograph of 60083 SIR HUGO is the year – given as 1957. The lighting suggests an up train rather than down. In the mid-1950s Heaton worked the 7.50 from Newcastle as far as Peterborough and the 7.53 from Sunderland as far as Grantham before returning north. The location is at a point where either a branch joins the main line, or where the up slow/goods converges. It is almost certainly not south of Grantham, but there are several such points to the north and Hougham, Claypole and Ranskill would be possibilities. The radio mast on the left might be a clue, indicating the proximity of a larger junction such as Retford or Doncaster. A small detail but unusually, the A3, originally built by North British as right-hand drive and fitted at that time with a cranked reversing rod to clear the Westinghouse pump fitted, now has a modified Doncaster reversing rod, forged in two parts to facilitate handling, no doubt fitted when the drive was changed to left-hand. The A3 has Diagram 94A boiler No.27033 and GN tender No.5282. (transport treasury.co.uk)

SIR HUGO with a northbound relief express late in the day, at some time in the 1930s whilst still an A1. The location is a puzzle, although the NER milepost gives a hint. The A1 has a Diagram 94 boiler and a GN tender No.5292.

2582 SIR HUGO, in Grantham yard after coming off a football special for Kings Cross, in the spring of 1930 when she was still being overhauled at Darlington Works, and before the Westinghouse equipment was removed. Note low position of cabside numbers. The A1 has a Diagram 94 boiler No.7803 and a GN tender No.5292. (Rev. A C Cawston, courtesy Brian Bailey)

TRIGO

Built	22/2/30
Works No.	1731
Wartime black livery	3/10/42
LNER Nos.	2595, 84 (27/10/46)
LNER livery	1/2/47
BR No.	60084 (31/5/48)
BR experimental purple livery	31/5/48
Withdrawn	23/11/64

Allocation

To Gateshead	22/2/30
To Heaton	28/3/43
To Gateshead	3/11/45
To Neville Hill	4/9/49
To Gateshead	8/12/63

TRIGO was the first of a batch of eight A3s built at Doncaster of which five were allocated to Gateshead. At the same time three went to Haymarket. The works numbers of the eight locos ran chronologically, the running numbers did not. 2595-2597 were followed by 2795-2797, and then 2598-2589. The first ten A3s had been shared between Carlisle and the Southern Area, and TRIGO was Gateshead's first A3. The five were often to be found on the midday Scottish express and the winter Flying Scotsman.

On March 22nd 1939 COMMONWEALTH OF AUSTRALIA, on the up Coronation, ran hot and was replaced at Newcastle by TRIGO. Driver Nash then ran the 268.35 miles in 229 minutes, 225 minutes net, regaining the time lost in changing locos. TRIGO was one of the post-war transfers to Neville Hill, only returning to Gateshead towards the end of steam. See also SINGAPORE.

The up Queen of Scots Pullman pulls away from Harrogate behind TRIGO on May 22nd 1959. The A3 has Diagram 94A boiler No.27026 and A4 non-corridor tender No.5645. (Brian Morrison)

The 13.20 Kings Cross-Edinburgh, the predecessor of the Heart of Midlothian of 1951, was a very heavy train. TRIGO is managing well over the last few hundred yards to Potters Bar on 18 June 1937. Boiler: Diagram 94HP No.8084, A3 non-corridor tender No.5476. (Rev. A C Cawston, courtesy Brian Bailey)

TRIGO breasts Stoke summit in February 1932 with the down Flying Scotsman. An O4 waits on the down goods with a freight. The A3 has her original Diagram 94HP boiler No.8223 and her original A3 non-corridor tender No.5476. (Rev. A C Cawston, courtesy Brian Bailey)

MANNA (originally intended to be named COMMON)

Built	22/2/30
Works No.	1733
Wartime black livery	2/4/43
LNER Nos.	2596, 85 (27/10/46)
LNER livery	24/12/47
BR No.	60085 (3/7/48)
BR blue livery	11/11/49
BR dark green livery	23/12/52
Double Kylchap fitted	5/11/58
Trough deflectors fitted	27/4/62
Withdrawn	12/10/64

Allocation	
To Gateshead	22/2/30
To Heaton	28/3/43
To Gateshead	14/2/45
To Heaton	31/8/44
To Gateshead	16/6/63

MANNA was always on Tyneside, and more of a Heaton resident post-war. She was hardworking but had an unspectacular history. TRIGO and MANNA, when new, were used in comparative trials of superheater elements.

A dishevelled MANNA pauses south of the station at York on February 6th 1964. It is not easy at first sight to tell which way the A3 is running as she appears to be in midgear, but the lamp on the buffer beam doesn't look like a tail lamp, indicating light engine. The smokebox door handrail has been altered as a result of lowering the top lamp iron, as with a number of A3s. Boiler: Diagram 94A(27039) Tender: GN No.5283.

The up Flying Scotsman has called at Grantham, and the A3 is MANNA. The date is winter 1932, and the A3 has her original Diagram 94HP boiler No.8224 and her original A3 non-corridor tender No.5477. (Rev. A C Cawston, courtesy Brian Bailey)

On the up Flying Scotsman, MANNA, magnificently turned out, speeds through Greenwood. When the train was running non-stop, the power was provided by Kings Cross and Haymarket. For the remainder of the summer book the power was the same. In the winter timetable, Gateshead took part in the working. The date would be between 1930 and 1932. The A3 has a Diagram 94HP boiler and an A3 non-corridor tender No.5477.

GAINSBOROUGH

Built	7/4/30
Works No.	1736
Wartime black livery	13/6/42
LNER Nos.	2597, 86 (27/10/46)
LNER livery	23/5/47
BR No.	60086 (16/9/48)
BR blue livery	13/5/49
BR dark green livery	18/6/52
Double Kylchap fitted	12/6/59
Trough deflectors not fitted	
Withdrawn	18/11/63

Allocation	
To Gateshead	7/4/30
To Doncaster	15/3/36
To Gateshead	17/7/36
To Heaton	30/9/39
To Neville Hill	2/12/39
To York	29/2/40
To Heaton	28/3/43
To Gateshead	30/11/44
To Neville Hill	6/2/49

GAINSBOROUGH was a Gateshead engine, but with the arrival of the A3s and A4s, she was one of the trio sent to Neville Hill in 1939. GAINSBOROUGH was also used for experiments with superheater elements, having been fitted with Sinuflo elements. The tubes had been cranked into a sine wave profile, which increased the heating surface. These had been used on the Mikados previously. After the war she was returned to Neville Hill, with COLOMBO, HARVESTER, SHOTOVER and TRIGO, which is where she was at the end.

In late 1961 five new Type 4 diesels were allocated to Neville Hill and set to work on high mileage diagrams. In the midst of BR's teething troubles with diesel traction, they lasted a few days before failing, and the diagrams were abandoned. Neville Hill's fleet of four A3s, COLOMBO having moved away earlier, together with other borrowed Pacifics, were pressed into an amended diagram, working from Leeds to Newcastle, London and back to Leeds. Post-war, Neville Hill A3s were very rare sights in London, Copley Hill having so many Pacifics that it was never without power. Deputising for a diesel one morning on the 19.15 Aberdeen-Kings Cross in old platform 5 was GAINSBOROUGH, an A3 that I had not seen before at the south end of the main line. Fortunately I had my camera with me to record the stranger. One of the 'Baby Deltics' stands in platform 2 on an outer suburban service. Boiler: Diagram 107 No.29317, tender: A3 non-corridor No.5478. (P J Coster)

The North Briton was the name given to the service to Glasgow from Leeds City. An immaculate GAINSBOROUGH, specially prepared for an official footplate trip, waits on March 25th 1961. She has been reboilered with Diagram 107 boiler No.29317 and A3 non-corridor tender No.5478. (G W Morrison)

GAINSBOROUGH, at an unidentified location, in the 1930s. She has a Diagram 94HP boiler, and was always coupled to A3 non-corridor tender No.5478.

BLENHEIM (originally intended to be named ROCK SAND)

Built	14/3/30
Works No.	1743
Wartime black livery	10/6/44
LNER Nos.	2598, 565 (21/3/46), 87 (27/10/46)
LNER livery	26/6/47
BR No.	60087 (20/10/48)
BR blue livery	17/8/50
BR dark green livery	4/7/52
Double Kylchap fitted	12/8/58
Trough deflectors fitted	2/2/62
Withdrawn	28/10/63

Allocation	
To Gateshead	14/3/30
To Doncaster	29/7/37
To Gateshead	13/10/37
To Haymarket	16/10/37
To Gateshead	8/2/38
To Haymarket	9/3/39
To Ferryhill	20/7/40
To Haymarket	18/10/41
To St.Margarets	13/7/60
To Haymarket	28/11/60
To St.Margarets	13/12/61

BLENHEIM was originally one of the Gateshead A3 quintet, no doubt something that would have surprised post-war enthusiasts. That was because BLENHEIM, in the south, was a name and a number which existed only in *abcs*; it was *believed* to exist north of the Border, but was never seen. I saw her once, ex-works, heading north with the Saturday evening Leeds goods, but never again south of Newcastle. Visiting Scotland, she was like all of Haymarket's Pacifics, at work somewhere, often to Newcastle. Of the ten highest average annual mileages, five were by Haymarket engines.

In 1954 BLENHEIM and SPEARMINT were tested on the Carlisle-Leeds route, the thinking being that Haymarket could work through from Edinburgh to Leeds. It was a good idea. Whether this was a precursor to closure of Canal or not, it fell at the consultation stage since the trade unions were opposed to what would almost certainly be a lodging turn and Haymarket was reluctant to disturb its manning and loco rostering. Ideally, Carlisle had one shed too many – possibly two - as Leeds certainly did, but amalgamations were rarely successful since whatever their faults, depots had a sort of team spirit. It was rather like amalgamating two football clubs in the same town!

BLENHEIM, in splendid external condition, gets under way with one of the principal Anglo-Scottish services, the 10.5 Kings Cross to Glasgow in what certainly is a very cold day. The location is Damdykes, one of Jim Smith's favoured spots, near Cramlington. No problems with smoke deflection! The date is February 1955. Boiler: Diagram 94A No.27027, tender: A3 non-corridor No.5572. (Jim Smith)

BLENHEIM is super power for the down Class D partly fitted freight, although the photograph suggests few fitted vehicles behind the engine. Haymarket sometimes used this duty for an A3 going to Doncaster for overhaul. The location is at Damdykes level crossing, near Cramlington, north of Newcastle. The date is July 13th 1955 and the A3 went into Doncaster for a general overhaul two weeks later. Boiler: Diagram 94A No.27027, tender: A3 non-corridor No.5572. (Jim Smith)

BOOK LAW

Built	12/7/30
Works No.	1744
Wartime black livery	11/3/43
LNER Nos.	2599, 88 (2/8/46)
LNER livery	12/6/47
BR No.	60088 (15/7/48)
BR blue livery	14/3/51
BR dark green livery	11/2/53
Double Kylchap fitted	1/7/59
Trough deflectors fitted	9/6/61
Withdrawn	14/10/63

Allocation
To Gateshead	12/7/30
To Haymarket	8/10/37
To Gateshead	23/1/38
To Heaton	28/3/43
To Gateshead	3/5/43
To Heaton	3/11/45
To Holbeck	8/5/60
To Heaton	16/7/61
To Gateshead	16/6/63

BOOK LAW spent half her time at Gateshead and half at Heaton. Having no turns to London for a while post-war, as mentioned elsewhere, Heaton's A3s were unusual visitors to the south. The adjustment of Regional boundaries in 1957 and the influx of diesels within a few years brought a return to through working, and it caused a considerable increase in the number of A3s in the West Riding, able to work to London, Newcastle, Carlisle. In fact they worked north and north-west of Carlisle as well.

The down Waverley at Carlisle behind BOOK LAW in summer 1960; it was about to be replaced, appropriately, by 60509 WAVERLEY for the run from Citadel to Edinburgh. The A3 already has the lamp attached denoting light engine status for its run to Canal for servicing. The A3 has a Diagram 94A boiler 27064, and her usual GN tender No.5263. (P J Coster)

Heaton's BOOK LAW between Gamston and Grove Road with the 15.00 Kings Cross-Newcastle relief, as confirmed by the WTT No.74 on the central lamp iron. It is August 7th 1956, the Diagram 94A boiler is No.27004, and the GN tender is No.5263. (B K B Green, Initial Photographics)

FELSTEAD

Built	22/8/28
Works No.	1693
Wartime black livery	10/5/42
LNER Nos.	2743, 89 (18/9/46)
LNER livery	18/9/46
BR No.	60089 (3/9/48)
BR blue livery	27/10/50
BR dark green livery	21/3/52
Double Kylchap fitted	9/10/59
Trough deflectors fitted	11/10/61
Withdrawn	14/10/63

Allocation	
To Doncaster	22/8/28
To Gateshead	15/3/46
To Doncaster	17/7/36
To Grantham	9/2/41
To Kings Cross	19/5/46
To Haymarket	18/2/51
To Tay Bridge	21/11/60
To St.Margarets	19/12/60

This was the first newly built A3 as distinct from a rebuilt A1. FELSTEAD was coupled initially to a corridor tender (5330) for six months, despite having been allocated to Doncaster. The tender was then transferred to FLAMINGO, then MERRY HAMPTON and then LADAS, behind which it was actually used on the Non-stop! At Doncaster she was a regular choice for the hardest turns, notably the up 'Breakfast Flyer' in the 1930s. She was a Southern Area engine until February 1951, a familiar sight working from Top Shed. Although Haymarket had swapped four A3s with Doncaster (2) and Kings Cross (2), another A3, FELSTEAD, went north. (See ORMONDE).

On October 26th 1959 FELSTEAD, fresh from overhaul, was hauling a freight near Ardsley when she ran into the rear of another standing ahead. It was the classic permissive block collision, and FELSTEAD sustained considerable front end damage. It is likely that the Scottish Region insisted on the return of their A3, for FELSTEAD was repaired by March 1960, using parts of SOLARIO, which had been the subject of debate over repairs. The renascent A3 contained parts of both as a sort of SOLSTEAD or FELARIO?

For many years FELSTEAD was a Southern Area A3, but she was sent to Haymarket in early 1951 as a left-and drive engine, and was rarely seen south of Doncaster afterwards. Here she is running-in on an early morning stopping service at Retford on May 28th 1958. The Diagram 94A boiler is No.27072, and the GN tender is No.5255. (B K B Green, Initial Photographics)

The 12.5 to Carlisle pulls away from Waverley behind FELSTEAD on March 24th 1951. The A3 is immaculate in BR blue livery, a truly superb picture. The Diagram 94A boiler is No.27004, and the GN tender is No.5255. (J Robertson, transporttreasury.co.uk)

A gleaming FELSTEAD, not long after overhaul at Doncaster, at Dundee Tay Bridge in April 1952. The fireman appears to be a former Royal Navy man, practising making smoke! Notice that even the boiler top has been cleaned. She has a Diagram 94HP boiler 27073 and GN tender No.5255.

GRAND PARADE

Built	23/8/28
Works No.	1694
Replacement A3 entered service	14/4/38
Wartime black livery	18/11/42
LNER Nos.	2744, 90 (9/12/46)
LNER livery	24/5/47
BR No.	60090 (16/2/49)
BR blue livery	1/11/50
BR dark green livery	15/5/52
Double Kylchap fitted	8/8/58
Trough deflectors fitted	21/1/63
Withdrawn	28/10/63

Allocation

To Kings Cross	23/8/28
To Haymarket	7/7/37
To Doncaster	31/3/38
To New England	11/4/44
To Leicester	16/2/49
To Grantham	16/5/49
To Doncaster	2/4/50
To Haymarket	2/7/50
To Tay Bridge	21/11/60
To St.Margarets	19/12/60
To St.Rollox	18/6/62
To Eastfield	31/12/62
To St.Rollox	14/1/63

GRAND PARADE was initially a London engine but was sent to Haymarket in July 1937. On December 10th that year, the driver of the 16.03 Edinburgh-Glasgow express overran danger signals in a heavy snowstorm, and smashed into a preceding express standing at a failed signal. Thirty-five people were killed, and the force of the collision was such that the A3 was written off, and a new one built in its place, almost completed before the original A3 reached Doncaster. The original nameplates were reversed. Haymarket flatly refused to have her back, considering her to be an unlucky locomotive. It may seem curious to us, but footplate men were not to know that the A3 was a replacement, and the thought of what had happened to her could be disturbing. We sometimes forget that footplatemen are the unwilling witnesses to horrifying accidents quite often, sadly.

Twelve years later, GRAND PARADE returned to Haymarket as part of the four engine exchange in 1950. With the arrival of diesel traction, Haymarket's Pacific fleet was dispersed and several found their way on to the Aberdeen-Glasgow service. GRAND PARADE eventually found her way to St Rollox, the old Caledonian shed at Glasgow.

The first GRAND PARADE stands at York in 1932 with an up express. The Diagram 94HP boiler is No.8029, and the A3 corridor tender is No.5331. The date must therefore be after August in that year. (J W Armstrong).

The second GRAND PARADE resplendent in apple green north of New Southgate with a down express. It is often difficult to distinguish between the original A3, destroyed in the Castlecary accident, and its April 1938 replacement, since at times both had 94HP boilers and GN pattern tenders. In April 1938 Doncaster commenced putting the class on the buffer beam below the number, which confirms that it is the replacement A3, when it was a Doncaster engine. The Diagram 94HP boiler is No.8029, and the GN tender is No.5263.

CAPTAIN CUTTLE

Built	8/9/28
Works No.	1695
Wartime black livery	16/2/42
LNER Nos.	2745, 91 (11/10/46).
LNER livery	11/10/46
BR No.	60091 (2/4/48)
BR experimental purple livery	2/4/48
BR blue livery	3/11/49
BR dark green livery	6/1/53
Double Kylchap fitted	14/3/59
Trough deflectors fitted	11/10/61
Withdrawn	12/10/64

Allocation	
To Doncaster	8/9/28
To Haymarket	24/10/28
To Carlisle	26/10/28
To Gateshead	30/5/48
To Heaton	13/6/48
To Gateshead	6/7/58
To Darlington	7/6/59
To Gateshead	6/12/59
To Darlington	17/12/61
To Gateshead	24/6/62
To Heaton	9/9/62
To Gateshead	16/6/63

CAPTAIN CUTTLE, after the customary month or so at Doncaster, was transferred to Haymarket for two days presumably in preparation for the Waverley route, before going on to Carlisle Canal. She was the first Pacific to work regularly on this difficult route. It was heavily graded and curved, much of it laid in ash and quite restricted in speed. She remained there for almost two decades.

There seems to have been a bureaucratic blunder in that she arrived at Carlisle coupled to a corridor tender, the last place where it would have been needed. It took nearly two years to swap tenders with SPEARMINT. Indeed communication between the people deciding the allocation of the new A3s and those coupling locos and tenders at Doncaster, from reading Yeadon's Register, seemed not to exist!

In an episode that has its comic aspects, CAPTAIN CUTTLE was selected as one of the seven A3s for the experimental livery, no doubt since she was in Doncaster at the time. It was soon realised that this was one of the few A3s that would not be widely seen. She was exchanged with BAYARDO, as described earlier, which resulted in all seven purple A3s gathered at Gateshead, a shed hardly noted for the cleanliness of its locomotives. CAPTAIN CUTTLE was almost immediately sent on to Heaton and soon appeared on the 17.35 Kings Cross-Newcastle. The exchange was extremely well received at the lineside; indeed one might indeed say it was Manna from Heaven.

CAPTAIN CUTTLE pounds up Falahill bank with an up express in August 1935. The express is bound for St Pancras, and will use the old MR route south of Carlisle. Also known as Borthwick bank, it was the hardest part of a hard route going from Edinburgh to Carlisle. The achievement of Haymarket men in 1948, tackling this long bank with their A4s with a big train, as part of a non-stop run to London, was amazing. The date is August 1935, and the A3 has her original Diagram 94HP boiler No.8028 and A3 non-corridor tender No.5480.

CAPTAIN CUTTLE at Darlington with the 9.10(SO) from Glasgow to Kings Cross on February 22nd 1953. The A3 has lost her experimental purple livery in favour of the less spectacular BR dark green, and has a Diagram 94HP boiler No.27084 and an A3 non corridor tender (No.5480). (R E Vincent, transporttreasury.co.uk)

CAPTAIN CUTTLE on shed at some time between 1930 and 1935. The shed is, I believe, Carlisle Canal. Three N2s of the 472X series were allocated there, but as Haymarket also had N2s it might easily be there. The tender was said to be the corridor tender (5332) initially attached, but it looks more like the A3 non-corridor tender 5480 that was coupled for the rest of the A3's working life. The corridor tender was 9 ins wider with no horizontal strip at the bottom of the side sheets. The boiler was a Diagram 94HP (8077 or 8028).

FAIRWAY (originally intended to be named CORONACH)

Built	26/10/28
Works No.	1700
Wartime black livery	9/7/42
LNER Nos.	2746, 92 (27/10/46)
LNER livery	14/6/47
BR No.	60092 (13/4/49)
BR blue livery	17/11/50
BR dark green livery	19/8/52
Double Kylchap fitted	13/11/59
Trough deflectors fitted	25/10/61
Withdrawn	12/10/64

Allocation	
To Kings Cross	26/10/28
To Gateshead	10/11/36
To Kings Cross	15/12/36
To Gateshead	14/1/37
To Heaton	28/3/43
To Holbeck	8/5/60
To Ardsley	11/6/61
To Gateshead	16/6/63

FAIRWAY was a Kings Cross engine, coupled to a corridor tender for nearly seven years, before she was sent to Gateshead, then Heaton. In each year, apart from 1929 and 1931, she was used on the non-stop Flying Scotsman. During her long stay at Heaton she was one of the least commonly seen from that shed. With the arrival of diesels around 1960, she was moved to Holbeck and Ardsley, before returning to Gateshead. She led an uneventful life in the north east and was withdrawn in 1964.

A heavy class C freight, or No.1 speed if that is your tradition, hauled by **FAIRWAY** at Grantshouse nearing the summit of the climb to Penmanshiel Tunnel. I would guess at the mid-1950s, and **FAIRWAY** looks as though a visit to Doncaster Works may not be far away. The A3 probably has Diagram 94A boiler 27042, and her A3 non-corridor tender is No.5574. (J Robertson, transporttreasury.co.uk).

FAIRWAY, bearing her 1946 LNER number 92, heads an express from Newcastle downhill towards Potters Bar Tunnel in April 1948. The Diagram 94A boiler is No.9485, and the tender is A3 non-corridor No.5574. (Rev. A C Cawston, courtesy Brian Bailey)

FAIRWAY at Kings Cross shed in the mid-1930s. The A3 was coupled to a corridor tender (No.5326) for over six years from 1929 to 1936. Her boiler was of course a Diagram 94HP.

E9315

The 11.00 departure to Glasgow from Kings Cross about to leave behind FAIRWAY on February 21st 1960. With the increased number of through workings between London and Newcastle, Heaton Pacifics began to supplement Gateshead's fleet. Although only three months out of a general overhaul, the A3 is already travel stained. She would have arrived at Kings Cross the previous evening with the afternoon Talisman. Kings Cross was changing with a spluttering of Type 4s in the Loco Yard, and a growling of 350HP shunters instead of the ubiquitous N2s. The Diagram 94A boiler is No.27079, and the tender is A3 non-corridor No.5574. (David Idle, transporttreasury.co.uk)

CORONACH (originally intended to be named COLORADO)

Built	24/11/28
Works No.	1703
Wartime black livery	28/2/42
LNER Nos.	2747, 93 (7/7/46)
LNER livery	8/8/47
BR No.	60093 (19/9/48)
BR blue livery	14/10/49
BR dark green livery	7/5/52
Double Kylchap fitted	19/12/58
Trough deflectors not fitted	
Withdrawn	24/4/62

Allocation	
To Doncaster	24/11/28
To Kings Cross	17/3/30
To Doncaster	31/5/30
To Haymarket	16/3/39
To Carlisle	23/1/41

CORONACH was allocated to Doncaster, during which time she was one of two A3s selected for smoke deflection trials following the accident at Leighton Buzzard on the LMSR in 1931, in which inadequate smoke deflection was held to be a contributory cause. Experiments were already in hand with the W1 10000 to overcome the problem of a soft exhaust with that particular locomotive. The smokebox crown of CORONACH was cut away at the front. A variety of arrangements with vents, double chimneys, etc were tried between 1931 and 1933, and the arrangements were sufficiently encouraging to be carried over into the P2s and A4s. Mercifully the A1s and A3s were spared the facial disfigurement! CORONACH herself was restored to normal A3 appearance subsequently. In 1941 CORONACH was transferred to Carlisle, where she and her sister A3s continued to slog over the Waverley hills until the diesels took over. (See also HUMORIST).

One of the Carlisle Canal quartet, 60093 CORONACH with the up Waverley pounding up the 10 miles of 1 in 72-80 from Hawick to Whitrope near Shankend station in remote and lonely country on May 13th 1961. The A3 is steaming well, but the driver appears to have just eased the regulator for some reason, probably for a temporary speed restriction (TSR), causing the safety valves to erupt. There was no signal or significant permanent speed restriction (PSR) here. Boiler: 107(29322) Tender: GN (5287) (John F Aylard)

CORONACH, now coasting with only eight coaches, heads the down Waverley near Stow in the valley of the Gala Water, May 31st 1961. The reflected sunlight on the smokebox door was unusual for a locomotive travelling north, but at this point the Waverley route swung westwards briefly, before climbing to Falahill. Boiler: 107(29322) Tender: GN (5287) (John F Aylard)

CORONACH with an up Pullman, either the West Riding or Harrogate services. The location is not clear: either A3 is climbing the bank to Abbots Ripton, or more likely coming up the long straight north of Cadwell, north of Hitchin. The date is uncertain, and the boiler, a 94HP, and GN tender might be one of several.

COLORADO (originally intended to be named FLAMINGO)

Built	20/12/28
Works No.	1705
Wartime black livery	28/5/43
LNER Nos.	2748/94 (1/12/46)
LNER livery	26/9/47
BR No	60094 (20/12/48)
BR blue livery	10/5/50
BR dark green livery	29/4/52
Double Kylchap fitted	26/8/59
Trough deflectors fitted	19/8/61
Withdrawn	24/2/64

Allocation	
To Doncaster	20/12/28
To Kings Cross	13/2/29
To Carlisle	5/4/29
To Haymarket	29/12/47
To St.Margarets	13/12/61
To St.Rollox	18/6/62
To Eastfield	31/12/62
To St.Rollox	14/1/63

COLORADO, after two months at Doncaster, moved to Kings Cross. After two more months she was moved to Carlisle Canal, to join CAPTAIN CUTTLE and FLAMINGO. During the 1939-45 war, two more Pacifics were added, but post-war COLORADO moved to Haymarket. She was a regular member of the Haymarket fleet but when displaced by diesel traction moved firstly to St.Margarets and then to St.Rollox. Like GRAND PARADE, she finished on the Aberdeen-Glasgow route, based at St Rollox.

A Saturday extra for London pulls out of Waverley suburban platforms behind **COLORADO** on July 3rd 1954. She has a Diagram 94A boiler No.27076 and a GN tender No.5279. (J Robertson, transporttreasury.co.uk).

2748 COLORADO, running light, at some time in the 1929-39 period. The loco appears to have been recently completed or overhauled, running in between Doncaster and Grantham. Initially at Doncaster, then Kings Cross, it was sent to Carlisle Canal as a replacement for ENTERPRISE. The boiler is a Diagram 94HP and the GN tender is No.5271.

COLORADO stands at Glasgow Queen Street in May 1950. She has not long returned from general overhaul in BR blue livery. The A3 has acquired Diagram 94HP boiler 9568 and GN tender No.5279.

FLAMINGO (originally intended to be named PAPYRUS)

Built	26/1/29
Works No.	1707
Wartime black livery	9/12/42
LNER Nos.	2749, 558 (13/3/46), 95 (5/5/46)
LNER livery	29/8/47
BR No.	60095 (19/9/48)
BR blue livery	15/12/50
BR dark green livery	28/5/52
Double Kylchap fitted	6/2/59
Trough deflectors not fitted	
Withdrawn	10/4/61

Allocation
To Doncaster	26/1/29
To Carlisle	6/2/29

FLAMINGO, after the initial fortnight at Carr Loco, went to Carlisle Canal and stayed there until withdrawal. In the south, she was one of the unholy trinity of unseen A3s – with BLENHEIM and CICERO, all stars of lineside fencing and station woodwork. Unsurprisingly she was fairly anonymous. In the early 1950s the CMEE at Doncaster, K.J. Cook, had introduced optical equipment as used at Swindon to impart a greater degree of precision in locomotive repairs. As a result, ex-works Pacifics sounded far quieter than hitherto. O.S. Nock was an engineer and commentator on railway performance, and he occasionally rode on the footplate. On one of his runs, FLAMINGO took over at Carlisle, and as she made her way north, Ossie was astonished at the quietness of the A3 as she accelerated her train northwards, seeming to float over the pointwork.

The four Carlisle A3s were not allocated budget provision by the LMR for heavy repairs in 1961 and 1962, and in March 1961 sister Carlisle A3 SIR VISTO was repaired at Doncaster. In April, FLAMINGO, having reached its shopping mileage and needing repair, was not so lucky and became an early withdrawal.

FLAMINGO stands at Carlisle on July 23rd 1959, waiting to take over the down Waverley from Jubilee 45657 TYRWHITT for the final stage of the journey to Edinburgh. The A3 has a Diagram 107 boiler 29299, and A4 non-corridor tender No.5637. (P J Coster)

FLAMINGO at Haymarket, standing next to an anonymous A4; 60009, 60012, 60027 or 60031 from the look of the tender. The A3 is out of steam and may have been repaired or inspected there. Carlisle Canal shed oscillated between the LM and Scottish Regions over the years, and Haymarket, a senior shed and of course familiar with the A3s, may have assisted the LM Region with special repairs or examinations. Boiler: Diagram 107 No.29299, and A4 non-corridor tender No.5637.

FLAMINGO splendid in LNER apple green, pounding up Borthwick Bank, otherwise known as Falahill Bank, with a stopping service. With ten miles of hard climbing, whether the train was class A or B didn't seem to matter so much: it was still hard work! The date must be in late summer 1947 or early summer 1948. Doncaster painted both class and allocation on the buffer beam and this is a good illustration of the practice. The photographer appears to have used a lens with a longer focal length than usual, probably the plate camera equivalent of 85mm. The engine has a Diagram 94A boiler No.9450 and a GN tender (5224). (transporttreasury.co.uk)

A delightful summer view on the Waverley route, looking across at Stow village. The train hardly seems to qualify as an express, but it has open lights despite its modest formation. The identity of the A3 is a puzzle that would baffle Poirot. It is said to be CICERO, but that reclusive engine was never coupled to a GN tender. Under a glass it appears to be one of the 60090s, CORONACH, COLORADO, FLAMINGO, PAPYRUS, or SPION KOP, immaculate in LNER apple green rather than BR blue, with a GN tender bearing the new owner's name. Most were shopped in the winter months, curiously. Although it looks most like PAPYRUS, shopped in August 1949 and well turned out by Haymarket, both the latter two can be dismissed as they were never coupled to a GN tender during the immediate post-war period and were at Kings Cross until July 1950. The former two were not seen in such condition very often, and both emerged from general overhaul in winter. So one concludes that it is FLAMINGO, probably in the 1948-50 period, reluctantly since there is that uneasy feeling that the evidence doesn't quite add up. However, it is a very pleasing picture, for once not dominated by the subject. Boiler: Diagram 94A and a GN tender. (A G Ellis, transporttreasury.co.uk).

PAPYRUS (originally intended to be named HUMORIST)

Built	23/2/29
Works No.	1708
Wartime black livery	8/5/43
LNER Nos.	2750, 96 (11/11/46)
LNER livery	15/12/47
BR No.	60096 (27/10/48)
BR blue livery	25/8/49
BR dark green livery	3/4/52
Double Kylchap fitted	23/7/58
Trough deflectors fitted	15/9/61
Withdrawn	9/9/63

Allocation
To Kings Cross	23/2/29
To Haymarket	14/8/37
To Kings Cross	8/9/37
To Doncaster	12/10/37
To Grantham	11/3/39
To Kings Cross	27/10/46
To Haymarket	2/7/50
To St.Margarets	13/12/61

PAPYRUS was the most famous of the A3s, mainly for one reason: 108mph, the highest speed for a non-streamlined steam loco in the UK. She worked the Non-stop from Kings Cross in six of the nine years that A1s and A3s were used. She was also the last A3 to work the non-stop Flying Scotsman, on August 6-7th 1937, after which she had a short spell at Haymarket. She gained an enviable reputation at Kings Cross, and was chosen for the March 5th 1935 high speed test run to Newcastle. The standard of running was superb, but the climax was the descent from Stoke, with its maximum of 108mph. The running times were 237 and 232 minutes down and up, and the net times down and up were 230 and 228 minutes respectively. The time from Peterborough to Kings Cross, 76.35 miles, was 62mins 5secs, the fastest achieved by 1935. A full record of her performance is included in the Appendix. After the war, PAPYRUS was one of the five A3s sent to Haymarket, and ran well there, although sadly she was seen hardly ever down south. There were some ideas at the time of her withdrawal of preserving the record holder, but alas, it was a dream too far. PAPYRUS was taken out of traffic with a badly cracked frame, and lay at Cowlairs, then Parkhead before being hauled with five other former Haymarket A3s to Arnott Young for scrap.

PAPYRUS was the fastest British steam locomotive of a traditional outline, and was a very popular machine by all accounts of the day, especially on the Non-stop. She was the last A3 to retain a corridor tender and work the non-stop Flying Scotsman, on August 6th and 7th 1937. This posed undated picture is on the Kings Cross station turntable after working the Non-stop. The boiler is a 94HP, and a corridor tender is coupled: the numbers of each depend on the date of the photograph.

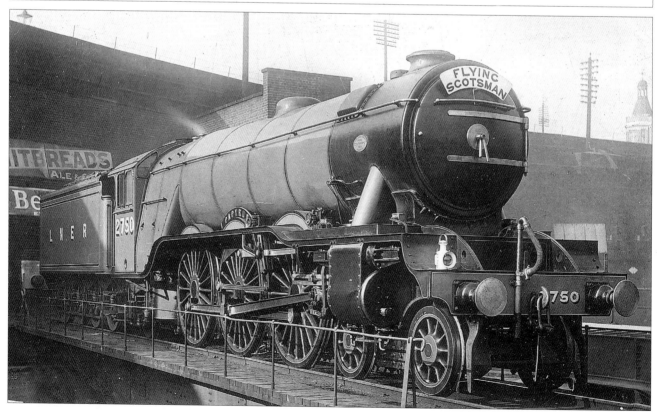

A classic view of the non-stop Flying Scotsman, racing into London past Greenwood behind an immaculate PAPYRUS in the first decade of through running. The A3 was a magnificent locomotive to look at, impressive yet superbly well proportioned and built for speed. The A3 has a Diagram 94HP boiler and an A3 corridor tender, 5329 or 5331.

HUMORIST (originally intended to be named SPION KOP)

Built	7/3/29
Works No.	1709
Double Kylchap fitted	
(with rimmed double chimney)	30/7/37
Stovepipe chimney and	
small deflectors fitted	11/2/38
Wartime black livery	7/8/42
LNER Nos.	2751, 97 (27/5/46)
LNER livery	26/9/46
Large deflectors fitted	25/4/47
BR No.	60097 (24/6/48)
BR blue livery	30/11/49
Rimmed double chimney fitted	19/4/51
BR dark green livery	20/11/52
Trough deflectors fitted	11/10/61
Withdrawn	14/10/63

Allocation

To Doncaster	7/3/29
To Grantham	7/8/42
To Kings Cross	27/10/46
To Haymarket	2/7/50
To Carlisle	6/1/54
To Haymarket	21/2/54
To St.Margarets	13/12/61

HUMORIST at Grantham during testing in May 1931 with the 16.30 slow train to Doncaster. The indicator shelter was necessary for the testing staff to travel on the front of the engine at speed safely while taking readings from gauges and indicators showing the actual steam pressure in the cylinders at different speeds. A number of tests were carried out, chiefly concerned with smoke deflection, but also with distribution of power between the three cylinders. The A3 has new Diagram 94A boiler No.8254 and GN tender No.5265. (Rev. A C Cawston, courtesy Brian Bailey)

HUMORIST was the second A3 selected for experiments in smoke deflection in 1933, when further permutations in smokebox alterations and chimney arrangements were tested. (See also CORONACH) The A3 was restored early in 1934. In 1937 HUMORIST was chosen for redraughting with a double Kylchap, together with the W1 10000 and A4 4468 MALLARD. The modified A3 had a rimmed double chimney that sat slightly forward due to the need to keep the exhaust assembly clear of the superheater header. It looked very much like the chimney used earlier in the smoke deflection experiments.

In an era when signal sighting was an art rather than a straightforward process, exhaust drifting down obscured the driver's view ahead, and the soft exhaust of the Kylchap allowed this more readily. A plain chimney was substituted instead with small wing or chimneyside deflectors, to avoid the vortexing of the soft exhaust and improve airflow. This was not a very effective arrangement, and Thompson and Peppercorn both opted for full size deflectors. In May 1947 large deflectors as used on Peppercorn's A2s replaced this arrangement, still with the stovepipe chimney. In April 1951 HUMORIST received a rimmed chimney as part of the practice of replacing stovepipe chimneys.

When one considers the fine lines of the A3, HUMORIST was something of an aesthetic disaster, as the deflectors, which suited the Peppercorn Pacifics well (although they were not very effective) did not fit the A3 visually at all. She was sent to Haymarket in August 1950, a loss to the south, but was appreciated in Scotland. Little is known of her work in Scotland although she was well liked as a fast and free steaming machine, but it is hard to avoid the conclusion that she would have done better at Top Shed, among the A4s. Although the exhaust beating down is annoying and an obvious safety hazard, it is perhaps surprising that little was done beyond fitting deflector plates of questionable efficacy. HUMORIST was withdrawn within a week of her old shedmate PAPYRUS, but she had gone to Doncaster where she was condemned and cut up.

HUMORIST during 1932 when smoke lifting experiments were being conducted. The A3 has a double chimney, the exhaust using the front orifice and the slipstream funnelled up through the rear orifice so as to lift the exhausting steam. The chimney was mounted further back than with the double Kylchap modification, requiring the anti-vacuum valve to be duplicated and the connections to the superheater header altered, as can be seen in the photograph. The location is Harringay. One feels for the occupants of the leading carriage! The A3 has new Diagram 94HP boiler 8254 and GN tender No.5265.

HUMORIST with the 14.00 from Kings Cross to Edinburgh on June 10th 1950, passing Abbots Ripton, just a few weeks before the transfer to Scotland. The A3 has Diagram 94A boiler 9516 and GN tender No.5265. It can be seen that the Peppercorn style smoke deflectors and stovepipe double chimney never suited the A3 as well as the A1s and A2s with their longer smokeboxes reaching much farther forward. 60097 was destined to be very much the ugly duckling, but her superior performance made her a favourite of drivers. This was taken in the days before prefabricated relaying, as the sleepers laying in the foreground show, when the track was re-laid by hand, a long and wearying process. (R E Vincent, transporttreasury.co.uk)

SPION KOP (originally intended to be named GAINSBOROUGH)

Built	20/4/29
Works No.	1710
Wartime black livery	24/2/43
LNER Nos.	2752, 561 (18/3/46), 98 (2/6/46)
LNER livery	1/3/47
BR No.	60098 (3/11/48)
BR blue livery	28/7/50
BR dark green livery	24/11/52
Double Kylchap fitted	17/7/59
Trough deflectors not fitted	
Withdrawn	28/10/63

Allocation

To Doncaster	20/4/29
To Haymarket	29/1/38
To St.Margarets	8/2/38
To Doncaster	2/3/38
To Grantham	1/7/43
To New England	2/4/44
To Grantham	16/4/44
To New England	29/5/44
To Kings Cross	18/8/46
To Doncaster	4/6/50
To Haymarket	6/8/50
To St.Margarets	6/1/63

SPION KOP, by contrast with several of the A3s, had an unremarkable history. It is characterised by a number of short term transfers between fairly long periods at Doncaster, Kings Cross and Haymarket. SPION KOP was one of the five Southern Area A3s that featured in the exchange with Haymarket in 1950-51. The A3 has memories for Harry Knox (*Steam Days at Haymarket*, Irwell Press) who fired her for Driver Peter Robertson on the Talisman in both directions. SPION KOP achieved some very fast running between Edinburgh and Newcastle.

SPION KOP waiting south of Grantham with the 16.30 local service to Doncaster in June 1931, probably running-in from Doncaster Works. The A3 has her original Diagram 94HP boiler No.8084 and GN tender No.5265.

SPION KOP runs light through Princes Street Gardens on the way to Haymarket shed in May 1959. The A3 has a Diagram 94A boiler No.27049 and an A3 non-corridor tender No.5481. This is an excellent view of the non-corridor standard tender that was introduced with the second batch of A3s in 1930.

CALL BOY

Built	19/4/30
Works No.	1738
Wartime black livery	20/12/41
LNER Nos.	2795, then 99 (21/7/46)
LNER livery	15/2/47
BR No.	E99 (5/3/48), 60099 (21/7/49)
BR blue livery	21/7/49
BR dark green livery	1/7/52
Double Kylchap fitted	29/7/58
Trough deflectors fitted	1/7/61
Withdrawn	28/10/63

Allocation
To Haymarket	19/4/30
To St.Margarets	12/1/40
To Haymarket	19/10/40
To St.Margarets	6/1/63

CALL BOY was Haymarket's first A3, and within two months was coupled to a corridor tender for non-stop operation. She worked on the Nonstop for seven years, from 1930 to 1936, usually with SPEARMINT, and was photographed several times. Haymarket's Pacifics were kept in excellent condition externally after the war, and their mechanical condition seemed to be good, to judge from the annual mileages achieved. CALL BOY was the only Scottish A3 of the 1928 and 1930 builds that was not fitted with tablet catching apparatus.

Curiously, CALL BOY often came south after general overhaul. I remember, whilst at Cemetery signalbox, seeing the first Hull fish, 579up, speed past behind Haymarket's KINGFISHER, only to be followed by the Doncaster goods, 1113up, hauled by the same shed's CALL BOY. It was sad to see her dumped in the long siding east of the shed in 1960. She was the one Scottish Pacific that I recall Gateshead borrowing to work to the south, on the up Talisman shortly before the ubiquitous English Electric Type 4s took over. Her life mileage was significantly higher than her sister A3s, pointing to an exceptionally reliable locomotive.

CALL BOY was the first A3 to be allocated to Haymarket, where she and sisters SPEARMINT and CICERO were popular and widely used. CALL BOY in particular had an enviable record of reliability and hard work. Here she is at Haymarket, ready for the Queen of Scots duty in April 1957. GRAND PARADE stands on the adjacent road, ready to go north. She has a Diagram 107 boiler No.29317 and an A3 non-corridor tender No.5568.

Haymarket's CALL BOY on shed at St Rollox. The date lays between July 1961 and late 1962 when she was sent to St Margarets. The A3 has Diagram 94A boiler No.27064 and A3 non-corridor tender No.5568.

Haymarket's CALL BOY, immaculately clean – even the boiler top is polished – sets off from Waverley for Dundee. It has been published before, but it is a magnificent photograph of a magnificent locomotive. The date is given as July 1950 but the evidence of livery and detail change suggests that it is 1953 or later. The boiler is a Diagram 94A, No.9982 fitted new a year previously, and the A3 non-corridor tender is No.5568. George Heiron.

SPEARMINT

Built	17/5/30
Works No.	1741
Wartime black livery	7/2/43
LNER Nos.	2796, 100 (20/7/46)
LNER livery	24/11/47
BR No.	60100 (13/4/49)
BR blue livery	15/11/50
BR dark green livery	3/9/52
Double Kylchap fitted	25/9/58
Trough deflectors fitted	17/8/61
Withdrawn	19/6/65

Allocation

To Haymarket	17/5/30
To Ferryhill	4/4/37
To Haymarket	6/3/38
To Eastfield	19/7/38
To Tay Bridge	5/10/40
To Haymarket	14/12/40
To St.Margarets	6/1/63

Much of what was said about CALL BOY applies equally to SPEARMINT, her companion on the Non-stop. Good work was recorded on the Flying Scotsman, and *The Railway Magazine* published an excellent run behind her. SPEARMINT gained fame as the regular engine of Norman McKillop, who rose through the links at Haymarket, and discovered a career as a writer, firstly in magazines, and then in a book or two. His A3 was a constant point of reference in his writings. No doubt SPEARMINT was a good engine, but I daresay other drivers would say much the same about theirs!

On a trip to Aberdeen in 1964, I was delighted to see SPEARMINT run into Tay Bridge station with the down train. It was nostalgic to lean out of the window, braving the occasional cinder, and listen to an A3 at work, probably for the last time, climbing the harder gradients of the Aberdeen road, the three cylinder exhaust fairly even and strong. SPEARMINT survived to 1965, one of the final three A3s.

Below. Having worked a stopping service over the Waverley route, SPEARMINT stands at Carlisle station. The picture must predate the larger tender normally coupled, so it is before August 1952. The A3 has a Diagram 94A boiler and a GN tender (No.5283 or 6). (J A C Kirke, transporttreasury.co.uk)

SPEARMINT at Doncaster, fresh from overhaul and provision of trough deflectors in August 1961. A WD and a new Brush diesel are in the background. The A3 has a Diagram 94A boiler No.27057and an A3 non-corridor tender (No.5566). (J Leaf, Colourrail.co.uk)

CICERO

Built	4/6/30
Works No.	1742
Wartime black livery	27/1/43
LNER Nos.	2797, 101(14/7/46)
LNER livery	22/5/47
BR No.	60101 (20/8/48)
BR blue livery	2/12/49
BR dark green livery	20/9/51
Double Kylchap fitted	20/2/59
Trough deflectors not fitted	
Withdrawn	11/4/63

Allocation

To Haymarket	4/6/30
To Tay Bridge	15/2/37
To Eastfield	20/11/38
To St.Margarets	2/2/40
To Haymarket	19/10/40
To St.Margarets	6/1/63

CICERO was something of a curiosity. Whereas the first two A3s at Haymarket were used on the Non-stop, the third was not; though one would have thought she would, even as a reserve. She kept to the services powered from Haymarket in post-war years, only coming south to go to Doncaster Works for overhaul. Her history was unremarkable although she seemed to have been reliable and hard working like most Haymarket Pacifics. In the late 1930s the up Queen of Scots was worked throughout from Edinburgh to Leeds, by Eastfield and Neville Hill Pacifics, but the working stopped with the war. CICERO was one of the rarest visitors to the south, if not the rarest. The world of the loco-spotter was frustrating: the reward for patience was the sight of a gleaming loco approaching, but the odds were on a local, rather than a strange visitor. But some strangers came south more often than others, and one can understand youthful annoyance at the appearance of such as GRAND PARADE yet again.

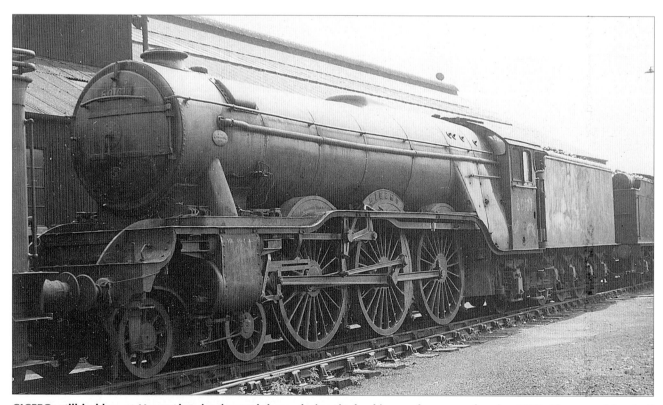

CICERO, still in blue, at Haymarket, by the workshops, during single chimney days around spring 1951. The curved handrail was unusual. The A3 has Diagram 94A boiler 27011 and A3 non-corridor tender (No.5571).

Haymarket's CICERO, looking spick and span, backs down to Waverley on June 25th 1959. She has a Diagram 94A boiler No.27083 and an A3 non-corridor tender No.5571. (J Robertson, transporttreasury.co.uk).

CICERO at Haymarket in the late 1930s, when the inspection doors were provided with covers. It is quite unusual to see an A3 with a single line tablet catcher. The A3 has Diagram 94HP boiler 8223 and an A3 non-corridor tender No.5571.

SIR FREDERICK BANBURY

Built	10/7/22
Works No.	1539
GNR No.	1471
LNER Nos.	1471N (14/12/23), 4471 (1/8/25), 102 (28/4/1946)
Long travel valves fitted	27/11/30
Rebuilt as an A3 with wartime black livery	16/10/42
LNER green livery	20/5/47
BR No.	60102 (13/5/49)
BR blue livery	13/5/49
BR dark green livery	10/8/51
Double Kylchap fitted	21/4/59
Trough deflectors not fitted	
Withdrawn	14/11/61

Allocation (A1)
To Doncaster	10/7/22
To Grantham	12/12/32
To Doncaster	5/5/33

(A3)
To Grantham	1/7/43
To New England	30/4/44
To Grantham	11/10/44
To Leicester	16/5/49
To Neasden	4/7/54
To Leicester	21/11/54
To Kings Cross	1/9/57
To Doncaster	13/10/57
To Grantham	14/6/59
To Kings Cross	9/10/60

The second GNR Pacific, SIR FREDERICK BANBURY was always in the shadow of her successive sisters. As much a Doncaster engine as anywhere, post-war she spent as long a spell as any on the GC section before the A3s were moved back to the main line when Regional boundaries changed. Her one moment of fame was on September 3rd 1922, when she hauled a 600 ton train from Kings Cross to Barkston and back, an awesome demonstration at the time. Like most of the A3s that spent much of their lives on the GC section its life mileage was below the average for its contemporaries.

The oldest and only GN Pacific to survive into BR days, SIR FREDERICK BANBURY coasts down light into Grantham in June 1960 past Saltersford. She has a Diagram 107 boiler 29285 and GN tender No.5292.

60102 at Neasden shed on September 12th 1954 during its short period allocated there. As the only surviving GN Pacific after 1945 she had attained a measure of celebrity. Sent to Leicester in May 1949 SIR FREDERICK BANBURY did not return to Kings Cross until September 1957 from where it was withdrawn in November 1961. (B K B Green, Initial Photographics)

FLYING SCOTSMAN

Built	24/2/23
Works No.	1564
GNR No.	1472
LNER Nos.	1472N (12/23), 4472 (2/3/23), 502 (20/1/46), 103 (5/5/46)
Long travel valves fitted	5/4/28
Wartime black livery	3/4/43
Rebuilt as an A3 with LNER green livery	4/1/47
BR No.	E103 (15/3/48), 60103 (30/12/48)
BR blue livery	16/12/49
BR dark green livery	14/3/52
Double Kylchap fitted	21/4/59
Trough deflectors fitted	16/12/61
Withdrawn	15/1/63
Preservation No.	LNER 4472

Allocation (A1)	
To Doncaster	24/2/23
To Kings Cross	11/4/28
To Doncaster	6/3/39
To New England	12/3/44
To Gorton	7/7/44
To Kings Cross	29/10/44
To New England	11/11/44
To Doncaster	5/12/44
(A3)	
To Leicester	4/6/50
To Grantham	15/11/53
To Kings Cross	20/6/54
To Grantham	29/8/54
To Kings Cross	7/4/57

Arguably one of the two most famous steam engines, the other being MALLARD, FLYING SCOTSMAN is the only preserved A3 for which, eternal thanks to Alan Pegler. Plucked from relative obscurity at Doncaster, 4472 worked the first non-stop Flying Scotsman express from London Kings Cross to Edinburgh Waverley in May 1928. She continued to work the duty until the A3s were replaced in 1937 by new A4s. She was selected for the high speed test run to Leeds in November 1934, during which 100mph was recorded for the first time, indisputably, by the dynamometer car. The record of the running is shown in the Appendix.

Feeling at Top Shed at the time was that VICTOR WILD, FLYING FOX or ROYAL LANCER would have done better. Although it seems close to blasphemy, FLYING SCOTSMAN was never one of the best of the class in the way that PAPYRUS, CALL BOY and the Tyneside Pacifics were. After the 1939-45 war she was rebuilt to class A3, and along with many of the A3s in the south, ran for a spell on the GC section. Relegated by the A4s and the newer A1s, the older Pacifics languished for a while, until the fitting of double Kylchaps breathed new life into the old favourites. The methods used in overhauling locomotives at Doncaster were improved in the 1950s by the CMEE, K.J. Cook, and as in the case of FLAMINGO, overhauled locomotives ran distinctly more quietly.

BR 60103 was one of those whose renaissance, in gleaming splendour, was enjoyed by many of us as she sped north with the Yorkshire Pullman in the evenings. Saved by the generosity of Alan, she returned to give us the incredible sight of the glorious apple green LNER livery once again. Her career in preservation is not within the scope of this book, but now she is safely in the hands of the National Railway Museum at York, to remind us of what a truly elegant and handsome machine was created by Sir Nigel and his team of engineers.

The location is Greenwood in days when it was in the country, and it looks very much as though FLYING SCOTSMAN is hauling the Flying Scotsman with its signature BG at the south end. The date is between 1928 and 1936, but there is little to fix it more accurately.

FLYING SCOTSMAN, a Grantham engine in the 1954-56 period, at Newcastle with an up express, ready for the Right Away. She would be deputising for one of the shed's A1s but it is difficult to hazard a guess at the service. The up Northumbrian would be the most likely at that time. This view shows the bogie axlebox shields, very much part of the A3's characteristic appearance before the introduction of AWS. The A3 has a Diagram 94A boiler No.27074 and an A4 non-corridor tender (No.5640). (J Robertson, transporttreasury.co.uk)

In 1959 the renaissance of the Gresley A3 Pacifics, now fitted with double Kylchap exhausts, was in full swing. One of the features of their revival was the prominence of the oldest locomotives. One might argue that with so much new or replacement material added periodically over their long career, their building date was of secondary importance. The veteran FLYING SCOTSMAN has been rostered for the Talisman on July 22nd 1959, and is seen here taking water on Werrington troughs. The A3 has Diagram 94A boiler was 27044 and A4 non-corridor tender No.5640. (D C Ovenden)

SOLARIO

Built	17/3/23
Works No.	1565
GNR No.	1473, possibly 1473N, date unknown.
Long travel valves fitted	15/12/27
LNER Nos.	4473 (14/6/24), 104 (12/5/46).
Wartime black livery	5/2/43
Rebuilt as an A3	11/10/41
LNER green livery	25/1/47
BR No.	60104 (28/7/48)
BR blue livery	13/1/50
BR dark green livery	17/6/53
Double Kylchap fitted	21/4/59
Trough deflectors not fitted	
Withdrawn	7/12/59

Allocation: (A1)

To Doncaster	17/3/23
To Copley Hill	25/9/37
To Doncaster	9/11/37
To Copley Hill	18/11/37
To Doncaster	3/1/38
To Gorton	1/5/39
(A3)	
To Kings Cross	5/2/43
To Leicester	4/6/50
To Neasden	4/7/54
To Leicester	26/12/54
To Kings Cross	1/9/57
To Doncaster	13/10/57
To Grantham	14/6/59
To Kings Cross	1/11/59

SOLARIO was, arguably, one of the most accomplished of the Gresley A1s, and one of the most famous A3s. That may sound strange when one considers FLYING SCOTSMAN, but BR 60103 is famous more because of her name rather than many outstanding feats of running. When LEMBERG, another prominent resident at Doncaster, was modified in 1927, she was tested against SOLARIO, both locomotives running well. Both were in the group that were used on the 'Breakfast Flyer' the sharply timed Leeds-Kings Cross morning express.

In the summer of 1936, Driver Joe Duddington had SOLARIO on the down Scarborough Flyer with a load of 395 tons. Delayed by a loose roofboard at Welwyn Garden City for 10½ minutes, Duddington kept SOLARIO to the Silver Jubilee timing between Hitchin and Selby with a load 50% heavier than the streamliner! The uphill work was slower than an A4, but Joe Duddington knew the Grantham-Doncaster road intimately, averaging 79.2mph over what one would hardly describe as a speedway in 1936.

Two years or so later, on May 17th 1938 SILVER FOX failed at Doncaster on the down Coronation with an overheated middle big end, and SOLARIO took over, running through to Waverley. Her tender had been fitted with a steam operated scoop, with which the Haymarket crew were unfamiliar, and therefore took water at Newcastle. Remarkably, Haymarket sent the A1 back with the Coronation on May 18th, despite the problems taking water. Driver Auger made a magnificent run, arriving at Kings Cross 16 mins late, despite the water stop and no less than four TSRs. This meant that SOLARIO, net, had more than kept to the Coronation timing. On March 14th 1939, WILD SWAN was unfit to return on the up West Riding Limited, and Kings Cross Driver Waite took SOLARIO, arriving 6 minutes late.

Post-war, she was a regular sight in the south as a Top Shed A3, before spending a long spell on the GC section and then a few years at Doncaster and Grantham. She had arrived back at Top Shed when she was sent to Doncaster Works for attention at the same time as the wrecked FELSTEAD arrived. She was in a poor state perhaps due to frame cracking, and was condemned, the front end components going to the restoration of FELSTEAD. So SOLARIO became the first A3 to be withdrawn, very sadly.

Another Leicester engine for a lengthy spell, SOLARIO is hauling the up South Yorkshireman at speed between Finmere and Calvert. The time is June 1957, and the A3 has Diagram 94A No.27052 and GN tender No.5254. (P J Coster)

The 13.00 to Edinburgh is about to get under way from Kings Cross. Then a Kings Cross loco, SOLARIO was still a right-hand drive engine. Roy Vincent was meticulous with the details on the back of the print, and gives the date as April 1950, when she would have been in BR blue livery. SOLARIO however is in apple green; this changed to BR blue in January 1950 so 1949 would seem more likely. One of the harder-working engines on the main line, she was the first to be withdrawn as a result of repair work needed. To those unfamiliar with the famous (old) platform 10 at Kings Cross, some idea of the crowd that gathered there at lunch time, indeed for much of the day, can be appreciated from this photograph. Many more would have been out of camera. It served as a sort of academy for those who wished to learn about railways, and also an information network, particularly for the south of the old LNER. Little happened on the railway that was missed by the characters who assembled there. (R E Vincent, transporttreasury.co.uk)

The southbound Leeds express at Potters Bar on June 18th 1937 is hauled by the Doncaster A1 SOLARIO. One of Doncaster's top link A1s, Driver Joe Duddington, of 126mph fame, made a magnificent run with her on the down Scarborough Flyer. I am sure she could be heard for miles from Carr Loco! SOLARIO was unique in that as an A1, she worked two out of the three streamliners in an emergency. The A1 has her Diagram 94 boiler No.7700 and GN tender No.5254. (Rev. A C Cawston, courtesy Brian Bailey)

VICTOR WILD

Built	24/3/23
Works No.	1566
GNR No.	1474
LNER Nos.	1474N (14/12/23), 4474 (15/11/23), 105 (12/5/46)
Long travel valves fitted	30/9/29
Rebuilt as an A3 with wartime black livery	1/10/42
LNER green livery	31/5/47
BR No.	60105 (18/8/48)
BR blue livery	17/3/50
BR dark green livery	20/2/53
Double Kylchap fitted	6/3/59
Trough deflectors fitted	9//12/60
Withdrawn	16/6/63

Allocation (A1)	
To Kings Cross	24/3/23
To Doncaster	9/11/37
To Gorton	25/2/39
To Leicester	19/8/39
To Gorton	2/12/39
(A3)	
To Kings Cross	22/11/42
To Grantham	9/9/51

VICTOR WILD was the first Pacific to be allocated to Kings Cross, and was always well regarded there. In 1925, when the exchange between the LNER and GWR took place, 4475 was selected for testing for two weeks on the GWR main line to Plymouth. As FLYING FOX had run hot, 4474 went as substitute. In the hands of Driver Alf Pibworth, she ran well, very well in the circumstances. The A1 was a large engine for the GWR road with its many winding miles, the fireman was unused to the Welsh coal, and the driver no doubt had a hard task learning the subtleties of a long and – to him – strange road. Nevertheless her performance improved steadily, and towards the end of the trials Alf Pibworth's growing confidence in tackling the South Devon banks equalled and exceeded the work of the Castle. The GWR CALDICOT CASTLE ran well, superbly on some runs, and was clearly the more powerful and economical. It was a great pity that the same team did not represent the LNER on the GN main line, as both the driver chosen and the engine used were not of the same quality.

VICTOR WILD had a corridor tender in 1933-34, apart from a two week break, and worked the Non-stop in both seasons. The Non-stop duty operated from May to October with the Summer Timetable, but the Flying Scotsman only ran non-stop in the middle 12-13 weeks of the summer. Outside that period the train stopped at Newcastle, but engines were not changed. VICTOR WILD was one of the Pacifics that worked that duty between London and Edinburgh and one run was recorded by O S Nock in September 1936. Curiously, remembering the general chaos among LNER Pacifics caused by changing tenders around, her original tender no.5225 was removed and returned throughout her working life.

After the war VICTOR WILD moved to Grantham where most of the A3s were second to the Peppercorn A1s, which worked nearly all regular main line turns. She stayed there nearly 12 years. With a double Kylchap, she became a more frequent visitor to Kings Cross, until steam operation ended.

A1 4474 with 3286 at Grantham Yard Box in 1930, in original condition as built. She was one of the last to be converted to group standard dimensions, in 1933, which explains its late use on the Non-stop by Kings Cross. (Rev. A C Cawston, courtesy Brian Bailey)

VICTOR WILD in her early years, before 1928, with an up express at Langley water troughs. With a square buffer beam and higher boiler fittings/cab, the A1 has not yet been modified to comply with the NE and NB structure gauges. The A1 has her original Diagram 94 boiler 7695 and GN tender (5225).

FLYING FOX

Built	4/23
Works No.	1567
GNR No.	1475
LNER Nos.	4475 (14/12/25), 106 (29/5/46)
Long travel valves fitted	24/7/28
Wartime black livery	6/2/42
Rebuilt as an A3 with LNER green livery	15/3/47
BR No.	60106 (3/12/48)
BR blue livery	24/5/50
BR dark green livery	20/4/52
Double Kylchap fitted	21/11/58
Trough deflectors fitted	7/10/61
Withdrawn	26/12/64

Allocation (A1)	
To Kings Cross	28/4/23
To New England	26/6/40
To Grantham	4/4/44
To Kings Cross	16/4/44
To Gorton	9/7/44
To Kings Cross	29/10/44
To Copley Hill	6/12/44
To New England	22/1/45
(A3)	
To Grantham	9/11/47
To Kings Cross	15/2/53
To Grantham	25/10/53
To Copley Hill	2/5/54
To Leicester	28/8/55
To Grantham	15/9/57
To Doncaster	8/9/63
To New England	20/10/63

FLYING FOX was the A3 that achieved the highest mileage of the class, close to 2.6 million miles by the end of 1962, and probably on the way to 2.7 million by withdrawal. She was an ever-present on the main line, although no particular events occur in her history. She had a corridor tender from 1928 to 1936, and was one of the regular engines used on the Non-stop before the A4s took over in 1937. On May 2nd 1964, FLYING FOX hauled a Gresley Society railtour from Kings Cross to Doncaster and back, with FLYING SCOTSMAN working the onward leg to Darlington and back. While at York, another tour arrived with BLINK BONNY to pose alongside 4472. It was the last day of A3s in service for many, and FLYING FOX ran superbly, with a final dash down Stoke at about 100mph with an average of 97mph between Corby Glen and Little Bytham.

The BTC Asst CME for design, E.S. Cox, rarely travelled on the East Coast, but on one occasion Kings Cross was advised that he wished to travel on the engine of the 17.15 from Leeds to Kings Cross, the heaviest train of the day. FLYING FOX was known to be the highest mileage A3 at Top Shed and in good condition. She was carefully prepared, and on the day worked down with the White Rose. Now fitted with a double Kylchap exhaust, the A3 ran perfectly. Peter Townend went to Kings Cross to meet Cox, who was impressed by the economy and quietness of the A3. Not having ridden on a Kylchap engine for many years, if at all, he did not realise that the A3 was well over 30 years old, and had gained the impression that FLYING FOX ran so well because she had not long emerged from general overhaul!

FLYING FOX nears the top of the climb from the Fens at Abbots Ripton with the 12.20 Hull-Kings Cross on June 10th 1950. The exhaust is clear although she must be working hard. The driver eyes the camera with interest, but it is also a good illustration of the value of the glass sight screen introduced from 1929 onwards, and the protection that it gave. Perhaps we forget what it was like to look out of the window behind a steam engine! The boiler is Diagram 94A No.9208 and GN tender No.5278. (R E Vincent, transporttreasury.co.uk)

It has been curiously difficult to find suitable photographs of FLYING FOX, another Top Shed favourite; almost a daily sight on the GN main line, and the Gresley Pacific with the highest accrued mileage, almost 2.7 million miles. Here is an early shot of the old favourite in original condition with the initially modified buffer beam, and the early nameplates that were later replaced. The single lamp suggests that the A1 is running in on a slow train after overhaul, but one cannot tell at this distance in time. Boiler: 94(7696) Tender: GN (5226)

FLYING FOX, in a disreputable state, leans to the curve past Red Hall with an up express. She was the A3 that achieved the highest mileage, approximating to 2.7 million miles, although the last three years or so could only be estimated as mileage recording for steam traction stopped in 1961. The date must lay between November 1958 (double Kylchap) and October 1961 (trough deflectors) and from the state of the A3 probably 1959/60. (There is confirmation in the absence of overhead warning flashes, introduced in 1961.) The A3 has Diagram 94A boiler No.27063 and one of the two actual GN tenders, No.5212 off SIR FREDERICK BANBURY when built.

ROYAL LANCER

Built	26/5/23
Works No.	1568
GNR No.	1476
LNER Nos.	4476 (7/2/25), 107 (4/10/46)
Long travel valves fitted	5/4/28
Wartime black livery	20/2/43
Rebuilt as an A3 with LNER green livery	4/10/46
BR No.	60107 (23/4/48)
BR blue livery	19/10/49
BR dark green livery	3/12/52
Double Kylchap fitted	2/6/59
Trough deflectors fitted	22/2/62
Withdrawn	1/9/63

Allocation (A1)	
To Grantham	26/5/23
To Kings Cross	11/4/28
To New England	26/6/40
To Grantham	11/4/44
To New England	11/6/44
To Gorton	7/7/44
To Kings Cross	29/10/44
To Grantham	16/12/44
To Kings Cross	19/5/46
(A3)	
To Leicester	4/6/50
To Copley Hill	27/7/52
To Leicester	10/8/52
To Grantham	15/9/57
To Kings Cross	9/10/60
To Grantham	16/6/63

ROYAL LANCER was another of the Kings Cross stud that worked the Non-stop in the 1928-36 period. Post-war, she spent a long spell on the GC section, and was said to be the pick of the fairly substantial group of A3s at Leicester. On return to the main line, she worked chiefly from Grantham, where she was one of the more regular sights on the Grantham turns. ROYAL LANCER was one of the highest mileage A3s of the class, one of that small group of locos that were always about on the main line. Some fast running was recorded in her last five years or so. In March 1962 she headed the 9.18 White Rose from Kings Cross. The A3 was fitted with a 'Wool Wins' headboard as part of an advertising campaign for the Yorkshire woollen industry.

ROYAL LANCER pulling out of the old, narrow platform 8 at Kings Cross with a train of GNR elliptical roof coaches with Gresley bogies; not main line stock so much as old non-corridor outer suburban stock. I would put the period at 1937-39, due to the A3 non-corridor tender and the inspection hole covers used at that time. The A1 has Diagram 94 boiler No.7701 or 2 and tender No.5481.

The first post-war Queen of Scots Pullman at the top of Holloway Bank by the North Down signalbox, headed by an immaculate apple green ROYAL LANCER. The old LNER headboard has been taken out of store, but within a few years would be replaced by a cast duralumin version. The A3 has Diagram 94A boiler No.9515 and GN tender No.5267.

LNER No.4476, probably after her first overhaul, but still awaiting both name and longer travel valves. The buffer beam is unmodified as well. The exact location is not stated and is impossible to guess at. The A1 was a Grantham engine, as can be seen from the reflection of the splashers under the boiler, and it might be anywhere between London and York.

GAY CRUSADER

Built	16/6/23
Works No.	1569
GNR No.	1477
LNER Nos.	1477N (25/9/23), 4477 (20/6/25), 507 (28/3/46), then 108 (5/5/46).
Long travel valves fitted	13/6/28
Rebuilt as an A3 with wartime black livery	30/1/43
LNER green livery	22/8/47
BR No.	60108 (23/3/49)
BR blue livery	1/9/50
BR dark green livery	21/2/52
Double Kylchap fitted	21/5/59
Trough deflectors fitted	17/11/61
Withdrawn	19/10/63

Allocation (A1)	
To Doncaster	16/6/23
To Grantham	12/11/34
To Doncaster	11/4/35
To Gorton	7/12/41
(A3)	
To Kings Cross	30/1/43
To Doncaster	7/1/51
To Kings Cross	22/6/52
To Neasden	28/9/52
To Kings Cross	29/3/53
To Neasden	29/11/53
To Kings Cross	10/7/55
To Neasden	2/10/55
To Kings Cross	27/1/57
To Doncaster	19/10/58
To Kings Cross	2/11/58
To New England	10/9/61
To Grantham	16/6/63
To Doncaster	8/9/63

GAY CRUSADER was one of the regular sights on the main line, mainly from Doncaster and, after the war, also from Kings Cross. She was used as a spare engine to help out at Neasden in the 1950s, but she returned to Top Shed between times, working on the principal services, particularly once converted to double Kylchap. I remember her on the down Morning Talisman in 1957, fitted with an experimental self-cleaning arrangement. The schedule was cut to ribbons by permanent way work as the continuous welded rail programme got under way, but with 290 tons, GAY CRUSADER was given her head where possible and picked up speed very quickly, reaching 90 mph and more several times. She was one of the regular sights on Kings Cross duties.

GAY CRUSADER backs down on to the 14.00 Tees-Thames in old platform 5 at Kings Cross, in 1960. Her Diagram 94A boiler was 27077 and GN tender No.5266. Unusually, in platform 8 a BTH Type 1 D8200 diesel has brought in ECS, while in platform 10 a Matisa Track Recording Trolley awaits the signal. Quite what it is doing in the middle of the day in Kings Cross station I cannot imagine. (P J Coster)

LNER No.1477N in her first year or so, unmodified, before naming as GAY CRUSADER, north of Wood Green station with a Pullman car train. It is not clear whether it is the Sheffield or Harrogate Pullman; probably it's the latter, although the 'West Riding Pullman' replaced the Sheffield train in September 1925. The tidy appearance of the tracks was due to the large scale use of ash ballast up to the top surface of the sleepers, of which there was an ample supply, but it also illustrates a time when people cleared waste materials away before leaving the site of work! Bounds Green carriage shed has not yet been built. Her Diagram 94 boiler was 7698 and GN tender No.5228.

GAY CRUSADER was another favourite at Kings Cross and fortunately it departed this world long before the name came to suggest something else. In this busy scene in 1952 she is pulling out with the down White Rose, while N2 69556 is setting the pace with a suburban train on the down slow. In the distance the New England A2/2 off the up Aberdonian stands in the loco yard, waiting for the 10.05 Glasgow. On the right one can see a lengthman, presumably trusting the lie of the points and his local knowledge! How many owe their lives to the high-visibility jacket! Boiler 94A (27068) Tender GN (5266) (John F Aylard)

HERMIT

Built	30/6/23
Works No.	1570
GNR No.	1478
LNER Nos.	1478N (26/9/23), 4478 (5/3/25)
	508 (20/1/46) then 109 (22/6/46)
Long travel valves fitted	12/4/30
Wartime black livery	7/3/42
Rebuilt as an A3	16/11/43
LNER green livery	15/3/47
BR No.	60109 (1/5/48)
BR blue livery	8/11/49
BR dark green livery	27/11/52
Double Kylchap fitted	12/3/59
Trough deflectors fitted	27/1/61
Withdrawn	29/12/62

Allocation (A1)	
To Doncaster	30/6/23
To Grantham	16/9/28
To Doncaster	26/4/38
To Gorton	4/3/39
To Kings Cross	22/11/42
(A3)	
To Copley Hill	3/12/43
To New England	29/5/44
To Kings Cross	24/9/44
To Grantham	9/9/51
To Doncaster	18/10/53
To Kings Cross	8/6/58
To Doncaster	19/10/58
To Kings Cross	5/4/59

HERMIT was another of the first batch of LNER Pacifics and a regular sight on the main line. She worked from Doncaster, Grantham and Kings Cross for much of the time. At Kings Cross briefly, in 1958, once through working was restored in 1956-57, she was used on Newcastle and Leeds turns, more often back at Kings Cross once the double Kylchap was fitted in 1959. She had an astonishingly long run on the Yorkshire Pullman duty, 73 consecutive return journeys. The remarkable feature of the fitting of double Kylchaps was the reinvigoration of many of the oldest A3s, all Southern Area locos, working the principal services, immaculately clean and reliable. This fine old engine was withdrawn in the catastrophic weekend at the end of 1962 when many old favourites were withdrawn.

HERMIT, now with a double Kylchap, heads an up express south of Hatfield past Red Hall box. The date must be between May 1959 and January 1961 when trough deflectors were fitted. Her Diagram 94A boiler was 27029 and GN tender No.5271.

This photograph was taken an hour earlier than that of MELTON (see page 61) north of Hitchin, with HERMIT on the 13.00 Heart of Midlothian. In exactly the same way, an attempt to catch the motion of HERMIT at top dead centre, precisely the reverse has been achieved, and the loco looks 'hobbled'. Once again, in fact the A3 was travelling very fast, but it looks as though it is restarting from a signal check! The A3 has Diagram 94A boiler 27029 and GN tender No.5271. (P J Coster)

HERMIT at Harringay with the up Scarborough Flyer on August 18th 1962, emerging from the rebuilt Harringay Flyover. The A3 would have been working through from York. She was withdrawn five months later. The A3 has a Diagram 107 boiler No.27973 and a GN tender (No.5268). (A Swain, transporttreasury.co.uk).

ROBERT THE DEVIL

Built	25/7/23
Works No.	1571
GNR No.	1479
LNER Nos.	1479N (19/10/23), 4479 (11/4/25)
	110 (24/8/46)
Long travel valves fitted	20/2/30
Rebuilt as an A3 with wartime	
black livery	8/8/42
LNER green livery	8/2/47
BR No.	60110 (2/3/49)
BR blue livery	3/8/50
BR dark green livery	28/8/51
Double Kylchap fitted	30/5/59
Trough deflectors fitted	7/61
Withdrawn	23/5/63

Allocation (A1)	
To Grantham	25/7/23
To New England	7/1/42
(A3)	
To Grantham	11/10/42
To Kings Cross	27/10/46
To Grantham	9/9/51
To Kings Cross	16/6/57

ROBERT THE DEVIL was very much the Grantham engine, spending more than 28 years there. The name was held to be a joke against the august person of Robert Thom, the Assistant CME at Doncaster. Despite being a regular sight on the main line, her history is fairly uncomplicated. A curious fact about this engine is that she retained the same GN tender, No.5230, for 40 years.

ROBERT THE DEVIL at Top Shed, alongside THANE OF FIFE being prepared for the Tees-Tyne Pullman, April 30th 1958. The A3 has Diagram 94A boiler 27025, and her original GN tender No.5230. (transporttreasury.co.uk).

ROBERT THE DEVIL strides north with the 10.54 from Kings Cross to Leeds on the 1 in 200 beyond New Southgate in summer, 1957. The A3 has recently been transferred to Top Shed. The engine has a Diagram 94A boiler (27025) and a GN tender (5230). (P J Coster)

The 10.00 from Leeds was the balancing turn for the previous night's Yorkshire Pullman, which is the reversed headboard carried by ROBERT THE DEVIL as she rolls into Kings Cross in 1961. One of the new Brush diesels is in the Station Loco yard. The engine has a Diagram 94A boiler (27052) and her original GN tender (5230). (P J Coster)

ENTERPRISE

Built	17/8/23
Works No.	1572
GNR No.	1480
LNER Nos.	1480N (25/8/23), 4480 (11/4/25)
	111(4/5/46)
Rebuilt as an A3/1	15/7/27
Long travel valves fitted	20/12/27
19in cylinders fitted	10/8/34
Wartime black livery	11/2/43
LNER green livery	26/11/47
BR No.	60111 (28/10/49)
BR blue livery	28/10/49
BR dark green livery	4/3/53
Double Kylchap fitted	5/6/59
Trough deflectors fitted	14/4/62
Withdrawn	29/12/62

Allocation (A1)	
To Grantham	17/8/23
(A3)	
To Doncaster	16/7/27
To Carlisle	18/12/28
To Kings Cross	5/4/29
To Doncaster	14/4/29
To Kings Cross	5/3/39
To Grantham	31/12/41
To Copley Hill	1/10/43
To Grantham	11/10/43
To New England	29/5/44
To Doncaster	12/12/48
To Neasden	20/2/49
To Leicester	27/3/55
To Grantham	15/9/57

ENTERPRISE was one of the two A1s to be reboilered in 1927 in order to assess the effect of higher boiler pressures. The other A1 was LEMBERG, which had its cylinders lined down to equate its tractive effort to the original A1s. ENTERPRISE retained its 20 ins cylinders, which increased the tractive effort by over 20%. ENTERPRISE was however omitted from the subsequent trials between LEMBERG and SOLARIO. Meanwhile the remaining three new 94HP boilers were fitted to three NE area A1s. The Scottish Area had experimented with Pacific haulage over the Waverley route in 1927 using WILLIAM WHITELAW, which was not successful. A year later, SHOTOVER, reboilered, was used successfully, which led to a new A3, CAPTAIN CUTTLE being allocated to Carlisle, and the transfer of ENTERPRISE. Two more A3s arrived, and ENTERPRISE was returned to Kings Cross, (as is discussed in greater detail earlier). She became a standard A3 with 19ins cylinders in August 1934, the last of the five 1927 rebuilds. Back on the main line ENTERPRISE was at a variety of sheds, before going to the GC section for a long spell. On returning to the main line she went to Grantham where she became one of the regular group of A3s replacing the Peppercorn A1s in the later 1950s.

ENTERPRISE spent a decade at Doncaster from 1929 to the outbreak of war. One of the top duties at Doncaster, apart from the Pullmans, was the Scarborough Flier, seen here at speed over Langley troughs during that period. Fashion is fickle, and it is strange to consider that, 70 years ago, Scarborough and its holiday traffic were commercially important to the LNER, and the train had considerable prestige. The boiler was a Diagram 94HP, and the tender was a GN pattern, No.5223 or 31.

Another up express with an A3 races round the curve past Red Hall box, in the distance. ENTERPRISE was one of the Southern Area engines that moved around, including a spell on the GC and even a brief spell at Carlisle Canal pre-war, but she was one of Grantham's fleet of speedy A3s in the double Kylchap years. From the electrification flashes (applied summer 1961) the period looks to be winter 1961/62. The A3 has Diagram 94A boiler No.27025 and A3 non-corridor tender No.5569.

ST. SIMON

Built	8/9/23
Works No.	1573
GNR No.	1481N
LNER Nos.	4481 (1/2/25), 511 (20/1/46),112 (11/5/46)
Long travel valves fitted	24/12/29
Wartime black livery	19/2/43
Rebuilt as an A3 with	
LNER green livery	30/8/46
BR No.	E112 (20/1/48), 60112 (25/3/49)
BR blue livery	10/2/51
BR dark green livery	24/10/52
Double Kylchap fitted	2/7/58
Small deflectors fitted	21/11/59
Trough deflectors fitted	5/10/62
Withdrawn	26/12/64

Allocation (A1)	
To Doncaster	8/9/23
To Gateshead	1/11/23
To Doncaster	10/4/24
To New England	4/11/27
To Doncaster	8/11/27
To Grantham	17/2/31
To Copley Hill	3/12/43
To Doncaster	29/5/44
To Grantham	28/10/45
To Kings Cross	19/5/46
(A3)	
To Copley Hill	4/6/50
To Doncaster	26/11/50
To Copley Hill	1/4/51
To Doncaster	9/9/51
To Grantham	7/10/51
To Doncaster	15/2/53
To Grantham	14/6/59
To Doncaster	8/9/63
To New England	30/10/63

ST. SIMON was the last of the batch ordered by the GNR and confirmed by the newly formed LNER. She was built with a lower roof to fit the NBR loading gauge, but with a taller ventilator which that gauge allowed. This led to the twenty A1s built by North British being allocated to Gateshead, Heaton and Haymarket. The initial reaction at Gateshead to the A1s was cool, which may have been partly due to the short travel valves of the A1, partisanship, or that the NB A1s had the Darlington valve setting. On the A1s, at Darlington and Cowlairs, the valves were set without expansion allowance, unlike Doncaster, which resulted in less freedom in running and might well have put the NE men off. When the class was taken over by Doncaster, the opposition had disappeared.

ST SIMON, as a single blast engine, was not one of the foremost of the class, largely due to limited steaming like many of the class post-war, but like other A3s that were only taken with some reluctance, once fitted with a double chimney, she was as good as the rest. Indeed the renaissance of the older A3s was as rewarding to see as it was surprising..

Below. Doncaster's ST. SIMON, recently fitted with a double Kylchap, at the head of the 13.25 to Leeds and Bradford at Kings Cross, September 1958. The older engines seemed to have a new lease of life with the improved draughting and were a much more common sight on the principal expresses than in single blast days. Two N2 0-6-2Ts stand in platform 2 ready for the empty stock of the lunchtime arrivals. She has a Diagram 94A boiler (27086) and the prototype GN tender (5211). (P J Coster)

The 9.40 departure from Kings Cross Goods to New Clee, No.1126 down, was a train of fish empties which ran for many years, and was the preserve of Immingham K3s. It usually ran as a Class C or D fast freight. In its last years before the fish traffic disappeared, the K3s were replaced by 9F 2-10-0s. So, on a sunny Saturday on April 6th, 1957, John Aylard was astonished to see not a K3 but an A3, 60112 ST. SIMON, and not on the down goods but the down main, between New Barnet and Greenwood. The fish empties appear to have been combined with general fast freight traffic, making an unusually large train of over 60 wagons, mainly but not exclusively vans. The 'bottleneck' was still in being at the time, and no doubt the crew had the luxury of a clear run for a change. It is sobering to think that out of approximately 600 tons load, the revenue earning portion could probably have been carried in just one of today's 100 ton vehicles! Boiler: 94A(27026), Tender GN (5211). (J F Aylard)

The ex-LNER Pacifics were seldom found off their native heath, and when it did occur, it was usually an A4, probably MALLARD. The A3s were the same, other than regular operations over Midland, G&SW and Caley main lines but even so, on August 25th 1963, the railtour over the SR hauled by ST. SIMON was something of an occasion. Two months later, of course, Alan Pegler's vision in apple green appeared, eventually to travel over many routes never remotely used by A3s. ST. SIMON was well turned out, and with her double chimney she acquitted herself well with several high speed sprints. Here she is at Waterloo with her train. She has a Diagram 107 boiler (29295) and a GN tender (5289). (P J Coster)

GREAT NORTHERN

Built	11/4/22
Works No.	1536
GNR No.	1470
LNER Nos.	1470N (9/10/23), 4470 (21/3/25), 113 (8/10/46)
Long travel valves fitted	2/8/30
Wartime black livery	14/2/42
Rebuilt as Thompson A1with GER blue livery, small deflectors and a double Kylchap	25/9/45
Large smoke deflectors fitted	13/12/45
LNER green livery	16/5/47
BR No.	60113 (1/10/48)
BR blue livery	6/1/50
BR dark green livery	21/8/52
Withdrawn	19/11/62

Allocation (A1)

To Doncaster	11/4/22
To Gorton	8/7/44
To Kings Cross	29/10/44
To Doncaster	11/11/44
(A, then A1, then A1/1)	
To Kings Cross	7/10/45
To Gateshead	24/7/47
To Haymarket	2/9/47
To Kings Cross	13/9/47
To New England	4/6/50
To Grantham	9/9/51
To Kings Cross	15/9/57
To Doncaster	13/10/57

The first Gresley Pacific, after her initial appearance had stunned the railway world in April 1922, continued to work from Doncaster for just over 22 years. Truth to tell, such a prestigious locomotive had a fairly humdrum if hard working existence there. By 1928 the first A3s at Doncaster had started to overshadow the A1s on the principal duty – the 'Breakfast Flyer' so called. Her one moment of glory as an A1 occurred when on 6/6/39, A4 4494 OSPREY was found unfit to return with the 'West Riding Limited' streamliner, and GREAT NORTHERN worked the up train, arriving two minutes late.

The rebuilding of GREAT NORTHERN is dealt with in the text. The rebuilt engine was tested against HERRING GULL in late 1945, and then against GOLDEN PLOVER when working from Gateshead and Haymarket. The resulting figures were very close, the slight differences favouring GREAT NORTHERN. The rebuild tended to be lighter on her feet, but was clearly better than the original A1.

The rebuilt GREAT NORTHERN was not an everyday sight since the Peppercorn A1s in the Grantham top link were very reliable, and when they were substituted, it was with another A1, sometimes GREAT NORTHERN or often one of the A3s. She returned to Kings Cross as part of the reorganisation of operations but was almost immediately reallocated to Doncaster. GREAT NORTHERN never actually got to Kings Cross as she was at Doncaster at the time, about to enter the works. She ran as well there as at any time, but as a non-standard locomotive she was likely to be an early withdrawal.

She must have been an incredible sight for those in 1922. What started in wonder gradually subsided, as newer designs surpassed her. Then came controversy, the new start, but again overshadowed by newer designs. As in 1922 she opened the way to the A4s, in 1945 she opened the way for the Peppercorn A1, and we have TORNADO to remind us of the outcome of what was started in 1945. However, when all is said and done, what was started in 1922 and finished with SAINT JOHNSTOUN was for the major part, a Gresley Pacific.

GREAT NORTHERN is hauling the 17.45 Kings Cross-Leeds north of Potters Bar in 1928. This was a heavy train and very popular. The A1 has Diagram 94 boiler No.7783 and GN tender No.5211 or 5227.

GREAT NORTHERN, newly renumbered and repainted as LNER 4470, pulls out of Kings Cross in summer 1925 with the 13.30 to Leeds and Bradford. The driver has the sanders on. Kings Cross was signalled at the time by the East and West signalboxes, with a forest of somersault signals. The power signalling scheme came to fruition in 1932 with the central box at the end of platforms 5 and 6. The A1 has her original Diagram 94 boiler, 7646, and GN style tender, 5211.

Appendix

GENERAL PERFORMANCE

The work of the A1s and A3s on the East Coast route could be followed over the years in the *Railway Magazine*, which continues to comment on performance today. Cecil J Allen, followed by O S Nock, wrote a monthly article entitled 'Locomotive Practice and Performance' in which the logs of correspondents were published. CJA was an employee of the LNER and was privy to 'inside' information in the 1930s. He was often invited to time special performances since his expertise had become well-known.

One has to realise that 80-90 years ago, travel was a far less common experience. The fares appear very cheap, but this was a time when for many, salaries of less than £10 per week were common, and for some as little as £4 was not unusual. Therefore the base information on which the work of locomotives could be judged was very small. For example, the work of the Mikados was exemplified by one return run by Ossie Nock, and one or two contributions by Allen himself and others. It would be difficult to find more than say 20 runs on the streamliners, although their operation was well documented.

With friend Brian Bailey's help I have gathered a number of examples showing the running of A1s and A3s on the East Coast route from 1930 up to 1940, and in the 'Indian Summer' when the engines had been re-draughted with double Kylchaps. Watches seem to have been read to the nearest 5 seconds in the earlier days, and only a few speeds were noted. What hits the eye at first is the size of trains that were operated in those days and, secondly, the generally low speeds that prevailed. The greater power of the A3s is evident, and one can imagine the enormous impact that the A4s and the streamliners had on enthusiasts and professionals alike.

The first tables cover typical to good running between Kings Cross and Peterborough. In fact the times would not have been markedly different from those experienced in post-war years. In the Kings Cross-Grantham section, the quality of the work on the 13.20 Scottish express is impressive, despite the huge loads. Indeed the work of COLOMBO on the first run was quite exceptional from Hatfield to Fletton, after which the run was cut to pieces by signal checks. The A3, with 545 tons, a load 2.4 times greater, had kept to the schedule of the Silver Jubilee from Hatfield to Huntingdon. Of course it says more about fast running than haulage power, but it was a remarkable run even so. A late 1950s run with KNIGHT OF THISTLE, with a lighter train, shows the fast running that was possible with the re-draughted A3s. Down runs tended to be some 10mins slower than the up due to the relative height of Grantham to London, and a net time of 97½mins was very good. In the up direction there are three good runs with the Flying Scotsman, and another on the heavy late morning Leeds express with Doncaster's LEMBERG. FELSTEAD's light train was a delayed Scarborough Flyer, without its Newcastle portion, and a very fast run was the result. There are two examples of the huge loads hauled during the war, coincidentally both by A1s. After that there are three runs on the down Talisman, demonstrating how the Scottish crews made excellent use of the re-draughted A3s, and fast running was not confined to the southern end of the main line. Pre-war, the Coronation was allowed 120 minutes with A4 haulage, which would have been well within the compass of an A3, especially with a double Kylchap.

Following this there are some copies of tables published in the *Railway Magazine* articles. The first table contains four runs on the Scarborough Flyer, three with A3s, and one with none other than the prototype herself, GREAT NORTHERN. There are very few records of 4470 in action, and this is an excellent run. The second table contains two runs, an admirable one with FLYING SCOTSMAN on the 13.20, and another on the Scarborough Flyer. The Flyer was an important train in the 1930s, timed to run non-stop to York in three hours with a load just below 400 tons, quite a formidable proposition.

On July 6th 1936 the train was headed by Doncaster's SOLARIO, driven by Joe Duddington. What followed is surely one of the finest runs by a 180psi Pacific, if not the very best. A roof-board had loosened and the train was stopped at Welwyn Garden City. Restarting, Duddington ran the 142.5 miles from Hitchin to Selby in 115½ minutes, 74mph, and ran SOLARIO into York eight minutes early. His net time from Kings Cross to York was 163 minutes. The remarkable feature of this run was that he kept to the schedule of the Silver Jubilee (net) between Hitchin and Selby with a load 68% heavier. His time of 38 minutes from Grantham to Doncaster was three minutes faster than the Jubilee, and probably a record at the time. No doubt it was due to the driver's close knowledge of the route. No speedometer, semaphore block signalling!

Next come two 1959 runs, the down Talisman and its return working, with TRACERY on the down run, and SANDWICH on the up. The next two tables are of the two famous high-speed runs of November 30th 1934 and March 5th 1935 with FLYING SCOTSMAN and PAPYRUS.

I finish with Brian's log of the last run in BR service of FLYING SCOTSMAN, and his analysis of the run of FLYING FOX on May 2nd 1964. I was fortunate to be on the footplate while Brian, a meticulous timer of many runs, was on the train. A steam loco speedometer was untrustworthy if not downright meretricious, although to attain 5% accuracy in the hostile environment of a footplate is quite creditable. However 100mph on the speedo usually meant 94-97mph. I made no record, but I can confirm that for at least six miles if not more the speedometer needle was on 100 mph unwaveringly. FLYING FOX was riding splendidly and was not being pressed unduly hard. Brian has compared passing times from his notes and compared them with other high speed descents of Stoke Bank. He makes the very good point that the runs of PAPYRUS and FLYING FOX are virtually the same.

So, Dear Reader, it is for you to judge whether that was the last 'Ton.'

Kings Cross-Peterborough

	LNER No.	2743		2597		2552		2751	4479	
		A3		A3		A1		A3	A1	
	Name	FELSTEAD		GAINSBOROUGH		SANSOVINO		HUMORIST	ROYAL LANCER	
	Load, tare	445		469		538		509	533	
	Load, gross	470		500		570		545	560	
	Departure	1.10		10.00		13.40		13.30*	19.25	
0.0	KINGS CROSS	0 00		0 00		0 00		0 00	0 00	
2.6	Finsbury Park	8 15		6 55		6 50		6 22	6 50	
5.0	Wood Green	12 25		10 15		10 05		9 31	10 05	
9.2	New Barnet	19 20	32	16 00		16 10	TSR	14 45	16 10	TSR
12.7	Potters Bar	25 15		22 05		21 40	35	19 35	21 40	35
17.7	HATFIELD	30 30	75	27 25	70.5	27 05		24 45	27 05	
23.5	Woolmer Green SB	35 50	52	32 50	56.5	32 55		30 10	32 55	
28.6	Stevenage	40 40		37 50	72.5	38 30		34 54	38 30	
31.9	HITCHIN	43 25		40 45	TSR	41 40		37 56	41 40	
37.0	Arlesey	47 10	86.5	47 35		46 00	76	41 55	46 00	76
44.1	Sandy	52 35	80	54 20	69	52 10	67	48 10	52 10	67
51.7	St.Neots	58 40	72.5	61 05	64	59 10	63	55 10	59 10	63
56.0	Offord	62 00	78.5	64 40	70	62 50	70.5	59 10	62 50	70.5
58.9	HUNTINGDON	64 20		67 15		65 25		61 42	65 25	
62	MP 62	67 10	62	70 30	53	68 35	54	64 56	68 35	54
69.4	Holme	73 20	80.5	77 05	76.5	75 05	76.5	71 45	75 05	76.5
75	Fletton Jct	78 00		82 10		79 55		76 55	79 55	
76.4	PETERBOROUGH	79 45		84 15	(pass)	81 50		79 08	81 50	
	Net time	79.75		80		81.75		79	80	

*No speeds were given with this run

Kings Cross-Peterborough-Grantham

	LNER No.	2501		2501		2744		2559		60065	
		A3		A3		A3		A1		A3	
	Name	COLOMBO		COLOMBO		GRAND PARADE		THE TETRARCH		KNIGHT OF THISTLE	
	Load, tare	514		533		506		505		356	
	Load, gross	545		570		540		545		375	
	Departure	13.20		13.20		13.20		13.30		9.40	
0.0	KINGS CROSS	0 00		0 00		0 00		0 00		0 00	
2.6	Finsbury Park	7 50		8 12		6 15		6 40			
5.0	Wood Green	11 28		11 40		9 34	TSR	9 50	55.5		
9.2	New Barnet	16 58		17 02		16 42	TSR	15 05	46.5		
12.7	Potters Bar	21 59		21 50		23 28		19 55	43		Sigs
17.7	HATFIELD	27 05	75	26 58		29 11		25 00	72		
23.5	Woolmer Green SB	32 21	58.5	32 23		35 01		30 30	55.5		
28.6	Stevenage	37 04		37 16		39 15		35 20			
31.9	HITCHIN	39 43	83.5	40 07		42 09		38 10		43 50	82
37.0	Arlesey	43 14	90	43 43		45 50	85	42 00	80.5	46 35	84
44.1	Sandy	48 12	86.5	48 56		51 06		47 55	75	52 40	83
51.7	St.Neots	53 52	76.5	54 54		57 07		54 55	57	58 10	78
56.0	Offord	57 03	83.5					58 55	66		
58.9	HUNTINGDON	59 16	77.5	60 46		63 05		61 45		63 36	80
62	MP 62	62 00	64	63 43		66 08		65 30	43	65 59	78
69.4	Holme	67 54	83.5	70 10		72 24		72 40	75	71 16	90
75	Fletton Jct	73 03	Sigs	75 06		77 04		78 10	58		
76.4	PETERBORO'	75 30	4.5BT	76 59		78 44		80 15	3BT	78 30	
79.5	Werrington Jct	80 13	Sigs	81 45		83 16		6 05	55.5	82 30	66
84.8	Tallington	86 11		87 05		88 27		11 30	64.5	87 20	69
88.6	Essendine	93 10	Sigs	90 31	66	92 05		15 10	61.5	90 38	72
92.2	Little Bytham	98 04		93 51	65	95 43		18 50	56	93 33	69
97.1	Corby Glen	104 41		99 06	56	101 49		24 45	52.5	98 08	64
100.1	Stoke SB	108 33		102 37	51	105 38	44.5	28 25	48	100 58	62
105.5	GRANTHAM	114 53	Sigs	110 17	Sigs	111 45		33 45	53	105 30	
								(pass)			
	Net time	107.5		109		106.5		114		97.5	

Peterborough - Kings Cross

		2744		4473		2743		2552	
	LNER No.	2744		4473		2743		2552	
		A3		A1		A3		A1	
	Name	GRAND PARADE		SOLARIO		FELSTEAD		SANSOVINO	
	Load, tare	409		413		415		499	
	Load, gross	435		440		440		525	
	Departure	17.30		10.15		10.15		18.21	
		Ex - Leeds		Ex - Leeds		Ex - Leeds		Ex-Doncaster	
0.0	PETERBOROUGH	0 00	-5	0 00		0 00		0 00	
3.8	Yaxley	7 10				6 10		6 20	
7.0	Holme	10 20	66.5	9 15	67	10 00	65	9 50	60
12.9	Abbots Ripton	16 00	53.5	15 05	52.5	16 10	49	16 20	
14.4	MP 62	17 40		16 50		17 55		18 20	43
17.5	HUNTINGDON	20 35	67	19 50	68	21 00	66	21 30	74
24.7	St.Neots	27 15	61	26 10	61	27 55	56	27 55	58.5
32.3	Sandy	33 50	72	33 00	69	35 20	66	35 00	67
35.3	Biggleswade	36 30		35 45		38 20		37 50	
40.7	Three Counties	41 45	64	41 00	64	43 40		43 20	60
44.5	HITCHIN	45 40	52.5	44 55	52.5	47 40		47 25	
47.8	Stevenage	49 50	45	48 55	49	51 35	48	51 20	48
51.4	Knebworth	54 00		52 50		55 30		55 30	
54.4	Welwyn North	57 00		55 50		58 30		58 35	
58.7	HATFIELD	60 35	77	59 25	76	62 00	76	62 15	75
63.7	Potters Bar	65 10	62.5	64 10	58.5	66 40	58	67 05	59
71.4	Wood Green	71 55		71 00		73 45	69	73 55	
73.8	Finsbury Park	74 10	Sigs	73 10		76 05	Sigs	76 05	
76.4	KINGS CROSS	79 35		77 05		82 45		81 00	Sigs
	Net time	78		77		80		80	

Grantham - Peterborough - Kings Cross

		4476		2503		2796		2544	
	LNER No.	4476		2503		2796		2544	
		A1		A3		A3		A3/1	
	Name	ROYAL LANCER		FIRDAUSSI		SPEARMINT		LEMBERG	
	Load, tare	439		479		506		494/519*	
	Load, gross	470		510		540		520/550*	
	Departure	10.00		10.00		10.00		10.15	
		Ex-Edin		Ex-Edin		Ex-Edin		Ex-Leeds	
								(pass)	
0.0	GRANTHAM	0 00		0 00		0 00		0 000	47.5
5.4	Stoke SB	9 11	45.5	9 07	48	9 55		8 10	37
8.4	Corby Glen	12 13		12 04		12 57		11 50	62
13.3	Little Bytham	16 02		15 53		16 40		16 10	75
16.9	Essendine	18 33	88	18 23	88	19 05	90	19 00	76.5
20.7	Tallington	21 18		20 59		21 41		22 05	73.5
26.0	Werrington Jct	25 18		24 51		25 32	Sigs	26 45	66
29.1	PETERBORO'	28 57		27 51		29 28	Sigs	31 55	
36.1	Holme	36 58		35 38		39 33			
42.0	Abbots Ripton	42 37		40 53		46 35		16 46	44
46.6	HUNTINGDON	47 17		45 21		51 17		21 56	
53.8	St.Neots	53 17		51 23		57 12		28 23	
61.4	Sandy	59 50		57 48		63 32	75	35 37	
68.5	Arlesey	66 25		64 00		69 43		42 48	
73.6	HITCHIN	71 33		68 25		74 17		48 37	46
76.9	Stevenage	75 45		71 50	56.5	77 47	55.5	53 26	43
80.5	Knebworth	79 50		75 24		81 22		57 00	
83.5	Welwyn North	82 55		78 11		84 09		60 33	
87.8	HATFIELD	86 38		81 29		87 28		64 11	71
92.8	Potters Bar	91 29		85 48		91 43	66	68 55	
96.3	New Barnet	94 50	80.5		Sigs	94 44			
100.5	Wood Green	98 05		94 39		98 06		75 27	78
102.9	Fin. Park	100 11		96 44	Sigs	100 38		77 50	Sigs
105.5	KINGS CROSS	104 14		102 50		104 45		84 10	
	Total							116 05	
	Net time	104		99		102		113**	

* Extra coach added at Peterborough
** Including stop at Peterborough

Grantham - Peterborough - Kings Cross (cont)

	LNER No.	2743		2557		2545		60046	
		A3		A1		A1		A3	
	Name	FELSTEAD		BLAIR ATHOL		DIAMOND JUBILEE		DIAMOND JUBILEE	
	Load, tare	242		695		644		267	
	Load, gross	255		750		720		290	
	Departure	11.35							
		Ex-York (pass)							
0.0	GRANTHAM	0 00	70	0 00		0 00		0 00	
5.4	Stoke SB	5 30	Sigs	13 22		12 00	32.5	7 37	57.5
8.4	Corby Glen	8 10		17 22		15 36	66	10 17	79
13.3	Little Bytham	11 37	89.5			19 53	72.5	13 43	93/98
16.9	Essendine			24 45		22 58	74	15 57	93/97
20.7	Tallington	16 39		28 14		26 11	71.5	18 21	92
26.0	Werrington Jct	est.21 00		32 48		30 48	Sigs	22 12	Sigs
29.1	PETERBORO'	24 21		36 17		43 33		31 24	
36.1	Holme		78	46 24		10 33	61	8 48	72
42.0	Abbots Ripton	37 44	69.5	53 00		16 58	44	13 48	64
46.6	HUNTINGDON	40 04	82	58 20		22 13	67	17 43	83.5
53.8	St.Neots	45 28		65 09		29 03	53	23 08	72
61.4	Sandy	51 10	83.5	72 56		36 50		28 45	80
68.5	Arlesey	56 28	76.5	80 40		45 00	53.5	34 16	75
73.6	HITCHIN	60 25	70	88 25	Sigs	50 58	42	38 33	66
76.9	Stevenage	63 29	66	93 52		56 10	38	41 49	60
80.5	Knebworth			98 28		60 38		45 08	65
83.5	Welwyn North	68 45			Sigs			49 10	79
87.8	HATFIELD	71 57	82	106 09		68 05	70.5	52 32	TSR
92.8	Potters Bar	76 03	70	111 45		73 33	51	59 27	59
96.3	New Barnet						Sigs	65 02	
100.5	Wood Green	82 12	78.5	119 09	Sigs	80 43	70.5	69 06	67
102.9	Finsbury Park	84 30		123 15		83 23	Sigs	72 00	Sigs
105.5	KINGS CROSS	89 56		129 03		89 10		79 55	
	Total					132 43		111 19	
	Net time	87		124.5		123**		100**	

** Including stop at Peterborough

NEWCASTLE-EDINBURGH

	BR No.		60043		60087		60101	
	Name		BROWN JACK		BLENHEIM		CICERO	
	Load, tare		311		312		307	
	Load, gross		325		320		320	
	Train		Talisman		Talisman		Talisman	
		Schedule	Mins	Speed	Mins	Speed	Mins	Speed
0.0	NEWCASTLE	0	0 00		0 00		0 00	
2.6	Benton Bank		5 27	49.5	6 53	42/49		
5.0	Forest Hall		8 06	53	10 05	Sigs	7 11	54
9.9	Cramlington		12 32	69	15 02	67/80	12 10	68
13.9	Stannington		15 33	85.5	18 13	76	15 19	78/82
16.6	MORPETH	20.5	18 10	40*	20 58	40*	17 15	45*
20.2	Longhirst		21 37	74/79	24 20	77	20 50	71
23.2	Widdrington		23 59	77	26 50	72		
25.6	Chevington		25 47	82.5	28 47	76/78	25 11	78
28.5	Acklington		27 51	87	31 04	61*		
31.9	Warkworth		30 24	73*/82	34 19	69/72	30 03	78/82
34.8	ALNMOUTH JCT	37	32 35	72*	36 48	67	32 20	75*
37.5	Longhoughton		34 48	68.5	39 19	57.5	34 27	66
39.5	Little Mill		36 31	66	41 20	58	36 19	64
43.0	Christon Bank		39 24	81	44 18	84	39 25	81
46.0	Chathill		41 26	92.5	46 23	88	41 33	86
51.6	BELFORD	52	45 15	87/95	50 29	81	45 40	80
54.9	Smeafield				52 53	90		
58.6	Beal		49 50	93	55 31	60*	50 12	94
60.8	Goswick		51 16	91	58 15	40*		
63.6	Scremerston		53 06	78.5	60 59	59	53 35	81
65.8	Tweedmouth		55 13	50*	63 15	55*	55 33	
67.0	BERWICK	69.5	56 44	40*	64 39	51*	57 35	25*
72.5	Burnmouth		63 56	53	70 44	66	64 53	59/70
74.2	Ay ton		65 36	63/71	72 10	70/74		
78.2	Reston Jct	82	69 04	66.5	75 28	67.5	69 55	67
83.2	Grantshouse	88	73 55	60	80 21	60/77	74 50	60
88.0	Cockburnspath		78 16	Sigs	84 23	71*	79 15	75
90.7	Innerwick		80 47	63.5	86 35	76	82 10	25*/72
95.2	DUNBAR	98	86 26	Sigs	90 33	68*	86 00	66*
101.0	East Linton		92 27	63	95 36	70/83	91 05	69
106.7	Drem	108	97 14	72	100 00	77	95 28	79/73
111.2	LONGNIDDRY		101 04	76	103 32	81/83	99 13	75
115.0	Prestonpans		104 07	TSR	106 20	82	102 23	68
119.8	New Hailes			Sigs	110 57	40*		Sigs
121.5	Portobello		112 24	Sigs	112 55	44*/50		Sigs
124.5	EDIN. WAVERLEY	129	122 04		118 50		120 45	
	Net time		111		117		113	

*TSR

L.N.E.R. KING'S CROSS—YORK

Distance.	Engine.—4-6-2 No. Name	Schedule.	2752 Spion Kop.	4470 Great Northern.	4480 Enterprise.	2747 Coronach.
	Load.—Coaches		10	10	11	12
	,, Tons tare		328	339	380	402
	,, Tons full		345	355	405	420
Miles.		min.	m. s.	m. s.	m. s.	m. s.
0·0	KING'S CROSS	0	0 00	0 00	0 00	0 0
2·5	FINSBURY PARK	—	5 50	6 03	5 22	6 03
5·0	Wood Green	—	8 43	8 47	8 08	8 59
12·7	Potter's Bar	—	16 40	16 22	16 16	17 23
17·7	HATFIELD	22	20 53	20 34	20 55	21 48
23·5	Woolmer Green	—	25 52	25 28	25 54	26 42
					sigs.	
28·6	Stevenage (28¼)	—	30 18†	29 54†	32 02	31 01
31·9	HITCHIN (32)	35	33 09†	32 44†	36 33	33 33
37·0	Arlesey	—	37 00	36 29	40 42	37 16
44·1	Sandy (44)	—	42 25†	41 56†	46 10	42 53
51·7	St. Neot's	—	48 44	48 06	52 09	49 08
58·9	HUNTINGDON (59)	56	54 40†	53 46†	57 53	55 08
62·0	Mile-post—62	—	57 35	56 19	60 35	58 16
69·4	Holme	—	63 33	62 27	66 35	64 35
				sigs.		
75·0	Fletton Junction	—	68 23	67 48	71 09	69 38
76·4	PETERBOROUGH¶	73	70 54	70 18	73 02	71 53
79·5	Werrington Junction	—	—	—	77 10	76 34
84·8	Tallington (85)	—	80 13†	79 26†	82 15	81 34
88·6	ESSENDINE	—	83 14	82 30	85 42	84 53
92·2	Little Bytham	—	86 18	85 38	89 01	88 13
97·1	Corby	—	90 48	90 18	93 50	92 58
100·1	Stoke	—	93 53	93 24	96 50	96 09
105·5	GRANTHAM‡	102	98 56	98 34	101 41	101 10
109·7	Barkstone	—	103 10	102 25	105 23	105 23
115·4	Claypole	—	—	—	109 41	109 53
				sigs.		sig. stop
120·1	NEWARK (120)	114	111 35†	110 48†	113 15	125 55
126·4	Carlton (126¼)	—	116 41†	116 37†	118 14	132 30
133·7	Markham (134¼)	—	124 11†	124 54†	125 09	139 23
138·6	RETFORD‡	132	127 34	128 38	129 36	143 35
143·9	Ranskill	—	132 30	133 07	133 56	148 27
147·7	Bawtry	—	135 46	136 10	136 59	151 38
149·5	Mile-post—149¼	—	137 39	137 44	138 36	153 12
153·2	Black Carr Junction	—	140 55	140 42	141 43	156 20
			sigs.		sigs.	
156·0	DONCASTER‡	147	144 51	143 19	144 40	158 48
160·2	Shaftholme Junction	—	149 21	147 19	148 52	162 38
166·0	Balne	—	154 19	152 06	154 01	167 48
169·8	Templehurst	—	157 39	155 18	157 21	171 14
174·4	SELBY (174¼)¶	164	162 20†	160 29†	161 53	176 02
178·5	Riccall	—	167 35	165 57	167 12	181 41
184·0	Naburn	—	172 34	170 48	172 15	186 55
				sigs.	sigs.	
188·2	YORK	180	177 57	177 29	178 35	192 19
188·2	Net times (min.)	180	175¾	175	172¼	178¼

† Timings in these cases to the mile-posts shown in brackets, and not to centres of stations or signal-boxes indicated in mileage column.   ‡ Service slack, slight or moderate.   ¶ Service slack, severe.

The Scarborough Flyer

Distance	Train	Scarborough Flyer.			1.20 p.m. ex King's Cross		
	Engine, 4-6-2 No.	4473, *Solario.*			4472, *Flying Scotsman.*		
	Driver	Duddington.			Sparshatt.		
	Load	11 = 371 tons tare.			15 = 500 tons tare.		
	Gross Load	395 tons.			530 tons.		
		Sched.	Actual.	Speeds.	Sched.	Actual.	Speeds.
Miles.		min.	m. s.	m.p.h.	min.	m. s.	m.p.h.
0·0	KING'S CROSS	0	0 00	—	0	0 00	—
2·5	Finsbury Park	—	6 16	—	—	6 10	—
5·0	Wood Green	—	9 11	—	—	9 13	—
9·2	New Barnet	—	13 45	—	—	14 18	—
12·7	Potter's Bar	—	17 37	—	—	19 04	43½
17·7	HATFIELD	22	21 55	77	25	24 08	74
			sig. stop				
23·5	*Woolmer Green*	—	35 20	51½	—	29 37	55
28·6	Stevenage	—	40 04	72	—	34 39	—
31·9	HITCHIN	35	42 38	80½	39	37 26	—
37·0	Arlesey	—	46 04	91	—	41 13	83½–79
44·1	Sandy	—	51 02	85½	—	46 36	80½–77
51·7	St. Neot's	—	56 41	76	—	52 47	66
56·0	Offord	—	59 51	81	—	56 23	74
58·9	HUNTINGDON	56	62 07	74	62	58 57	—
62·0	*Milepost 62*	—	64 49	65½	—	62 07	52½
69·1	Holme	—	70 30	83½	—	68 46	77½
			sigs.				
75·0	*Fletton Junction*	—	75 21	38	—	73 46	—
76·4	PETERBOROUGH	73	77 23	26*	80	75 34	20*
79·5	*Werrington Junction*	—	81 27	60	—	80 48	—
84·8	Tallington	—	86 18	—	—	86 08	—
88·6	Essendine	—	89 36	68	—	89 52	61½
92·2	Little Bytham	—	92 47	—	—	93 37	—
97·1	Corby	—	97 30	60	—	99 55	43½
100·1	*Stoke Summit*	—	100 27	57½	—	103 58	42
105·5	GRANTHAM	102	104 44	81½	114	110 49	—
109·7	Barkston	—	107 49	—	—	6 37	—
115·4	Claypole	—	111 40	90	—	11 24	77½
120·1	NEWARK	114	114 56	85	15	15 12	—
126·4	Carlton	—	119 33	82	—	20 26	72
133·7	*Markham Summit*	—	125 45	64	—	27 41	51
138·6	RETFORD	132	129 40	84†	35	32 23	75
143·9	Ranskill	—	133 31	81½	—	36 48	76½
147·7	Bawtry	—	136 19	—	—	39 58	—
149·5	*Piper's Wood Summit*	—	137 48	71–83½	—	41 43	57–70
156·0	DONCASTER	147	142 55	67*	53	48 31	40*
160·2	*Shaftholme Junction*	151	146 20	—	58	53 40	—
166·0	Balne	—	150 51	76	—	59 34	—
169·8	Temple Hirst	—	153 48	—	—	63 23	—
174·4	SELBY	164	157 53	34*	73	68 47	30*
178·5	Riccall	—	162 31	62	—	75 34	—
184·0	Naburn	—	167 14	72	—	82 02	48*
186·2	*Chaloner's Whin Junc.*	—	169 08	—	—	84 22	—
						sig. stop	
188·2	YORK	180	172 06	—	90	89 50	—
189·8	*Poppleton Junction*	—	—	—	4	3 54	—
193·7	Beningbrough	—	—	—	—	8 16	—
199·4	Alne	—	—	—	14	13 30	69
204·3	Pilmoor	—	—	—	—	17 52	67
210·4	THIRSK	—	—	—	25	23 13	71½
218·2	NORTHALLERTON	—	—	—	33	30 04	65
221·9	Danby Wiske	—	—	—	—	33 28	71½
227·1	*Eryholme*	—	—	—	42	38 03	66
229·7	Croft Spa	—	—	—	—	40 22	71½
						sigs.	
232·3	DARLINGTON	—	—	—	48	46 38	—

"THE TALISMAN"

Engine: "A3" No. 60059.
Train: 7.50 a.m. Kings Cross–Newcastle.
Load: 9/299 tons tare.

Driver: A. Austin.
Fireman: E. Colton.
Loco Inspector: G. Harland.
Weather: Fine–moderate wind.

1959

Dis-tance		Sched.	Actual	Speed	Boiler pressure/ steamchest pressure	Regu-lator/ cut-off
miles		min.	m. s.	m.p.h.	lb./ sq. in.	
0.0	KINGS CROSS ..	0	0 00	—	220/–	—
2.5	Finsbury Park ..	—	6 20	37	210/200	F/20
5.0	Wood Green ..	—	9 36	40*	220/–	S/–
6.4	New Southgate ..	—	11 40	40*	200/190	F/25
9.2	New Barnet ..	—	15 15	51	205/195	F/22
10.6	Hadley Wood ..	—	16 50	53	210/205	F/20
12.7	Potters Bar.. ..	17	19 15	52	210/205	F/17
17.7	Hatfield	22	24 00	69	210/205	F/14
20.3	Welwyn Gdn. City	—	26 12	64	210/205	F/14
25.0	Knebworth.. ..	—	30 45	60	200/195	F/14
28.6	Stevenage	—	34 00	66	215/200 §	¾/14
31.9	HITCHIN	35	36 46	75	210/195 §	¾/14
35.7	Three Counties ..	—	39 40	83	210/195 §	¾/14
41.1	Biggleswade ..	—	43 40	82	210/205	F/14
44.1	Sandy.. ..	44	45 58	78	210/205	F/14
47.5	Tempsford ..	—	48 29	82	205/200	F/14
51.7	St. Neots	—	51 36	80	205/200	F/14
56.0	Offord	—	54 39	72	220/– §	S
58.9	HUNTINGDON ..	55	57 05	75	205/200	F/17
62.0	Milepost 62 ..	—	59 40	67	200/195	F/20
63.5	Abbots Ripton ..	—	60 52	74	210/205	F/15–20
69.4	Holme	(3) †	65 20	84	210/205	F/20¶
72.6	Yaxley	—	67 35	77	190/185	F/15
75.0	Fletton Junc. ..	—	69 52	65/10*	185/–	S
76.4	PETERBOROUGH	73	74 00	20	190/–	S–F/25
79.5	Werrington Junc. ..	—	78 15	65	200/195	F/17
84.8	Tallington ..	—	82 30	71	200/195	F/23
88.6	Essendine	85	86 15	62‡	200/195	F/23
91.0	Milepost 91 ..	—	88 20	66	205/200	F/25
92.2	Little Bytham ..	—	89 25	65	205/200	F/25
97.1	Corby Glen ..	—	94 00	62	205/200	F/25
100.1	Stoke Box ..	95 (3) †	96 52	61	205/200	F/25
105.5	GRANTHAM ..	102	101 05	74	210/–	S
109.7	Barkston S. Junc. ..	106	104 20	76	200/195	F/14
115.4	Claypole	—	108 40	83/40*	210/200	⅞/14
120.1	NEWARK	114	113 50	60	200/195	F/25
126.4	Carlton	(1) †	119 10	75	200/180	¾/25¶
131.3	Dukeries Junc. ..	—	123 20	68	180/170	F/17
138.6	RETFORD	131	129 50	61	200/–	S
143.9	Ranskill	—	134 20	73/40*	210/190	¾/17
147.7	Bawtry	—	138 35	48	180/175	S–F/25
149.5	Milepost 149½ ..	(6) †	141 05	50	200/195	F/23
153.2	Black Carr Junct.	—	145 20	58	210/–	S
156.0	DONCASTER ..	153 (3) †	148 55	32	200/160	¾/25
160.2	Shaftholme Junc. ..	161	154 10	58	185/175	⅘/17
167.3	Heck	—	160 30	69	205/185	⅘/17
174.4	SELBY	173½	167 20	40	200/195	S–F/25
184.0	Naburn	—	177 30	61	210/–	S
186.2	Chaloners Whin Jc.	—	180 20	42	215/	S
188.2	YORK	188½	183 30	30	210/–	S
189.8	Skelton Junc. ..	191½	186 25	35	180/175	F/27
193.7	Beningborough ..	—	191 15	61	205/200	F/23
197.9	Tollerton	—	194 45	76	215/210	F/15
199.4	Alne	200	196 00	75	210/205	F/15
204.3	Pilmoor	—	200 00	76	210/205	F/15
210.4	Thirsk	209	205 00	70	200/195	F/20
214.8	Otterington	—	208 40	71	200/195	F/20
218.2	NORTHALLERTON	215	211 30	69	200/195	F/17
225.4	Cawton	(3) †	218 45	64	180/175	F/15
227.1	Eryholme Junc. ..	224½	220 15	64	180/175	F/15
232.3	DARLINGTON ..	231	226 00	—	200/–	S

* P.W.S.   † Recovery margin.   ‡ Signals.   § Blowing off.
¶ Driver blinded by drifting steam. Cut-off lengthened to overcome this.
Notes : Coal poor and dusty from Tallington to Doncaster. Strong east wind between Tollerton and Northallerton caused drifting steam to obscure driver's view badly.

Engine: "A3" No. 60039
Train: 9.55 a.m. ex-Newcastle.
Load: 10/361 tons tare to York;
 11/394 tons tare beyond.

Driver: A. Davis.
Fireman: P. F. Roberts.   1959
Loco. Inspector: G. Harland.

Distance		Sched.	Actual	Speed	Boiler press.*	Regulator/cut-off
miles.		min.	m. s.	m.p.h.	lb./sq. in.	
0.0	NEWCASTLE C.	0	0 00	—	220	—
0.6	King Edward B. J.	3	2 50		220	½/25
2.5	Low Fell	—	6 00	50	210	½/17
5.4	Birtley	—	9 30	51	200	/20
11.1	Milepost 69	—	15 55	42/20‡	190	¾/25
14.0	DURHAM	19	20 00	—	210	
0.0		0	0 00	—	220	—
1.0	Relly Mill Junc.	—	3 00	33	215	¾-F/25
4.2	Croxdale	—	7 30	60	200	F/17
9.1	Ferryhill	13	12 20	62	200	½/17
16.6	Aycliffe	(4)†	19 00	68	200	S
22.0	DARLINGTON	31	25 40	—	220§	S
0.0		0	0 00	—	220	—
5.2	Eryholme Junc.	6	7 20	53	200	F/15
10.4	Danby Wiske	—	12 15	68	210	F/17
14.1	Northallerton	14	15 35	70	215	F/15
21.9	Thirsk	21	21 45	78	210	F/15
28.0	Pilmoor	—	26 15	82	205	F/15
32.9	Alne	30	30 00	78	215	F/15
38.6	Beningborough	—	34 20	79	220	F/15
44.1	YORK	42	40 20	—	220	
0.0		0	0 00	—	220	—
2.0	Chaloners Whin Jc.	—	4 00	42	210	¾/17
9.7	Riccall	—	11 20	69	220	F/15
13.8	Selby	16	15 40	38	200	¾/25
22.2	Balne	(4)†	24 10	69	220§	F/15
28.0	Shaftholme Junc.	34	29 10	73	220§	S
32.2	DONCASTER	39	34 00	40	205	F/22
35.0	Black Carr Junc.	—	37 15	56	220§	F/17
38.7	Milepost 149½	—	41 10	55¶	220	F/20
40.5	Bawtry	—	43 30	40‡	220§	S
44.3	Ranskill	—	48 00	56	210	F/15
49.6	RETFORD	56	52 42	62	210	F/15
54.5	Milepost 133¾	—	57 40	56	210	F/22
56.9	Dukeries Junc.	—	59 55	68	220	½/12½
60.8	Crow Park	—	63 35	71	210	½/12½
68.1	NEWARK	73	69 55	64	215	½/12½
72.8	Claypole	(3)†	74 25	63	215	½/12½
78.5	Barkston S. Junc.	86	80 00	56	200	½/12½
82.7	GRANTHAM	91	85 15	—	210	
0.0		0	0 00	—	215	—
5.4	Stoke Box	8	8 30	45	200	F/30
8.4	Corby Glen	—	11 30	69	210	F/15
13.3	Little Bytham	—	15 05	88	210	F/15
16.9	Essendine	17	17 32	82	215	½/15
20.7	Tallington	(4)†	20 05	81	215	½/15
26.0	Werrington Junc.	28	24 30	64	215	S
29.1	PETERBOROUGH	33	29 25	20/10‡	220	S
30.5	Fletton Junc.	—	33 00	34	185	F/30
32.9	Yaxley	—	36 15	49	205	F/17
36.1	Holme	—	39 30	64	205	F/17
46.6	Huntingdon	51	50 30	20¶	220	S
49.5	Offord	—	54 47	59	210	F/20
53.2	St. Neots	—	59 05	60	220	F/17
58.0	Tempsford	—	62 58	69	220	F/15
61.4	Sandy	63	66 00	68	210	F/15
64.4	Biggleswade	(6)†	68 40	67	200	F/15
68.5	Arlesey	—	72 15	67	210	F/15
73.6	Hitchin	80	76 52	64	210	F/22
76.9	Stevenage	—	80 42	53/20‡	200	F/25
80.5	Knebworth	87	86 55	41	200	F/30
85.2	Welwyn Gdn. City	(1)†	91 45	66	220§	S
87.8	Hatfield	95	94 05	64	210	F/17
92.8	Potter's Bar	101	98 48	60	205	F/17
96.3	New Barnet	—	102 13	64¶	200	S
100.5	Wood Green	(2)†	108 05	30¶	205	S
103.0	Finsbury Park	113	113 00	—¶	—	S
105.5	KINGS CROSS	118	122 00	—	—	S

* Steamchest pressure gauge was not functioning.   † Recovery margin.
‡ P.W.S.   § Blowing off.   ¶ Signal checks.
Notes : Newcastle start in drizzle, and engine slips repeatedly. At Selby poor and dusty coal encountered. From Crow Park engine eased to avoid too early arrival at Grantham.

L.N.E.R. Experimental Runs, London to Leeds and Back. November 30, 1934

Engine, 4-6-2 No. 4472, *Flying Scotsman.* Driver W. Sparshatt, Fireman Webster

Down Journey 4 coaches, 144¾ t. tare, 147 t. gross					Up Journey 6 coaches, 205¼ t. tare, 207½ t. gross			
Distance	Schedule	Actual Times	**Max. and Min. Speeds	Stations	Distance	Schedule	Actual Times	**Max. and Min. Speeds
Miles	Min.	Min. Sec.	M.p.h.		Miles	Min.	Min. Sec.	M.p.h.
0·0	0	0 00	—	KING'S CROSS	185·8	165	157 17	—
2·5	—	4 04	55	FINSBURY PARK	183·3	—	153 22	—
3·4	—	4 59	—	Harringay	182·4	—	152 28	—
4·0	—	5 34	—	Hornsey	181·8	—	151 58	—
5·0	—	6 25	71½	Wood Green	180·8	—	151 13	81
6·4	—	7 40	67	New Southgate	179·4	—	150 09	83¾
9·2	—	10 07	68½	New Barnet	176·6	—	148 08	79¾
10·6	—	11 22	68	Hadley Wood	175·2	—	147 03	77½
12·7	—	13 16	67	Potter's Bar	173·1	—	145 16	69¾
14·6	—	14 41	—	Brookman's Park	171·2	—	143 47	72¼
17·7	19	17 03	83¼	HATFIELD	168·1	148	141 11	85
20·3	—	19 09	60‡	Welwyn Garden City	165·5	—	139 16	80
22·0	—	20 45	—	Welwyn North	163·8	—	137 58	77
23·5	—	22 06	68½	*Woolmer Green*	162·3	—	136 48	72
25·0	—	23 26	†81¾	Knebworth	160·8	—	135 31	†76¼
28·6	—	26 05	80¼	Stevenage	157·2	—	132 37	70¼
31·9	30	28 22	93½	HITCHIN	153·9	137	129 50	72½
35·7	—	30 48	94¾	Three Counties	150·1	—	126 43	76¼
37·0	—	31 40	††85¾	Arlesey	148·8	—	125 38	75
41·1	—	34 27	91¾	Biggleswade	144·7	—	122 00	62¼
44·1	—	36 24	92¾	Sandy	141·7	—	118 33	‖40
47·5	—	38 38	93¼	Tempsford	138·3	—	115 55	80¾
51·7	—	41 29	85	St. Neot's	134·1	—	112 38	71½
56·0	—	44 24	§90	Offord	129·8	—	109 08	eased
58·9	50	46 31	81¾	HUNTINGDON	126·9	116	106 42	80½
62·0	—	48 58	72½	*Mile-post 62*	123·8	—	104 13	—
63·5	—	50 11	—	Abbots Ripton	122·3	—	102 57	72
69·4	—	54 28	83¼	Holme	116·4	—	98 31	83¼
72·6	—	56 57	75	Yaxley	113·2	—	96 05	72½
75·0	—	58 57	—	*Fletton Junction*	110·8	—	93 52	—
76·4	66	60 39	¶21	PETERBOROUGH	109·4	100	92 00	¶25
78·0	—	63 29	—	*Mile-post 78*	107·8	—	90 10	—
79·5	—	64 20	71½	*Werrington Junction*	106·3	—	89 00	80¼
81·9	—	66 14	79	*Helpston*	103·9	—	87 14	84
84·8	—	68 26	80¼	Tallington	101·0	—	85 10	86½
88·6	—	71 13	84	ESSENDINE	97·2	—	82 38	98
92·2	—	73 47	83¾	Little Bytham	93·6	—	80 25	95½
97·1	—	77 21	82½	Corby	88·7	—	77 11	85¾
100·1	—	79 33	81¼	*Stoke*	85·7	—	74 54	68½
102·0	—	80 58	*87¼	Great Ponton	83·8	—	73 14	68¼
105·5	92	83 39	¶62	GRANTHAM	80·3	74	70 18	73¾
109·7	—	87 16	—	Barkstone	76·1	—	66 45	‡‡69
111·5	—	88 41	77½	Hougham	74·3	—	65 13	75
115·4	—	91 24	90	Claypole	70·4	—	62 13	78
120·1	103	94 38	86½	NEWARK	65·7	62	58 28	77½
126·4	—	99 10	82½	Carlton	59·4	—	53 44	—
127·4	—	99 54	81	Crow Park	58·4	—	53 01	81¾
131·3	—	102 56	—	Dukeries Junction	54·5	—	50 08	81¾
131·9	—	103 29	—	Tuxford	53·9	—	49 42	81¾
133·7	—	104 53	76½	*Markham*	52·1	—	48 23	73¾
135·5	—	—	83¾	*Gamston*	50·3	—	46 55	73¼
138·6	119	108 44	¶69	RETFORD	47·2	47	44 28	81½
141·7	—	111 19	81¾	Sutton	44·1	—	42 14	85
143·9	—	112 53	87	Ranskill	41·9	—	40 41	86½
145·8	—	114 11	88¼	Scrooby	40·0	—	39 23	88¼
147·7	—	115 30	—	Bawtry	38·1	—	38 04	83¾
149·5	—	116 50	79	*Piper's Wood*	36·3	—	36 44	73
151·3	—	118 08	87¼	Rossington	34·5	—	35 18	*77½
153·2	—	119 31	—	*Black Carr Junction*	32·6	—	33 49	75
156·0	133	122 27	¶40	DONCASTER	29·8	32	30 58	¶35
158·8	—	124 29	—	Castle Hills	27·0	—	28 58	—
160·0	—	126 38	76¼	Carcroft	25·8	—	27 01	¶72
162·5	—	128 37	79	Hampole	23·3	—	25 03	81¾
164·7	—	130 17	80¼	South Elmsall	21·1	—	23 25	77½
—	—	—	77½	—				
167·9	—	132 41	81	Hemsworth	17·9	—	20 47	74½
170·4	—	134 37	77½	Nostell	15·4	—	18 33	61½
171·9	—	135 43	83¼	Hare Park	13·9	—	17 05	64½
174·2	—	137 26	—	Sandal	11·6	—	14 55	63¼
175·9	151	139 28	¶35	WAKEFIELD	9·9	14	12 42	¶39
177·0	—	—	57	*Wrenthorpe North*	8·8	—	11 16	—
178·3	—	141 22	¶40	Lofthouse	7·5	—	9 46	¶48
180·2	157	144 39	55½	Ardsley	5·6	9	7 46	54
183·3	—	147 46	68	Beeston	2·5	—	4 17	56
185·3	—	150 15	¶10	Holbeck	0·5	—	1 36	—
185·8	165	151 56	—	LEEDS (CENTRAL)	0·0	0	0 00	—

Down journey: Left King's Cross 9.8 a.m. Arrived Leeds (Central) 11.40 a.m.
Up journey: Left Leeds (Central) 2.0 p.m. Arrived King's Cross 4.37 p.m.

¶ Service slack; * Maximum before shutting off steam; † Maximum at Langley; ‡ Minimum by brakes leaking on from Hatfield to mile-post 20; § Maximum before easing for curves; †† Minimum at Langford. ‖ Permanent-way relaying slack; ‡‡ Minimum at Peascliffe tunnel.
** At or at changes of gradient near station shown in centre column.

L.N.E.R. Experimental Runs, King's Cross to Newcastle and Back
March 5, 1935

Engine: 4-6-2 No. 2750, *Papyrus*
Load: 6 coaches, 213½ tons, 217 tons gross

DOWN JOURNEY
Driver: H. Gutteridge. Fireman: A. Wightman

UP JOURNEY
Driver: W. Sparshatt. Fireman: R. Webster

Distance	Schedule	Actual	Speeds‖	Station	Distance	Schedule	Actual	Speeds‖
miles	min.	min. sec.	m.p.h.		miles	min.	min. sec.	m.p.h.
0·0	0	0 00	—	KING'S CROSS	268·3	240	231 48	—
2·5	—	4 47	—	FINSBURY PARK	265·8	—	227 58	—
5·0	—	7 11	72	Wood Green	263·3	—	225 54	81¾
9·2	—	10 41	74½	New Barnet	259·1	—	222 52	85
12·7	—	13 42	64	Potter's Bar	255·6	—	220 12	77½
17·7	19	18 03	80§	HATFIELD	250·6	223	216 23	85§
23·5	—	22 48	68	*Woolmer Green*	244·8	—	211 52	71½
25·0	—	24 08	—	Knebworth	243·3	—	210 36	—
28·6	—	26 48	76½	Stevenage	239·7	—	207 46	78½
31·9	30	29 19	82½	HITCHIN	236·4	212	205 17	79
35·7	—	31 59	88½	Three Counties..	232·6	—	202 28	85
37·0	—	32 53	83½*	Arlesey	231·3	—	201 31	80*
41·1	—	35 47	85	Biggleswade	227·2	—	198 29	85¾
44·1	—	37 53	83¾	Sandy	224·2	—	196 23	87½
47·5	—	40 18	86	Tempsford	220·8	—	194 02	85¾
51·7	—	43 19	82½	St. Neot's	216·6	—	191 02	76½
56·0	—	46 28	70¶	Offord	212·3	—	187 31	68¶
58·9	50	48 52	78½	HUNTINGDON	209·4	191	185 00	75
63·5	—	52 30	74½†	Abbot's Ripton	204·8	—	181 16	72
69·4	—	56 40	86½	Holme	198·9	—	176 47	83½
72·6	—	59 14	71	Yaxley	195·7	—	174 18	72
75·0	—	61 15	—	*Fletton Junction*	193·3	—	172 07	—
76·4	66	63 21	20½¶	PETERBOROUGH	191·9	175	169 43	22¶
79·5	—	67 13	73½	*Werrington Junction*	188·8	—	166 26	—
81·9	—	69 05	—	*Helpston*	186·4	—	164 43	—
84·8	—	71 19	81	Tallington	183·5	—	162 48	98½
88·6	—	74 19	75½	Essendine	179·7	—	160 32	102
—		—	77½		—	—	—	108
92·2	—	77 05	77	Little Bytham	176·1	—	158 29	106
97·1	—	80 58	75½	Corby	171·2	—	155 28	91
100·1	—	83 21	75½	*Stoke*	168·2	—	153 16	69½
102·0	—	84 52	76	Great Ponton	166·3	—	151 38	70½
105·5	92	87 42	64¶	GRANTHAM	162·8	149	148 42	71½
109·7	—	91 16	79	Barkstone	158·6	—	144 37	59½
115·4	—	95 32	83½	Claypole	152·9	—	139 37	73
120·1	103	99 10	71	NEWARK	148·2	137	135 52	77
126·4	—	104 23	76½	Carlton	141·9	—	130 53	75
131·3	—	108 36	62½	Dukeries Junction	137·0	—	126 59	72½
133·7	—	110 53	64	*Markham*	134·6	—	124 56	64½
135·5	—	—	80	*Gamston*	132·8	—	123 13	—
138·6	119	115 18	58¶	RETFORD	129·7	122	120 25	78½
143·9	—	120 11	75	Ranskill	124·4	—	116 21	80½
145·8	—	121 41	77½	Scrooby..	122·5	—	114 55	86½
147·7	—	123 13	72½	Bawtry	120·6	—	113 33	81¾
149·5	—	124 46	69½	*Mile-post* 149½	119·0	—	112 18	72
153·2	—	127 39	80	*Black Carr Junction*	115·1	—	109 13	77½
:		*sigs.*						
156·0	133	132 00	5¶	DONCASTER	112·3	107	106 40	53
		sig. stop	0¶				*p.w.s.*	15
158·1	—	138 30	—	Arksey	110·2	—	103 13	16¶
							p.w.s.	
160·2	137	141 01	68½	*Shaftholme Junction*	108·1	103	99 03	—
163·0	—	143 20	77½	Moss	105·3	—	96 38	74½
166·0	—	145 31	85	Balne	102·3	—	94 16	79
169·8	—	148 15	83½	Templehirst	98·5	—	91 15	72½
173·0	—	150 35	86½	*Brayton Junction*	95·3	—	88 33	—
174·3	150	152 05	38¶	SELBY	94·0	89	86 38	32¶
178·5	—	156 21	77	Riccall	89·8	—	82 24	73
181·1	—	158 21	80	Escrick	87·2	—	80 18	75
184·0	—	160 28	83½	Naburn	84·3	—	77 55	65
186·2	—	162 25	52¶	*Chaloner's Whin Junction* ..	82·1	—	75 31	—
188·1	164	165 11	23½¶	YORK	80·1	75½	72 17	19½¶
189·8	—	167 25	64½	*Poppleton Junction*	78·5	—	69 40	80
193·7	—	170 36	79½	Beningbrough	74·6	—	66 48	82½
199·3	175	174 43	83	Alne	69·0	65	62 43	84½
201·5	—	176 21	82½	Raskelf	66·8	—	61 11	88
204·2	—	178 22	80¾	Pilmoor	64·1	—	59 18	86
206·1	—	179 47	80	Sessay	62·2	—	57 58	82½
210·3	185	182 50	85	THIRSK	58·0	56½	54 53	84½
214·6	—	185 57	82¾	Otterington	53·7	—	51 48	81½
218·1	191	188 34	79½	NORTHALLERTON.. ..	50·2	50½	49 15	80
221·9	—	191 24	81½	Danby Wiske	46·4	—	46 31	87
227·1	198	195 17	76	*Eryholme*	41·2	43	42 52	78½
229·7	—	197 28	68½	Croft Spa	38·6	—	40 55	81½
232·3	203	199 47	67	DARLINGTON	36·0	38½	38 53	70½
237·7	—	204 39	62	Aycliffe	30·6	—	34 04	63¶
242·3	—	208 42	73	Bradbury	26·0	—	30 23	84
245·2	215	211 06	65¶	FERRYHILL	23·1	26½	28 12	74½

Cont over.

Distance	Schedule	Actual	Speeds‖	Station	Distance	Schedule	Actual	Speeds‖
miles	min.	min. sec.	m.p.h.		miles	min.	min. sec.	m.p.h.
247·2	—	213 02	68	*Tursdale Junction*	21·1	—	26 18	—
250·0	—	215 36	64	Croxdale	18·3	—	23 27	64
		p.w.s.	45¶				*p.w.s.*	47¶
253·2	—	219 27	—	*Kelly Mill Junction* ..	15·1	—	19 58	39½
254·2	225	221 07	32¶	DURHAM	14·1	17	18 07	31¶
255·6	—	222 50	—	*Newton Hall Junction*	12·7	—	16 25	—
258·1	—	225 28	66	Plawsworth	10·2	—	13 15	—
							p.w.s.	34¶
260·0	—	227 01	75	Chester-le-Street	8·3	—	11 02	68½
262·8	233	229 23	70½	Birtley	5·5	8	8 22	62½
		p.w.s.	46¶				*p.w.s.*	
265·7	—	232 28	49½	Low Fell	2·6	—	5 03	57
267·7	—	235 10	24¶	*King Edward Bridge Junction*	0·6	—	2 35	—
268·3	240	237 07	—	NEWCASTLE	0·0	0	0 00	—

* Speed at Langford (38½ mile-post).
† Minimum at mile-post 62.
‡ Speed at top of 1 in 200 (95½ miles); increased to 78 at 97 miles.
§ At Lea Valley (19 mile-post).
‖ The figures given in speed columns indicate maximum or minimum speeds at or near the stations shown.
¶ Indicates speed reduced by brakes for service, permanent way or signal checks.
p.w.s. Permanent-way slow.

Above. FLYING SCOTSMAN on her final run in BR service, in the snow on January 15th 1963, before purchase by Alan Pegler, on the 13.15 express from Kings Cross. The A3 has a Diagram 94A boiler No.27058 and an A4 non-corridor tender (No.5640).

Left. The end of the line. SIR FREDERICK BANBURY stands at Doncaster Works in late 1961 in very different circumstances from those of the earlier pictures. The only Great Northern Pacific is condemned, no longer wanted, sadly. The engine has a Diagram 107 boiler (29285) and a GN tender (5292).

THE LAST 'TON'

Between 1951 and 1964 Brian Bailey timed 46 southbound journeys between Grantham and Kings Cross, including the famous descent from Stoke box towards Peterborough. Indelibly imprinted on the minds of those interested in locomotive performance were names like Little Bytham, Essendine, and Tallington, vital timing points when hoping to record some spectacular run by an East Coast Pacific making up time on its way south to London. From time to time the railway management itself facilitated an outstanding show, either in earlier days with official test runs and in the post-war years to mark a significant anniversary, to provide Railway Societies with high speed runs and finally to commemorate the end of the Steam Era and especially that of the Gresley Pacifics. On the final staged A3 run on 2 May 1964 with 60106 FLYING FOX there must have been many others recording the runs in detail, but only this one seems to have seen the light of day, and unfortunately in the original article nearly 50 years ago there was a misprint that added 10 seconds to the timing for Little Bytham. The correct recorded time is only *one second slower* than the record breaking time achieved by 2750 in 1935! The average speed of 2750 between Corby Glen and Little Bytham was 97.5 mph with the dynamometer car recording speeds between 91 and 104 mph. With 60106 the average speed was 97 mph, varying between 92 and one reading of 101 mph, with a note at the time containing nine speed readings until the signal check by Essendine North Distant.

There is little doubt that 60106 did indeed reach 100 mph down Stoke bank on that final 'great hurrah' of the class on 2 May 1964, looking at the comparative evidence of other authenticated runs. First, is the much overlooked run by 2750 (later 60096) PAPYRUS on 5 March 1935 compared with the passing times of 60106 and other runs in the last decade of steam. In addition the rough notebook still exists in which was recorded 60106's run as it happened, so a transcript of the original is still accessible to remind us of the climax, when the brakes suddenly were applied on Driver Green seeing the signals for Essendine North at caution, and speed came down to 20mph before they cleared. Most likely the signalmen at Greatford and Tallington had difficulty in closing the crossing gates when Essendine gave them train on line.

In the light of the subsequent eras that have supplanted FLYING FOX and its sisters, their performances may seem very small beer. Over the past 50 years we have come to take for granted the everyday performance of first the Deltics, and now both the Class 91 electrics and the venerable HSTs. As examples from recent years: in March 1994 class 91 91019 ran from a Peterborough start to passing Grantham in 16¾ minutes, while later that year 91003 took 15 minutes 50 seconds to cover the same distance in the opposite direction. In September 2009 HST 43315/43319 ran from Kings Cross to passing Grantham in 57 minutes 25 seconds: including climbing Stoke Bank from Peterborough to MP 100 in 11 minutes 35 seconds and taking 15 minutes 10 seconds Peterborough to Grantham pass to pass. In the southbound direction in August 2008 HST 43238/43307 took 19½ minutes Grantham pass to stopping at Peterborough, including a speed restriction for trackwork at Stoke and coming to a stand for signals outside Peterborough for 30 seconds. It still seems strange in the northbound direction to feel the brakes going on to check the speed as a train tops Stoke bank and approaches the tunnel entrance.

However, it is hoped that this memoir will enable everyone who remembers 2 May 1964 with a mixture of nostalgia and regret to feel satisfied that 4475 of blessed memory did indeed achieve a final 'ton' for the honour of the class before the final curtain fell.

TRANSCRIPT of notebook of the run of A3 60106 on 2 May 1964 between Grantham and Little Bytham prior to the signal check on the approach to Essendine

GRANTHAM	pass 0.00 stop watch 12.4 sec 73.2 mph
Great Ponton	2.54 stop watch 12.7 sec 70.9 mph
Stoke Summit	4.38 70 (railbeats over 41 sec)
MP 98	stop watch 10.8 sec 83.3 mph
Corby Glen	6.55 92 (railbeats over 20½ sec)
MP 97	stop watch 9.8 sec 91.8 mph
MP 96½	stop watch 9.8 sec 91.8 mph
MP 96	stop watch 9.6 sec 93.8 mph
MP 95½	7.57 stop watch 9.5 sec 94.7 mph
MP 94	8.52 stop watch 9.2 sec 97.7 mph
MP 93½	100 (railbeats over 20½ sec)
Little Bytham	9.57 101 (railbeats immediately before station)
MP 91¾	100 (railbeats over 20½ sec)
MP 91¼	distant sighted shut off steam
ESSENDINE	16.44 signals 20 mph

14 January 1963: A3 60103 last run in BR service 13 15 Kings Cross- Leeds Locomotive: A3 60103 *Flying Scotsman*
Load: 11 coaches 369/400 tons

0.00 KINGS CROSS		00.00	RT
Finsbury Park		07.32	
Wood Green		10.47	53
New Southgate		12.32	50
New Barnet		15.56	50
Potters Bar		20.33	47
HATFIELD	23	25.31	70
Welwyn North		29.33	62
Woolmer Green		31.08	56/ TLS 20
Stevenage		38.11	57/76
31.9 HITCHIN	38	41.07	78
Three Counties		43.48	86/90 Arlesey
Biggleswade		47.42	81/86
Sandy		49.48	84
Tempsford		52.15	82
St Neots		55.56	76/signals 54 distant Everton*
Offord		60.00	72
58.9 HUNTINGDON	59	62.31	69
MP 62		65.27	60 minimum at summit
Holme		71.42	82/ eased 65 for TLS
Fletton Junction		76.26	TLS 20
76.4 PETERBOROUGH 79	80.39	arrive -1½ minutes	
0.00 PETERBOROUGH	00.00	RT	
Werrington Junction		06.00	62
Tallington		11.10	66
Essendine		14.39	69/66
Little Bytham		18.05	60
Corby Glen		23.06	58/52
Stoke Summit		26.31	50
Great Ponton		28.36	67
29.1 GRANTHAM	32	31.37	64
Barkston South		36.20	70/signals 20 distant Claypole*
Claypole		41.21	75/80
NEWARK		47.23	TLS 20
Carlton		53.23	74
Dukeries Junction		57.40	66/60
62.2 RETFORD	65	64.23	74/67 eased for crossing
Ranskill		69.13	72-78
Bawtry		73.26	Slack 30 subsidence on viaduct
Rossington		78.09	70
Black Carr Junction		79.48	72
79.6 DONCASTER	90	84.07	arrive +6 minutes.

Net times 73 minutes to Peterborough: 77 minutes to Doncaster. Combined running times 164 % minutes gross: 150 minutes net

	Loco	4472		2750		60006		60005		60111		60111		60034	60106		
	Load	207		217		495		330		345		345		330	320		
	Driver	Sp		Sp		Ha		Ho		35B		35B		34A	Green*		
	Exhaust	S		S		S		K		K		K		K	K		
									Sigs								
0.0	GRANTHAM	pass	74	pass	71		start	pass	5		start		start	pass	73	pass	73
3.4	Gt. Ponton	2 56	69			6 39		5 33		6 03	54	6 27	51		2 54	71	
5.4	Stoke SB	4 36	68	4 34	69	9 02	52	8 05	52	8 05	60	8 32	55	4 45	64	4 38	70
8.4	Corby Glen	6 53	86	6 46	91	11 55	70	10 54	77	10 35	86	11 05	82	7 12	83	6 55	92
13.3	Little Bytham	10 07	96	9 47	104	15 34	82	14 17	92	13 53	92	14 27	98	10 23	103	9 57	101
16.9	Essendine	12 20	100	11 50	108	18 06	90	16 35	96	16 11	95	16 39	94	12 32	100	16 44	Sigs
20.7	Tallington	14 52	86	14 06	108	21 00	80	19 05	88	19 00	78	18 58	100	15 05		20 55	78
26.0	Werrington Jct	18 42	84	17 44		25 31	72	22 56		23 22	60	23 55	TSR	19 05	Sigs	25 49	Sigs
29.1	PETERBOROUGH	21 42		21 01	**	30 50	**	26 18	**	27 35	stop	32 39	stop	26 30	**	31 17	stop
	Corby-L Bytham	3 14		3 01		3 39		3 23		3 18		3 22		3 11		3 02	
		91		97 5		80.5		87		89.1		87.2		92.2		97.1	
S=Single Blast K=Kylchap *36A Sp=Sparshatt Ha=Hailstone Ho=Hoole																	

EPILOGUE

The most important attributes of great engineers are determination, open-mindedness and a lack of prejudice. Nigel Gresley excelled in this respect, especially the ability to use the ideas of others for the benefit of his own work. He applied superheating to Henry Ivatt's Atlantics and transformed them into one of our best four-coupled locomotives. He continued Ivatt's approach to boiler design, and none of Gresley's designs could be described as under-boilered. With GREAT NORTHERN his adoption of the Pennsylvania Railroad Pacific boiler proportions was a stroke of genius, one which serves us today in TORNADO. The Doncaster boiler was a faithful servant that was used on another 387 locomotives. Gresley saw no need to use the more expensive and complicated Belpaire firebox, perhaps due to weight and structure gauge restrictions. Gresley was restricted to 20 ton coupled axle loads, and it needed skilful design to avoid exceeding the limit with GREAT NORTHERN. I would imagine that the robustness of the locomotive chassis would have been compromised by weight considerations, leading to frame fractures.

In the same way, Gresley pursued his idea of conjugating the outside valve gears in order to drive the middle cylinder. In theory it was possible and enabled considerable simplification between the frames – although the two most important bearings, the big and little ends remained. Here, H Holcroft assisted in simplifying the design. To many locomotive engineers it was somewhere between unadvisable and anathema, but as we saw later in the 1950s, if correctly set up and maintained, it worked. It did so in the 1930s when the skills were available. However, given the shortcomings of history leading to the 1939-45 war and its consequences, that was no longer possible. Post-war the A3s seemed to be less vulnerable to big end trouble than their newer sisters, although the hardest duties were usually taken by Peppercorn A1s and A4s. His use of Bugatti's streamlined shape gave us the A4, the natural development of the A3, and all that followed with those remarkable locomotives. That streamlined envelope was also the most successful answer to the problems of exhaust deflection in the steam era.

In looking at the history of the A3s, it is ironic that the design of the express locos that wrested supremacy from Swindon was actually improved by Swindon. The 1925 Exchanges were born out of a light-hearted challenge, but they were not of any great length, although quite long enough to show the superiority of the Castle. Driver Pibworth and No.1474 did well on the GWR, and were beginning to give the Castle a run for its money on the South Devon banks, but the shambles on the LNER must have been embarrassing. However, it is the lessons learnt from that contest that transformed the A1, and one may reflect on what might have happened had there never been an exchange. Development would have seeped through eventually, especially through Gresley's friendship with André Chapelon, and the persistence of Bert Spencer.

But it is curious to reflect that the events of 1925 led to the non-stop Flying Scotsman in 1928, the Breakfast Flyer, 100mph in 1934 by FLYING SCOTSMAN, and 108mph in 1935 . The A4, with its astonishing tour de force in September 1935, tended to obliterate the feat of PAPYRUS, which remains the highest authenticated speed by a non-streamlined steam locomotive in the UK. The records of the two famous runs by FLYING SCOTSMAN and PAPYRUS are reproduced in the Appendix. There were surely other feats of speed, many of which were unknown, together with those of SOLARIO, TRIGO, SINGAPORE and ST. FRUSQUIN which were known but unrecorded, sadly.

FLYING SCOTSMAN is now where she should be, in the National Railway Museum. It is a great pity that the whole business of conserving representative items of our engineering heritage was in its infancy in the late 1950s-early 1960s period. Modernisation was a necessary process for our rail system, but it was undertaken with impatience in an industry that was uncomfortable with change. As a result we lost the Euston Arch, the Great Hall (a more worthy candidate) and, nearly, St.Pancras station. At a time when much was being thrown out and cut up, it would have been quite a simple matter to preserve GREAT NORTHERN, one of the most historic of our steam locomotive fleet. By any rationale, the prototype A1 and A4 should be part of the National Collection. The first A3s were being withdrawn, and it would have been possible to recreate a non-working prototype A1 for a future NRM. That strange front end could have been removed and a conventional A3 boiler and front end could have been substituted. Within five years of building the A1s and A3s were kits of parts rather than the original unique machines. At a time when the new Deltics were entering service at £200,000 each, the cost would have been relatively small. Maybe No.4470 was not the best Gresley Pacific, but she was the first.

Gresley's Pacific was, to any engineer, the perfect marriage of balance and proportion to functionality and performance. A wonderful epitaph to a great engineer.